Building Family Business Champions

Building Family Business Champions

Eric G. Flamholtz and Yvonne Randle

STANFORD BUSINESS BOOKS
An Imprint of Stanford University Press
Stanford, California

Stanford University Press
Stanford, California

Special discounts for bulk quantities of Stanford Business Books are available to corporations, professional associations, and other organizations. For details and discount information, contact the special sales department of Stanford University Press. Tel: (650) 736-1782, Fax: (650) 736-1784

Printed in the United States of America on acid-free, archival-quality paper

Library of Congress Cataloging-in-Publication Data

Flamholtz, Eric, author.
  Building family business champions / Eric G. Flamholtz and Yvonne Randle.
     pages cm
  Includes bibliographical references and index.
  ISBN 978-0-8047-8419-1 (cloth : alk. paper) — ISBN 978-0-8047-9802-0 (electronic)
  1. Family-owned business enterprises—Management. 2. Success in business.
I. Randle, Yvonne, author. II. Title.
  HD62.25.F58 2016
  658.4—dc23

                              2015028101

Typeset at Stanford University Press in 10.5/15 Minion

*To the family behind Bell-Carter Foods,
in particular Tim Carter; his brother, Jud Carter;
and Tim's son, Tim T. Carter*

Contents

Preface

We wrote this book to help businesses understand what to do to become a "family business champion"—that is, a family business that has undergone at least two successful *leadership transitions from one generation to the next*, while simultaneously growing and remaining profitable. Research has shown that only one-third of family businesses are passed successfully to a second generation of family leadership.[1] In addition, "only 13 percent of successful family businesses last through the third generation."[2] Maintaining family business success for more than one generation is clearly a difficult task. Nevertheless, many companies have achieved this, including Simon Property Group (a NYSE-listed shopping mall developer and operator), Westfield (an Australian and U.S. shopping mall developer and operator), GOJO™ (developer and manufacturer of Purell™), and Heineken (the Dutch beer brewer).

The number of family businesses that have been highly successful for more than one generation and can therefore be called family business champions is quite small, and there are even fewer family businesses that have been successful for *four or more generations*. Any family business that has been successful for four generations can be called a "family business dynasty." Companies that have achieved this special status include Bechtel, SC Johnson & Son, and Bank Santander in Spain.[3] Throughout this book, we describe the evolution of another company that has achieved this elite status—Bell-Carter Foods. We use Bell-Carter (which has had four generations of successful family leaders over a 100-year period) as a unifying case to illustrate the concepts, frameworks, and methods we advocate for building family business champions.

A Look at One Family Business Champion: Heineken

Heineken, a true family business champion, has prospered over four generations of family leadership and more than 150 years.[4] Heineken was founded when Gerard Adriaan Heineken, then 22 years of age, bought a brewery in the heart of Amsterdam in 1864.[5] The young Heineken had no experience in brewing, but brewing was to become his passion and his life's work.

He had vision, treated customers and employees well, and strived for consistently high quality in his product. His vision was to expand the brewery to become the largest and best in Europe.[6] He was also committed to experimentation and continuous improvement, not only in product quality but also in methods of brewing alternative types of beers. On January 11, 1873, he officially incorporated "Heineken Bierbrouwerji Maatschappij NV" also known as "HBM." It should be noted that this resulted in the transition of Heineken from a pure family business to a quasi-family business.

Four Generations

Gerard died unexpectedly in 1893, at the age of 51. Although Gerard's widow was the majority shareholder, she was not prepared to run the company herself, so she appointed a family friend, J. D. A. Peterson, as a director of HBM. One year later she married Peterson, who became stepfather to Henry Pierre Heineken, Gerard's son.[7] In effect, Peterson became caretaker of the business until Gerard's son, Henry Pierre, could assume leadership.

On October 1, 1914, Henry Pierre Heineken became a director of HBM, and three years later he was appointed chairman. Henry Pierre Heineken, who held a doctorate in chemistry, managed the company from 1917 to 1940 and continued his involvement with the company until 1951. Under his leadership, HBM developed techniques to maintain consistent beer quality in large-scale production. During their tenure at HBM, Peterson worked alongside two other directors, and Heineken worked with three others in what has been described as a "very close-knit team."[8]

Henry Pierre's son, Alfred Henry Heineken, who was born in 1923, began working at the company in 1941 at the age of 18. Freddy, as he preferred to be called, was not originally interested in the business except as an owner and left the running of the business to the company's directors.[9] Freddy preferred artistic pursuits and at first seemed to be a classic third-generation scion under whose "leadership" the business would likely decline. After World War II, when the company began to focus more on exports and becoming a global brand, the brewery management "asked Leo Van Munching, Heineken's U.S. importer, to teach 'little Freddy' the finer points of the business."[10]

To the surprise of management, Freddy emerged as a successful salesman and with a new-found interest in the family business. During the prior generation's leadership, the family's share of stock ownership had been diluted. Freddy's mission was to return majority ownership to the family. When he succeeded in doing so by 1954, Freddy described it as "the masterpiece of my working life."[11]

One of Freddy's strengths was his ability to think strategically, and this was a key ingredient in Heineken's continued global expansion. As he stated: "I am a generational thinker and I think in terms of 25 to 50 years ahead. It is an entirely different way of thinking than, for example, the way a director thinks in maximum periods of 5 years." He used a chess metaphor to describe his business dealings, stating: "It is fun to checkmate people."[12] Freddy retired from the executive board in 1989 but maintained involvement with the company until his death in 2002.

Freddy's daughter, Charlene de Carvalho-Heineken, born on June 30, 1954, is the fourth generation of the Heineken family to be involved in the business. At this writing, she owns a controlling interest in the world's third-largest brewer, Heineken International, and sits on the company's board of management. Her mark on the company is a work in progress. Her husband is also a member of the board.

Today, Heineken is a family business dynasty and one of the leading brewing groups in the world. Although we are not privy to the internal Heineken family dynamics, the firm's success suggests a healthy functional family, generation after generation.

Becoming a Family Business Champion

Since its founding in 1978, our firm has worked with hundreds of companies, approximately 45 percent of them family businesses—including some of the family business champions mentioned here (Simon Property Group, GOJO™, Westfield, Techmer PM, and Bell-Carter Foods). Drawing on this experience and on our research, this book provides a framework for understanding what must be done to become a family business champion. We provide a set of concepts and managerial tools to help achieve this challenging objective including planning, performance management, and culture management. We also provide a unique set of questionnaires to facilitate the self-assessment of the extent to which a specific family business is positioned for long-term success.

Throughout the book, we examine both successful and unsuccessful family businesses and analyze the lessons that can be derived from each one. All of the unsuccessful companies are disguised unless they are in the public domain.

. . .

The book is organized in four parts. Part I consists of two framework chapters. Chapter 1 defines family business and family business champions and presents a "formula" for family business success that is based on managing what we call "family functionality" and the development of the company's "infrastructure." Chapter 2 provides a framework for understanding and identifying the stages of family business development.

Part II describes the managerial tools needed to manage and develop a family business successfully—strategic planning (chapter 3), organizational structure (chapter 4), performance management (chapter 5), and culture management (chapter 6). We examine each topic from a dual perspective: the technical aspects of the tools and the family business issues involved in their application.

Part III deals with the unique issues facing family businesses. Chapter 7 focuses on the "dark side" or dysfunctional aspects of family businesses. Chapter 8 deals with effective leadership. Chapter 9 presents a process for managing leadership succession.

In chapter 10 we step back from our discussion of individual companies and tools and offer insights and conclusions about what is required to become a family business champion.

The appendix contains a self-scored questionnaire that a family business can use to evaluate the extent to which it has developed the four essential managerial tools—strategic planning, structure, performance management, and culture management.

· · ·

This book makes several significant contributions to the family business literature. First, our overall approach is unique because we focus on what must be done holistically to create a successful family business. Specifically, we deal with the issues of family business from the perspective of the family *and* the business. We provide a framework or template for building family businesses capable of lasting multiple generations. The framework also is helpful in understanding and analyzing family business issues in relation to business issues more broadly.

Second, we make several important conceptual contributions to thinking about family business with constructs such as "family business functionality and dysfunctionality," the "family business foundation," "family business equilibrium," and the "family business success formula." We offer some new analytical frameworks, including six factors that must be managed to achieve a high degree of family functionality and a set of dysfunctional family business syndromes (see chapter 7).

Third, we provide assessment tools that can be used to improve family businesses. In chapter 1, we present two self-scored questionnaires for assessing the two key aspects of the family business success formula: (1) organizational development and (2) family functionality. Using the results of these questionnaires, the family business can identify which "type" it is (chapter 2). Chapter 2 also describes the "conditional stages" of family business development (which are based, in part, on the family business type) that will help leaders understand how to increase their company's effectiveness at the current stage and prepare for the next. The appendix provides methods for assessing the effectiveness of key family business management tools.

Our Unique Perspective

We believe that we offer a virtually unique perspective on family business for several reasons. First, as noted earlier, a large percentage of the companies that our firm, Management Systems (based in Los Angeles, but with global affiliates), has worked with since its founding in 1978 have been family businesses. Second, we are ourselves a family business, albeit first generation. As a husband-and-wife team (with the occasional involvement of other family members), we understand the unique challenges of making a family business work. Third, we have had the rare opportunity to be consultants to one family business, Bell-Carter Foods, for more than twenty years, since 1993.[13] The confidence of the Carter family in bringing us back several times during that period presented an opportunity to conduct longitudinal research in our role as both participant and observer. We are not aware of any other published in-depth study of a family business' development and transfer of leadership from one generation to the next over such an extended period. Our involvement was similar to research by anthropologists who visit tribes or communities over time.

Acknowledgments

While we present a number of case examples throughout this book, four of our clients allowed us to share their stories in more depth. We owe them a special thank you. We thank Jim Goodwin, CEO of Taylor-Dunn, for sharing his company's values and the story of how they were developed. John Manuck, founder and CEO, and his son, Ryan Howley, president, of Techmer PM, are an example of successful family business succession; we thank John, Ryan, and David Turner, managing director of Techmer's Fiber Division, for their time in helping us prepare this case study. Joe Kanfer, CEO, and his daughter, Marcella Kanfer Rolnick, vice chair, of GOJO™ Industries, shared their family business story with us over the course of several interviews. They also provided extensive input on the case study of GOJO™ and on the description of Marcella's transition to her leadership role. We are grateful to both for their time and for allowing us to present their story. A very special thank you goes to the Carter family, whose family business, Bell-Carter Foods, Inc., serves as a case study throughout this book. Both Tim Carter, retired CEO, and his son, Tim T. Carter, spent hours with us telling their family's story.

We have always enjoyed the self-deprecating humor of the Carter family. When asked if they would be willing to serve as a case study for two books we were considering writing—one dealing with successful organizations and the other with troubled or failing companies—Tim replied, "Sure. Which book will we be in?" When we asked Tim T. (now CEO) for permission to include his company as a case study, he said, "Yes, and I hope we will still be in business when it is published!"

One of our favorite stories about Tim and Jud occurred in our early years of working with the company. En route to dinner one evening after a management development session, Jud, who was driving the car everyone referred to as the "Love Boat," stopped for gas and a quick car wash. As the four of us began to go through the car wash, Tim said to Jud, "I hope you've closed your window." At that very second, water began streaming through the window adjacent to Jud's seat, drenching both of the Carter brothers. Tim, in his best straight-man voice, turned to us in the back seat and said simply, "See what I have to deal with?"

Without the Carters' permission to use Bell-Carter as our unifying case, the richness of this book would have been greatly diminished. They are the apotheosis of a functional family and a true family business champion. While not a perfect company—and they would be the first to say so—they are our role model for a successful family business, and a worthy model for any business. We are virtually certain that, after reading this, one of them will ask us, "Who were you talking about in that book?"

Another heartfelt thank you goes to Margo Beth Fleming, our editor at Stanford University Press. This is our second book with Margo, and we have worked well together because she is a consummate professional. When we proposed this book, we knew she had been looking for a book dealing with family business for a number of years, but had not found exactly the right concept. Margo not only trusted us to write the book, but also made important contributions to its development. When Margo went on maternity leave, Geoffrey Burn not only fully embraced the project, but also contributed to it. He was a great partner for the final leg of the book's three-year journey to publication. We were blessed to have these two wonderful editors as our partners in this writing project.

Building Family Business Champions

Part I

Building Family Business Champions

1 A Framework for Building Family Business Champions

Arthur Bell, born in 1888, and his older brother Henry were sons of a California doctor. Both brothers left home to work in a cotton factory at a time when doing so was an opportunity to make a good living. After a few years of this work, Arthur and Henry moved back to California and purchased an olive grove. The year was 1912, and this was the beginning of what would become Bell-Carter Foods—a family business that has grown and thrived for more than 100 years.

Like Bell-Carter, some families succeed in building family businesses that are "sustainably successful" over many generations. Cargill, Mars, Bechtel, Bank Santander, Heineken, Samsung Electronics, and TATA Steel are among the largest and most successful businesses in the world. These are true family business champions. Other families, at some point, sell all or a part of the business to nonfamily members—sometimes remaining active in the business (on the board, in specific management positions, etc.) and sometimes exiting the business entirely. Ford Motor Company, Simon Property Group, Samsung Electronics, Bank Santander, and 99 Cents Only Stores, for example, made the transition from family-held to publicly held, with family members remaining active in the business. Other family businesses last no more than one generation. Like a rock band with one hit song, these companies are a "one-generation wonder."

What are the secrets of those family businesses that grow and thrive over multiple generations to become family business champions? Is there a formula for long-term success? What can be learned from businesses that experience difficulties and last only one generation or decide to sell and exit (sometimes because family members cannot work effectively together)? Do they point to pitfalls that can be avoided?

This chapter provides a framework for understanding the challenges of building family businesses that last for generations. As we shall see, family businesses face all of the challenges and problems that other businesses do, but they also have problems and challenges that are unique to their "species." Here we provide criteria for assessing the extent to which a family business has the systems, processes, structure, and family dynamics needed to ensure its long-term success. We build on this framework throughout the book and explain how it can be used to promote successful family business development and create family business champions.

What Is a Family Business?

The typical perception or stereotype is of a small and unsophisticated company. Small family businesses are sometimes referred to as "mom and pop." However, as we shall see below, this stereotypical archetype is rarely accurate.

It should be noted that no "generally accepted" definition of a family business exists in the literature. For the purposes of this book, we define a family business as any business in which there is an owner, entrepreneur, or founder that employs one or more family members.[1] These other members might be spouses, children, siblings, cousins, parents, in-laws, and others. An organization can begin life as a family business or can evolve into one. Bell-Carter and Simon Property Group are examples of companies that began as family businesses—with brothers (two at Bell-Carter and three at Simon) as the founders. In Bell-Carter's case, the company was a family business from the very beginning, jointly owned by brothers Henry and Arthur Bell. Simon Property Group was founded by Mel Simon, who later invited his younger brothers Herb and Fred to join the firm.

The unique challenge facing a family business can be summed up simply: dealing effectively with family in a business context.[2] This challenge raises a dizzying array of issues, including:

- The role of family members in the business
- The effect of interpersonal conflict among family members as it plays out in day-to-day business activities

- The perception by other employees of favoritism, nepotism, or incompetence of family members
- Discomfort of nonfamily employees in working with, confiding in, criticizing, managing, or challenging the performance or ideas of family members
- Separating family financial needs from business needs
- Financial compensation of family members
- Management and leadership succession among family members
- Differences in motivation and ability across generations
- The complexity of managing a family business as family members come of age across generations
- The perception of "the family" as an entity in the minds of non-family member employees

This list is not exhaustive. Nevertheless, it suggests the added layers of complexity that must be dealt with in managing and growing a family business effectively. Running a family business may not be more complicated than running a giant like General Electric, Microsoft, or Nestlé. However, family-related challenges may explain why so few family businesses achieve the status of giant while continuing to operate as family-owned enterprises.[3] Research indicates that a family that perpetuates its business from generation to generation is rare. One study finds that only 13 percent of family businesses last through the third generation.[4]

The Family Business "Success Formula"

Our focus in this book is how a family business can become a "family business champion"—that is, a family business that operates successfully over multiple (at least two) generations. The question of how to become a "sustainably successful" family business is best answered through a combination of research and the analysis of the actual experience of family businesses. That is the approach we take in this book. Having worked with family businesses since 1978, we have developed our own formula for achieving family business success.

Perhaps not surprisingly, most of the literature on family business success has focused on family characteristics and dynamics (both within and outside the business), and sometimes on the characteristics of the business as it exists apart from the family. One study found that family enterprises that treat the family and the business as a holistic unit have better family results (and similar business results) than enterprises that pay attention only to the business in running their companies.[5]

Our approach to understanding family business success is based on a different perspective. Rather than focus only on the characteristics and attributes of a family business per se, we believe that there are two dimensions of family business success that need to be explicitly recognized and managed: (1) organizational or business development and (2) family functionality. Our approach is supported by our own experience and research on organizational effectiveness, and to some extent by the research of Mark Leenders and Eric Waarts.[6]

The first dimension, organizational development, is defined as the systems, processes, and structure that support effective and efficient operations. The second dimension, family functionality, is defined as the way family members relate to and work with one another within the business—categorized as either "functional" or "dysfunctional." A functional family is one whose dynamics are "healthy" in a social or psychological sense. A dysfunctional family is one whose dynamics are "unhealthy" in a social or psychological sense.

The relationship between these two dimensions (or "family business success factors") and long-term family business success is shown in Figure 1.1

A Framework for Successful Organizational Development

Based on our work and research with organizations of all sizes and types—including family-owned businesses—we have developed a framework for building the "infrastructure" (systems, processes, structure) needed to pro-

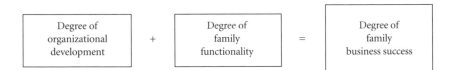

Figure 1.1. "Formula" for Family Business Success

mote long-term success, which we call the Pyramid of Organizational Development (Figure 1.2). This pyramid consists of a "business foundation" and six "building blocks for organizational success."[7]

The Business Foundation

All organizations are built on what we call a "business foundation," which consists of three components: (1) a business concept, (2) a strategic mission, and (3) a core strategy. Like the foundation of a house, this foundation—whether explicit (stated) or implicit (existing only in the mind of the business leader)—is what everything else in the business is built on. We briefly review the three components of the business foundation here (for more detail see chapter 3).

The *business concept* defines the purpose of the business—that is, what the organization is in business to do. For example, McDonald's is in the fast-food business; Disney (a family business) is in the entertainment business; Southwest Airlines is in the transportation business; Starbucks in in the business of providing a "coffee experience" to customers in its stores; and 99 Cents Only Stores (which began as a family business) sells all products for 99 cents.[8]

The *strategic mission* specifies what the company will try to achieve over a defined period of time (typically three to five years, sometimes longer). For example, the strategic mission of Starbucks, developed in 1994, was "to become the leading brand of specialty coffee in North America by the year 2000." Later, once the initial strategic mission was accomplished, the strategic mission became "to be recognized as the leading brand of specialty retail coffee in the world."

The *core strategy* is the central theme around which the company plans to compete to achieve its strategic mission. For Starbucks, the core strategy of its retail business unit was "ubiquity"—to be everywhere. A related aspect of its core strategy (or phase 2 of that strategy) was to become "the Coca Cola of coffee," a virtually ubiquitous lifestyle-based brand.

Six Key Building Blocks of Successful Organizations

Once an organization has identified the nature of its business (either implicitly or explicitly), it needs to develop an infrastructure to support the

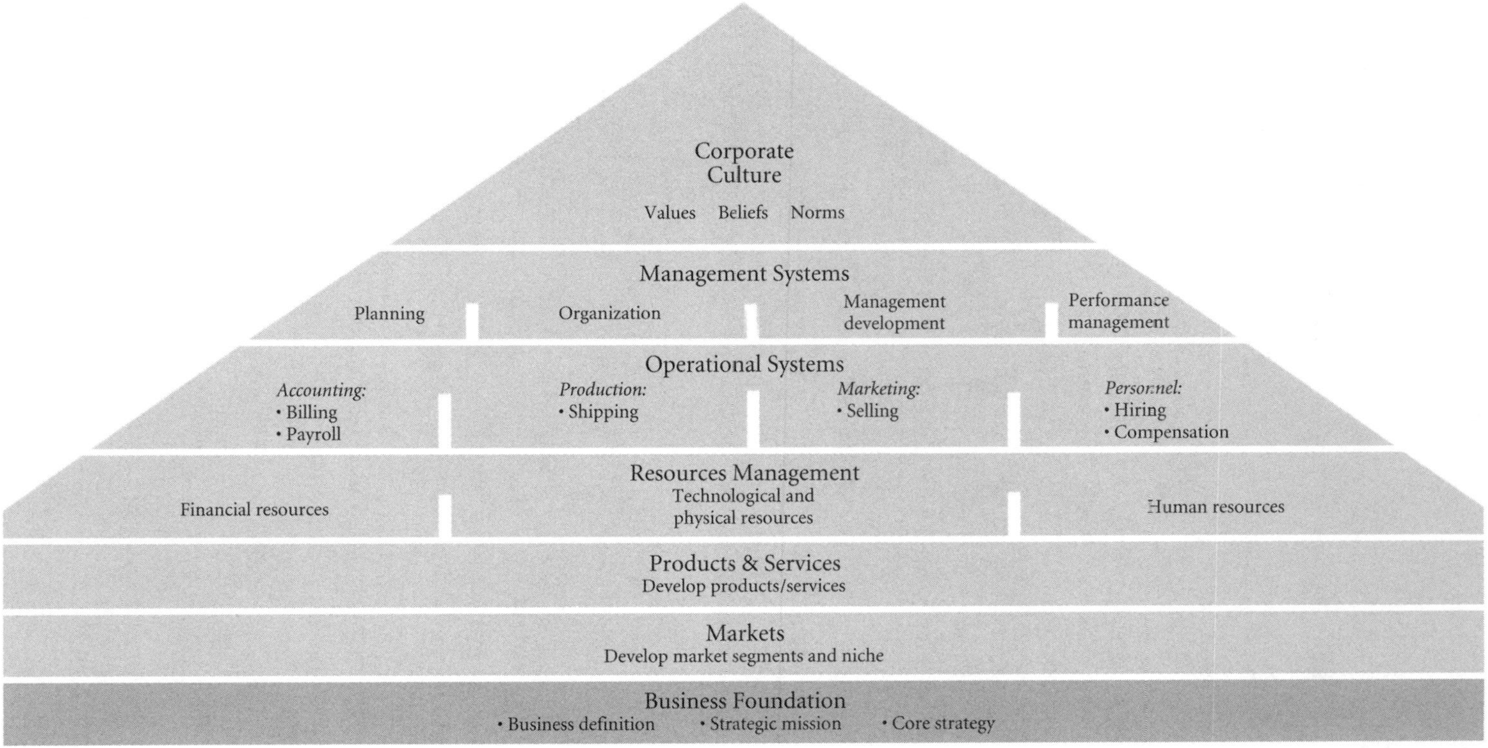

Figure 1.2. Pyramid of Organizational Development

business concept and promote the achievement of the strategic mission. Our research and consulting experience suggest that there are six organizational development factors a company needs to focus on to promote long-term success. These are:

Markets: Identifying present and potential customers that the organization wants to serve and developing an understanding of the needs (and changing needs) of these customers.

Products and Services: Developing products and/or services that will meet targeted customers' needs, monitoring the extent to which products and/or services actually meet customers' needs, and adjusting the product offering based on changes in customers' needs and wants.

Resources: Acquiring and effectively managing the human, physical (facilities, space), technological, and financial resources that the company needs to support its ongoing operations and continued growth.

Operational Systems: Developing, implementing, and working to maximize the effectiveness and efficiency of the processes that the company has in place (e.g., training, communication, product development, production, sales, and marketing) to support day-to-day operations and delivery of products/services to customers.

Management Systems: Developing, implementing, and working to maximize the effectiveness of the systems that the company has in place to support its long-term growth—planning, performance management, leadership development at all levels, and organizational structure.

Corporate Culture: Clearly defining, communicating, and managing the company's values—which trickle down to influence how the other levels of the pyramid function.[9]

These six factors are simultaneously strategic building blocks of organizational success and drivers of financial performance. Empirical research has tested and confirmed that there is a statistically significant relationship between these variables and financial performance, suggesting that the model has predictive validity.[10] For an organization to have the highest probability of long-term success, the six factors need to be designed and managed individually and as an integrated system (that supports the business foundation). Thus the most effective family businesses will have developed and will be effectively managing the pyramid on both a long-term (strategic) and short-term (operational) basis.

Evaluating the Strength of Organizational Development

It is possible to assess or measure the strength of the organizational development of a family business (or for that matter any business). Table 1.1 presents a self-scored tool—the Organizational Development Assessment

Table 1.1. Organizational Development Assessment Questionnaire

Organizational Development Component	A To a very great extent	B To a great extent	C To some extent	D To a slight extent	E To a very slight extent
To what extent is each of these developed?					
1. Business concept			X		
2. Strategic mission			X		
3. Core strategy	X				
4. Market understanding/ strength			X		
5. Products and services		X			
6. Resources			X		
7. Operational systems				X	
8. Management systems		X			
9. Culture management				X	
Scoring					
10. Add up the number of responses in each column.	1	2	4	2	0
11. Multiply the number on line 10 by the number on line 11 and record the result on line 12.	5	4	3	2	1
12. Result of line 10 times line 11.	5	8	12	4	0
13. Add up the numbers on line 12 in columns A–E and place the result on this line.	29				
14. Divide total on line 13 by 9.	3.22				

Questionnaire—that uses a five-point Likert-type scale. We believe that a minimum score of 3.5 is needed to be a sustainably successful company. To be a leading company, the score must exceed 4.0, and to be the industry leader or dominant company (business champion) the score must be greater than 4.5.

The general impression of family businesses is that they are relatively unsophisticated. However, our thirty-five years of data on "organizational growing pains" and fifteen years of data on businesses' "strategic development," including many family businesses, suggest that this impression is false. We have found *no statistically significant difference* between the organizational development strength of family businesses and nonfamily businesses (see Table 1.2). Family businesses are *not* behind the curve and are no less sophisticated than other companies in developing the systems, processes, and structure needed to support current and anticipated future operations.

Family Functionality: Developing and Managing the Family Aspects of Successful Businesses

The second dimension of building a successful family business is the functionality of the family as it exists and operates within the business. We are not suggesting a psychological diagnosis. Rather, this dimension reflects how family members behave and how the family interacts with each other

Table 1.2. Organizational Development Strength in Family and Nonfamily Businesses

	Markets	*Products/ Services*	*Resources*	*Operational Systems*	*Management Systems*	*Culture*	*Financial Results Management*	*Overall*
Family businesses	3.6	3.4	3.5	3.3	3.2	3.2	3.5	3.3
Nonfamily businesses	3.5	3.4	3.3	3.1	3.0	3.1	3.3	3.2

NOTE: The scores in this table are based on results obtained from a validated survey instrument that is used to assess the extent to which an organization has built the systems, processes, and structure needed at each level in the Pyramid of Organizational Development, as well as the extent to which its leadership is effectively managing financial results. Scores are on a five-point Likert scale, where 5 is high ("to a very great extent") and 1 is low ("to a very slight extent"). Although the data collection method differs from that discussed in this chapter, it uses the same scale.

when they are in the business, which is more specific and useful than the general notion of "family dynamics." Unfortunately, most families are unable to separate family dynamics and family issues from their business. The family business becomes just another arena in which family issues are played out.

We have identified six factors that need to be managed to promote a high level of family functionality and support the business's development. These are:

- Treatment of family members
- Treatment of nonfamily members
- Expectations of performance and accountability within the family
- Family rewards and recognition
- Willingness of the family to learn and to change
- Family and company leadership

Although other factors may play a role as well, we believe that these are the most important.

Treatment of Family Members

In functional families, there is a high level of respect for family members that is accompanied by a sense of trust. Communication between family members is open and honest; all members of the family feel valued and appreciated.[11] In dysfunctional families, there may be distrust among family members—sometimes to the point that there is a covert or not-so-covert "civil war" between individual family members or between family factions. If family members do not trust one another, their ability to communicate will suffer. In dysfunctional families, favoritism or preferential treatment may cause some family members to feel devalued. In dysfunctional families, mistreatment of family members is sometimes based on deep resentments that have nothing to do with the business. This "dark side" of family business is discussed in chapter 7.

Treatment of Nonfamily Members

In functional families, nonfamily members are treated in many respects as an extension of the family. Everyone—both family and nonfamily members—

feels valued.[12] In dysfunctional families, nonfamily members are treated as outsiders and as less valued than the family. Nonfamily members may not feel respected and, in the extreme, believe that they are viewed as "expendable." In such organizations, "the family" tends to be viewed as an entity whose wishes trump whatever any nonfamily member says or proposes. In these businesses, the term "the family" clearly suggests that there are two entities in the company: family members and everyone else. Family members are seen to hold a special status in the business.

Expectations of Performance and Accountability within the Family

In functional families, members are expected to fulfill their roles and responsibilities, achieve goals, complete projects and tasks in an effective and timely manner, and behave as if they are working for someone other than their family. In brief, they are expected to behave as professional business people, not as the children, spouses, siblings, in-laws, or other relatives of the founder, owner, or entrepreneur. Family members hold themselves and each other accountable for achieving results, modeling the company culture, and supporting the growth and development of the business.

In dysfunctional families, expectations for performance can differ; that is, some family members may be expected to achieve specific goals, while others do whatever they want regardless of the impact on the business. Other dysfunctional family businesses may give free rein to all family members and not hold them accountable for their behavior or their performance.

Family Rewards and Recognition

In functional families, the focus is on earning rewards based on performance. All family members feel comfortable giving and receiving feedback from one another. Highly functional families recognize individual successes and offer encouragement; they are also willing to listen to, encourage, and provide constructive criticism.[13]

In dysfunctional families, rewards and recognition are based on something other than performance. At the extreme, individuals receive rewards simply because they are members of the family, even if their contributions are limited and sometimes even when they adversely affect the company's performance. In dysfunctional families, there may also be competition between family members for rewards. Feedback in dysfunctional families can be nonexistent, or, if it exists, ineffective. Sometimes, the leader of the family provides feedback in a manner that could be likened to scolding a child. Family members may believe they should be recognized by others simply because they are family members, which leads to dysfunctional competition for "position" (typically for leadership roles).

Willingness of the Family to Learn and Change

In functional families, family members are open to learning from other family members, from nonfamily members, and from outsiders. Functional families strive for personal and business development, and there is a strong focus on continuous improvement.[14]

Dysfunctional families sometimes believe they "know it all" or that others have nothing of real value to contribute conceptually or strategically. Dysfunctional families can be so consumed with their own dynamics that they have no time to focus on learning, improving themselves, or enhancing their company's effectiveness.

Family and Company Leadership

In functional families, the founder, owner, or entrepreneur adopts the role of CEO and treats family members as employees. He or she understands and embraces the fact that roles "on the job" need to be different from those that play out in the home. If the business is fairly large, a team of family or family and nonfamily members may share the company leadership role. In functional families, all family members support those in leadership roles, whether or not they are family members.[15]

In dysfunctional families, the owner or entrepreneur treats family members as special (rather than as "mere" employees), in both positive and not-so-positive ways. Decisions are based on what is best for the leader or the family (or both), rather than what is best for the family *and* the business. Sometimes the leader uses his or her position (somewhat like a Roman emperor) to pit one family member against another in ways that have little to do with the business. In dysfunctional family businesses, the battle for leadership positions can be no less bitter than any war.

The Family Functionality Continuum

Family functionality can be viewed on a continuum. At one extreme are families that are "functional" on all six of the factors we have identified. At the other extreme are families that are "dysfunctional" on all six factors. In between are families that are functional on some, but not all factors. A dysfunctional family can negatively impact organizational success even if the company has developed an appropriate infrastructure. In chapter 7 we will discuss how the failure to manage one or more of the six factors can cause different dysfunctional family business syndromes.

A highly functional family can help to create organizational success even when the company has not developed an appropriate infrastructure. A functional family does not waste time and energy on intrafamily battles; rather, the focus is on getting things done and solving the problems of the business. As Bell-Carter Foods grew, for example, the family's openness to new ideas and willingness to work together to solve problems as they arose helped minimize the not-so-positive impact that its underdeveloped infrastructure could have had on company success. There did come a time, however, when Arthur's grandsons, Tim and Jud Carter (along with their family board) recognized that, as well as the family had managed the company, it had become too large to continue doing "business as usual." As we describe later in this book, they began to build the infrastructure that would take Bell-Carter into the future.

Assessing and Measuring the Degree of Family Functionality

It is possible to assess or measure the degree of family functionality within a family business. The Family Functionality Assessment Questionnaire uses a five-point Likert-type scale to measure family functionality (see Table 1.3). We believe that a minimum score of 3.5 is needed to support successful family business development. A score of 4.0 and above suggests that the family is highly functional, and its functionality could even compensate (up to a point) for an underdeveloped infrastructure.

Table 1.3. Family Functionality Assessment Questionnaire

Family Functionality Component	A *To a very great extent*	B *To a great extent*	C *To some extent*	D *To a slight extent*	E *To a very slight extent*
To what extent is each of these functional?					
1. Treatment of family members			X		
2. Treatment of nonfamily members			X		
3. Expectations of performance and accountability within the family	X				
4. Family rewards and recognition			X		
5. Willingness of the family to learn and change		X			
6. Family and company leadership			X		
Scoring					
7. Add up the number of responses in each column.	1	1	4	0	0
8. Multiply the number on line 7 by the number on line 8 and record the result on line 9.	5	4	3	2	1
9. Result of line 7 times line 8.	5	4	12	0	0
10. Add up the numbers on line 9 in columns A–E and place the result on this line.	21				
11. Divide the score on line 10 by 6.	3.5				

Bringing It All Together: A Two-Dimensional Framework for Building a Successful Family Business

This section brings business development and family functionality—together with what we call the "family business foundation"—into a single framework that can be used to understand, develop, and manage family businesses. This framework provides the perspective for the remainder of this book (see Figure 1.3).

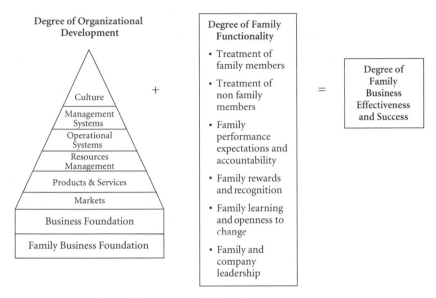

Figure 1.3. Model for Building a Successful Family Business

The Foundation of a Family Business

Think of the family business foundation as a sub-basement—it lies below the business foundation and influences every aspect of the company's business concept, strategic mission, and core strategy. It is the bedrock of the family business. Although it is invisible to the naked eye, the family business foundation affects virtually all behavior in a family business, for better or for worse.

The family business foundation is identical in composition to the business foundation. Each component of a business foundation has a counterpart in the *family* business foundation: (1) the family business concept, (2) the family strategic mission, and (3) the family core strategy. However, their purposes are different. The business foundation and its components are all about the business per se; the *family* business foundation is all about the *role of the business in relation to the family*.

The Family Business Concept

The "family business concept" is the view that the family holds of the business in relation to the family. Some families believe that the business is purely an extension of the family, while others see significant separation between the business and the family. This "family business concept" has profound consequences for the way the business is run. Everyone in the family needs to understand and embrace the same family business concept or it will be a source of conflict and a potential barrier to organizational success. For example, in one retail business listed on the New York Stock Exchange with more than $1 billion in revenues, in which the founding family still held a controlling amount of stock ownership, part of the family viewed the business as a business—separate and distinct from the family—where leadership succession was based on merit. The founder's wife, however, viewed the business as an extension of the family and believed succession should be based on birth order. She believed that the eldest son should be the CEO, regardless of his experience or ability. Understandably, these differing positions led to conflict among family and nonfamily members, particularly when the decision was made (by family vote) that the eldest son would *not* become CEO upon his father's retirement.

The Family Strategic Mission

The "family strategic mission" refers to what the family wants to achieve with the business in relation to the family over a defined time period. The family strategic mission can take many forms. It can reflect the family's desire to grow or strengthen the business or the family's desire to exit the business. It can reflect the desire to transition the business from family management to professional management or the desire to employ a new generation (or generations) of family members. It defines the family's overarching objective with respect to the business.

The Family Core Strategy

The "family core strategy" refers to how the family wants to use the business for the benefit of the family. The key word in the core strategy is "how." *How* will the business serve the family? Some families want to use the business as a cash cow to provide for family members' immediate needs. Others want to invest in the business so that it grows. Just as some businesses do not have core strategies, some families do not have explicit family core strategies.

The Interaction of the Family Business Foundation
with the Business Foundation

In a family business, the business foundation builds on or is influenced by the family business foundation. If, for example, the family views the business as an extension of the family and as a "family piggy bank" (core strategy), this will have a very different impact on the *company's* strategic mission than if the family views the business as quasi-independent of the family. These differences in perspective will affect such things as whether the family chooses to invest in developing the business for the long term. It will also affect decisions about compensation of family members in the business. Some families will "milk" the business, exploiting it for their own personal benefit; others will act as stewards or protectors of the "golden goose." The family business foundation must be explicit so that all can understand the family's perspective about the business. If it is not explicit, the underlying source of any conflict might be invisible.

The Interaction of Family Functionality
with the Pyramid of Organizational Development

How the family manages the six dimensions of family functionality will affect not only the development of the business foundation, but also the *execution* of the six building blocks of organizational success. As mentioned earlier, a high level of family functionality can actually compensate for an underdeveloped infrastructure. For example, highly functional families tend to have a high or even open-ended commitment to their business. Their commitment and tendency to work long hours can help overcome limitations associated with a lack of systems, a key component of infrastructure. One illustration of this is Bell-Carter Foods in the 1980s: the family had a high level of functionality but (at that time) a relatively low level of organizational development.

A low level of family functionality will undermine the organization's ability to implement even a well-developed organizational infrastructure. The business will be just another arena in which to play out family problems. In one reasonably successful family business we worked with, there was an open conflict between two brothers that manifested itself in everything from strategy to decisions about day-to-day operations. Although polite on the surface, there was an underlying tension throughout the organization as these "battling brothers" debated and argued about virtually everything.[16] Their inability to make decisions did not lead to organizational failure, but clearly prevented the company from growing to its potential. As a result, a once smaller competitor was able to surpass the embattled firm and become the dominant force in the industry. The company with the battling brothers could have been a contender for industry leadership, but its dysfunctionality prevented it from reaching its potential.

Table 1.4 shows how family business success factors—family functionality and organizational development—interact. Different combinations of the factors lead to four distinct family business "profiles," which can be used to diagnose the health of a family business.

Building Family Business Champions

How do we know when a family business has the potential to be, or is, a "champion"—that is, is built to be *sustainably* successful? The key operational (empirical) criterion of a family business champion is that it has survived for more than one family leadership generation. Clearly, the greater the number of successful transitions from one generation to another, the greater the evidence that the company is, or is becoming, a champion.

The transition from the founding generation to the next generation is a challenge; but the transition from a second to a third, and then a third to a fourth generation of family leadership is even more complex, and as a result is relatively infrequent. There are relatively few family businesses that have survived for several generations. But one excellent example is Bell-Carter Foods, a family business that has successfully transitioned to the fourth generation of family leadership and has built a family business to last.

The final section of this chapter presents a brief history of Bell-Carter's evolution. We use Bell-Carter to show how our model provides insight into the process of building sustainably successful family businesses. The firm's story (which we continue to tell throughout the remainder of this book) provides an in-depth look at how the company became a true family business champion by managing both the organizational development and family functionality of its business.

Bell-Carter Foods, Inc.: Company Overview

Bell-Carter Foods has had a well-defined business concept and has stayed close to its roots for much of its 100-plus-year history: its primary business is canning and distributing ripe table olives through retailers throughout the United States. The company is the largest table olive producer in the country and the second largest in the world. In its 100-plus-year existence, the company has undergone numerous transitions—both in family leadership and in the business itself. According to Tim Carter, former CEO, not all of the firm's transitions were easy.

Early History: The First and Second Generations

From 1912 until the start of the Great Depression, Arthur and Henry Bell were olive growers in Reedley, California, just south of Fresno. (Growing olives was the company's initial business concept.) They harvested and sold olives to processors in central California. Arthur also worked for Kings County Packing, where he learned how to pack olives. The start of the Depression in 1930 brought with it both problems and opportunity: the brothers found that their customer base had disappeared; but the opportunity was to begin processing the olives themselves. (Thus their business concept changed from growing olives to growing and processing olives.)

Arthur began searching for someplace with a boiler (required for processing the olives) and found one in a dry cleaning company in Berkeley, California. In 1930, the brothers began packing, distributing, and marketing their own olives under the "Bell's" brand. Their chopped olives were used in olive sandwiches (popular at the time) and were the islands in Thousand Island salad dressing. It was also in the 1930s that Arthur Bell worked with the engineering department at the University of California to develop the "pitter-chopper," which removed pits and chopped olives—equipment that became the industry standard.

According to Tim, after the Depression, the two brothers decided to "go their separate ways," with Arthur "getting the plant" and Henry "getting the orchard." The plant became the foundation for the business that Bell-Carter has become—that is, a processor of olives purchased from independent growers (the foundational business concept).

Table 1.4. Family Business Profiles Based on the Interaction of Family Functionality and the Degree of Organizational Development

High Family Functionality, High Organizational Development
• Family members are aligned about the business concept, strategic mission, and core strategy of the business, both for the business itself and in relation to the family.
• Systems are used to track customers' changing needs; the information collected about customer needs is used in the development and delivery of products/services.
• Systems are in place and are effectively used to acquire, allocate, and manage human, technological, physical, and financial resources.
• Day-to-day operational systems are designed to meet company needs and are effectively utilized by management.
• Planning systems are designed and effectively used by management (including family members) to identify where the company needs to go and how it will get there.
• Overall company structure is aligned with company strategy and is built around what is best for the business.
• Leadership development systems (including succession planning) are in place for both family and nonfamily members.
• Performance management systems— including individual performance evaluation systems—focus employees on achieving company goals and reward/recognize individuals for performance against goals.
• Organizational culture supports the development of the business and is well managed.

High Family Functionality, Low Organizational Development
• Family members are aligned about the business concept, strategic mission, and core strategy of the business, both for the business itself and in relation to the family.
• While formal systems are lacking, family and nonfamily members work effectively together to solve problems as they arise.
• Decisions about company growth and development are made based on what is best for the business and for the family.
• Roles and responsibilities may be designed more around people than around what is needed to support the business, but family membership is not a significant consideration when filling roles.
• Planning is informal, but the planning team extends beyond the family.
• There are limited leadership/management development processes in place, but family and nonfamily members have a clear idea about succession.
• Although the performance management system is underdeveloped, family and nonfamily members are held to the same standards of performance and levels of accountability (even though they may be ill-defined).
• Everyone feels a part of the "family" and is willing to work together to support the growth of the business.
• The family's willingness to learn and grow supports the continued development of the company's infrastructure— assuming that the family has the resources (including time) to invest in this process.

Low Family Functionality, High Organizational Development

- Family members are NOT aligned about aspects of the business concept, strategic mission, and core strategy either for the business or in relation to the family.
- Even though there are systems in place to collect and analyze information about customers' needs and then use this information in product development decisions, family members may ignore this information and/or may not be able to reach agreement on what it means.
- While there is a resource management process in place, acquisition, allocation, and investment of resources is based more on position within the family than on what is best for the business.
- Conflict within the family or between the family and nonfamily members undermines the effectiveness of well-developed operational systems. Family members may ignore the systems that are in place and instead do things the way that they want to do them.
- The family as a whole and/or individual members do whatever they want to do, even though there is a well-developed strategic planning process, structure, and performance management system in place.
- Management/leadership development processes are in place, but family members either do not participate in or do not support them.
- The company's culture may be well-defined, managed, and embraced by employees, but there are times when the family as a whole or individual members behave in ways that are inconsistent with stated values.

Low Family Functionality, Low Organizational Development

- Family members are NOT aligned about aspects of the business concept, strategic mission, and core strategy either for the business or in relation to the family.
- Decisions about which customers to pursue and which products/services to offer them are based on the family's and/or family leader's beliefs.
- Conflict between family members and/or between family and nonfamily members impedes the ability to pursue new opportunities as they arise.
- Resource allocation is based on status within the family and on what is best for the family rather than for the business.
- The lack of or underdevelopment of operational systems, combined with a high level of family conflict results in an inability to effectively and efficiently meet customer needs.
- Planning is informal and built around what is best for the family and/or individual family members.
- Roles are ill-defined and are based on status within the family.
- It is difficult to hold both family and nonfamily members accountable due to the lack of performance standards.
- There is no or limited focus on developing the company's management/leadership capabilities, and succession decisions are based on the role within the family rather than on capabilities.
- The dysfunctionality of the family creates a dysfunctional organizational culture. Because people—especially nonfamily members—do not feel valued, there is high turnover.

As Bell-Carter continued to grow and develop, another generation of family entered the business. Daniel Carter, Arthur's stepson, had dropped out of the University of California, Berkeley, and had just started managing a gas station under the umbrella of an entrepreneur named George Hill. This was, according to his son Tim, a "whole new business" at that time that promised to be very lucrative. But when Daniel's mother asked him to help with Arthur's business, in 1938 he left gasoline to focus on building the family olive business.

In 1945, Daniel returned from the Navy and began to take on more responsibilities within the company. Under Daniel's leadership, Bell-Carter expanded the presence of its Bell's brand of olives in grocery stores, delicatessens, and supermarkets. The company also continued to refine its operating systems to increase efficiency. The family "board" (though not called this at the time) consisted of Arthur, Arthur's wife, Daniel, and Daniel's wife. Board meetings were more like family gatherings, although the focus of the meeting was on the business. As he was approaching retirement, Arthur decided that Daniel and his half-sister, Mary, would each own 50 percent of the business, although Mary and her husband, Bill, were not interested in working in the company on a day-to-day basis. The board then consisted of Arthur, Daniel, Daniel's mother, and Mary.

The early years of the California olive industry were dominated by families who had low expectations of profits yet high hopes of living well (the family mission). According to Tim, many companies were operating with a "fly by the seat of your pants" mentality and a belief that each year would simply "take care of itself." Long-range planning focused on "what could be achieved in the next twenty minutes." The reason behind this, according to Tim, was that the management of most companies viewed themselves as "growers" (a business concept). They ran their business from crop to crop instead of taking a future-oriented perspective. They were operating, for the most part, as small, family-owned businesses.

The Third Generation Enters the Business

Daniel's sons, Tim and Jud, had grown up in the business. But Tim did not necessarily want to stay with the family business. Tim says, "I always worked there and hated it. . . . Anything was better than [working in a cannery]."

While Jud continued to work in the business, Tim pursued work outside of Bell-Carter, including selling Kirby vacuum cleaners door-to-door. He discovered that he "really liked sales." During his time away from the family business, Tim also attended San Jose State University. His father advised him that the two most important things to learn in college were "how to spend your time and how to solve problems." This advice would serve him well when he and Jud became Bell-Carter's leaders.

During Tim's first semester at San Jose State, his father, Daniel, contacted him and said, "I've got a problem. You and Jud are the only people who know how to process fruit." So in 1964, Tim returned to the business, where Jud joined him full-time in 1965. Annual revenues at the time were about $1 million. Tim says the family goal (or in our terms the "family strategic mission") was simply to "stay in business." This was supported by shifting the company's business concept from being a "branded" company to being a "private-label" company where the margins were significantly better. Private-label olives are sold under another company's own brand or house names through grocery store chains and are also distributed by food-service companies like Sysco that supply olives to restaurants and industrial customers with their own brand.

The company had several growth opportunities, but its culture did not fully support taking advantage of these opportunities. Everyone in the company operated as "one big family"; family and nonfamily members were treated in a similar manner, and people liked being a part of the Bell-Carter family. (This is a characteristic of a functional family business.) Many also liked things the way they were. Tim and Jud found a number of employees asking: "Wouldn't it be nice to keep the company small?"

Even though some employees were anxious about what growth might mean to them and to the company, the two brothers decided they wanted to grow the firm. To do so, however, they knew that they had to pay attention to building the infrastructure needed to support a larger company (a key aspect of organizational development). In particular, according to Tim, they realized that they needed to invest in those things that would make the company "the most efficient and low-cost producer that we could be." (This is both a strategic mission—what we want to become—and the foundation for a core strategy—how we will compete, by being "the most efficient and low cost producer" in their space.) As a result, they reinvested nearly all the firm's profits in the plant.

The Third Generation Assumes Leadership

By the time Tim and Jud Carter took over day-to-day management of the company from their father in 1973 (with Tim managing the sales and administrative side of the business and Jud focusing on production and on developing and maintaining grower relationships), the company's annual sales had grown to $6 million, with a record profit of $208,000. While the Carters recognized that they had to continue focusing on building production capabilities, they also identified a new opportunity within their market: to become a branded company with the acquisition of the Lindsay brand in 1992. This was an implicit new strategic mission and change in business concept—to transition from a private-label business to a branded *and* private-label business. The brothers turned to creating an infrastructure to support the new business concept.

During their more than thirty years as leaders of Bell-Carter, Jud and Tim demonstrated many of the characteristics of functional families and functional family businesses. They operated as true partners with a high level of respect for each other and for all members of their company team. They treated family and nonfamily members with respect, and people genuinely liked working for and being a part of the company. Turnover was low, and those who did not embrace the company's culture and values (which reflected those of the family) were asked to leave. Family and nonfamily members were held to the same standards of performance accountability for achieving their goals.

There was a strong focus in the company on learning and a desire for continuous improvement that was reflected in, among other things, the two brothers' willingness to solicit ideas and feedback from their team about how to improve their own and the company's effectiveness. Tim and Jud's attention to and active participation in their own development became the basis for ongoing management and leadership development for their entire management team.

The leadership of the company was shared by the two brothers, and while they occasionally had differing opinions about the business and its direction, they effectively resolved conflicts in a way that did not interfere with the company's operations and continued development. Finally, it was not a given at Bell-Carter that Tim's son, Tim T. Carter, would become the next CEO. (Of the four Carter children—Tim's children Christine and Tim T.; and Jud's children Amy and Kevin—Tim T. was the only one involved in the business.) Tim made it very clear that Tim T. would need to earn this position through education within and outside the company and through experience. Tim and Jud Carter did not view the business as purely an extension of the family where positions in the business were an entitlement of family membership. They maintained a healthy separation between the business and the family.

The Fourth Generation Prepares for and Assumes Company Leadership

Tim T. had worked in various capacities at Bell-Carter in his teens and early twenties, had gone to college, and then worked outside of Bell-Carter for several years. He returned to Bell-Carter in a sales management position and worked to complete his MBA.

In 2005, Tim and Jud Carter retired from day-to-day operations and appointed Ken Wienholz, who was not a family member, as CEO. It was understood that Ken would lead the company and serve as a "bridge" between generations of Carters. In 2006, Tim T. left the company for a senior management position at another food-processing company. He left, in part, to gain management experience outside of Bell-Carter, but also because he was having some difficulty making the transition to a senior leadership role within the family business. When Tim T. returned in 2009, Tim, Jud, and the other members of the family's board, with input from Bell-Carter's nonfamily senior leadership team, soon decided that Tim T. would become CEO upon Ken's retirement. In August 2012, the company transitioned to its fourth generation of family leadership when Tim T. became CEO.

Summary

This chapter outlines a unique framework or template for building family business champions capable of lasting multiple generations. Family business champions have:

- established strong business and family business foundations—that is, family members have a high level of agreement about the business they are in, the role the business plays for the family, what they want to achieve with the business, and how they want to achieve it;

- developed the "infrastructure" needed to support current and anticipated future operations (met the challenges of organizational development); and

- a high level of family functionality (family dynamics in the business promote, rather than detract from, effectively managing and growing the company).

The chapter offers two tools for assessing the level of family business success based on its organizational development (the extent to which the company has successfully built and managed the six levels in the Pyramid of Organizational Development) and family functionality. It also provides a typology of family business profiles based on the level (high or low) of organizational development and family functionality. Although some companies, like Bell-Carter Foods during the early stages of its development, are built without explicitly using this template, family businesses of all sizes and types will benefit from its use.

Building on this conceptual foundation, chapter 2 examines the stages of family business development and the nature of the transitions needed to maximize success over the long term.

2 The Evolution of Family Businesses

Bell-Carter Foods is quite different today from the company that Henry and Arthur Bell founded in 1912. Like other successful family businesses, it has evolved and grown through a series of business and family transitions. The first business transition was from being an olive growing company to being both an olive growing and processing company. The first family transition was from being a one company owned by two brothers to being two separate companies with one brother (Henry) owning the olive orchards and the other brother (Arthur) owning the olive processing company. Henry's side of the business went through one more family transition, when his adopted daughter inherited the orchard, converted it to pistachios, and eventually sold it to an outsider. On the processing side, there were several significant business transitions, as well as family transitions as Arthur's son, grandsons, and eventually great-grandson assumed the CEO role of the company that he founded. While these transitions were not always smooth, the family, along with the members of the company's senior leadership team, were able to successfully manage these stages of family business growth.

This chapter describes the nature of family business transitions and presents a life-cycle model of family business growth. The model is intended to serve family business leaders and their advisors by providing a conceptual framework or "road map" for understanding the different stages of family business growth as well as the key issues that are typically encountered at each stage. The chapter is inevitably conceptual, but wherever feasible we illustrate the model with real-life examples. Previous authors have presented alternative models with the same objective; but we believe the model presented in this chapter is superior in its validity and usefulness.

Our approach is consistent with other "life-cycle" models of family business in that it includes both family development and business development dimensions,[1] but our approach is unique both in its definition of these dimensions and in how they are brought together. In other models, the family dimension usually focuses on factors such as age of parents, age of children, family goals, and family roles (including ownership). The business dimension is typically based on the work of organizational life-cycle theorists.[2] Some models treat the two dimensions separately.[3] Others create business types based on linking the stages of organizational growth with the evolution of the family (e.g., first generation, founder-run business owned and managed by the entrepreneur; established business owned by a sibling partnership and experiencing rapid growth).[4]

We believe that the reason it has been so difficult to identify a family business "life cycle" in which the family life cycle exactly matches the stages-of-growth model is that all families evolve differently within the business; there is no predictable pattern for when ownership is transferred to a new generation, when family members are added to the business, what their relationship is to the founder, when the family decides to exit, etc. In addition, while we agree that factors related to family growth and development (marriage, children, transfer to a new generation) are important in a family business, the lack of a pattern to when these events occur makes them difficult to include in a specific, orderly, and predictive model.

Therefore our model of family business evolution and development focuses on identifying the impact that family dynamics—what we call "family functionality"—has on a company's ability to successfully transition from one stage of growth to the next. Our model uses a three-dimensional approach to identifying how family businesses should and do evolve over time. The three dimensions are:

- the company's nominal stage of growth;
- the extent to which the company deals effectively with the challenges presented at that stage of growth and is preparing for the next stage;
- the degree of family functionality.

In our model, we refer to a family business's "conditional stage," which combines family functionality, the level of organizational development, and the stage of business growth and development. This model helps leaders of family businesses understand where they are in their evolution and identify what they need to do or do differently to promote long-term success.

We begin this chapter by describing the family business stages of organizational growth and development. Next we identify the types of family businesses that can exist at any stage of organizational development—based on their degree of functionality and degree of organizational development. Finally, we illustrate what family businesses at each conditional stage might look like.

Stages of Organizational Growth

Organizational life-cycle theorists suggest that all companies pass through a series of stages, with each stage characterized by a different organizational structure or form (what we described in chapter 1 as "infrastructure")— from the founding of the business to the maturity of the business and beyond. The goal of life-cycle models is (or should be) to provide a company's leadership with a road map for the successful development of their businesses; these models should help company leadership understand and plan for the challenges they will face at each stage of development.

Unfortunately, many models are difficult to apply in practice because the definition of each stage (or parameters identifying the stages) is not clear. Some life-cycle models use the relationship between age and form,[5] some use the relationship between size and form,[6] and others use the relationship between form, age, and size to define the stage of growth.[7] However, many models do not adequately operationalize age and size. Most define both age and size in relative terms—with age ranging from "young to mature" and size ranging from "small to large." As a result, the timeline of organizational development remains vague, making it difficult for company leaders to use these approaches in a practical way. Another problem with models that use both age and size is the assumption that, as a company ages, it also grows in size. As is the case in trying to link family development with organizational development, this connection does not reflect what occurs in reality. Many companies that have been in business for twenty years or more have not grown beyond $5 million in revenue, while others, like Wal-Mart (initially a family business), Simon Property Group (a family business), and Starbucks grew into multi-billion-dollar enterprises over the same time period.

Based on our work and research, we have created a life-cycle model of organizational development that clearly defines when each stage of development should typically occur, using revenue as a measurement of size.[8] As in other life-cycle models, success requires meeting specific challenges and goals at each stage. In our model, the areas of focus are one or more levels in the Pyramid of Organizational Development—that is, one or more aspects of the company's infrastructure.[9] The stages of organizational growth in our approach are identified in Table 2.1.

Although the model identifies when each stage should occur, there are exceptions to every rule. In a highly competitive environment, a company may need to pass through the stages more quickly (for example, it may need to develop the infrastructure required at the Consolidation stage even though its revenues are those of an Expansion stage company). When there is no or very limited competition, a company may be able to delay developing a given level of infrastructure.

There is a key nuance worth noting in Table 2.1. We use different revenue ranges to reflect the greater relative complexity of a service company

Table 2.1. Stages of Organizational Growth

		Approximate Size (in $ revenues)	
Stage	Areas of Focus (Levels in the Pyramid)	Manufacturing Company	Service Company
I. New Venture	Markets and products/services	< $1 million	< $.3 million
II. Expansion	Resources and operational systems	$1 to $10 million	$.3 to $3.3 million
III. Professionalization	Management systems	$10 to $100 million	$3.3 to $33 million
IV. Consolidation	Corporate culture	$100 to $500 million	$33 to $167 million
V. Diversification	Markets and products/services	$500 million to $1 billion	$167 million to $333 million
VI. Institutionalization	Resources, operational systems, management systems, culture	$1 billion +	$333 million +
VII. Decline	All levels simultaneously	Any size	Any size

versus a manufacturing company. A service company with no raw materials to be recouped as a part of sales has a relatively more complex operation than a comparably sized company dealing in products.

In this model, the successful progression from one stage to another involves building the Pyramid of Organizational Development from the base up. Stated differently, an organization cannot move from one stage to another until it has successfully met the challenge of the previous stage. Leaders can thus pinpoint where their company stands, as well as the key developmental issue(s) that the company will face at each stage of its growth. For example, a $100 million business that has found a market and has products and services that customers want, but has underdeveloped resources, operational systems, management systems, and culture management processes, is a Stage IV (Consolidation) company with a Stage I (New Venture) infrastructure. When there is a gap between where the company is and where it should be with respect to its infrastructure (given its size), its effectiveness will suffer and it will be at risk.

Unlike many life-cycle models, our model creates a road map for long-term organizational success by providing leaders with information about what to focus on at each stage of development and giving them a preview of the next challenges. Its application helps company leaders understand where they are, what they need to do to improve their company's effectiveness, and what they need to do to plan for and manage the next stage of development.

Identifying Family Business Types

Bringing together the two family business success factors described in chapter 1—organizational development and family functionality—we have identified four types of family businesses that can exist at any one of the six primary stages (excluding Decline, which is a special case) of organizational development. These four types, shown in Table 2.2, build on the family business profiles presented in Table 1.4. However, we now provide names or labels for each family business type: superstar, high-potential, feuding family, and sinking ship.

Superstars are the optimal family businesses; they are strong on both the family and organizational infrastructure development dimensions. Superstar family businesses have the greatest probability of long-term suc-

Table 2.2. The Family Business Typology

Family Functionality	Degree of Organizational Development	
	Low	High
Functional	High-Potentials Functional families with underdeveloped organizational infrastructures	Superstars Functional families with well-developed organizational infrastructures
Dysfunctional	Sinking Ships Dysfunctional families with underdeveloped organizational infrastructures	Feuding Families Dysfunctional families with well-developed organizational infrastructures

cess and of becoming family business champions. Their challenge is to create systems and processes to help ensure that what they are doing right—as a business and as a family—will continue into the future. They also need to develop ways to adapt their strengths to new generations of family members, new generations of employees, and their environments. Bell-Carter is an example of a company that has become a superstar *and* a family business champion. It has had a high level of family functionality throughout its history and has successfully built the infrastructure that it needs—including effective operational systems, a well-developed planning process, a formal leadership development process, a structure that works, a performance management system that focuses employees on company goals, and a well-managed corporate culture. Other family businesses of this type include Simon Property Group and Westfield. It should be pointed out, however, that superstar family businesses do not start out that way. They typically begin as "high-potentials" and become superstars by building the internal organizational capabilities needed to support their size.

High-potentials, as their name implies, have high potential for success as a family business. They are functional as a family but have not developed the business capabilities or infrastructure of a highly effective enterprise. Their challenge is to develop the processes, systems, and structures needed to support effective and efficient operations. They also need to guard against the tendency on the part of the family to believe that it can continue operating as it always has as the business continues to grow. Bell-Carter was a high-potential for the first eighty years of its operation.

By 1994, the company had reached $85 million in revenue (from the $1 million in revenue it had in 1965), having grown into the largest private-label (house brand) olive company, and having acquired (in 1992) the Lindsay brand. CEO Tim Carter (grandson of the founder) and his younger brother, Jud, were jointly managing the business. They, the members of their senior leadership team, and their family board recognized that, as Tim puts it, "We just needed to start managing better." To achieve this goal, the company implemented a more formal strategic planning process, designed and implemented a leadership development program, refined performance management systems, and put a structure in place that would support being both a branded and a private-label business. In the chapters that follow we describe in more detail how Tim, Jud, and their team built the capabilities needed to become a superstar.

Another example of a high-potential was Melvin Simon & Associates up until the late 1980s. The owners of the firm were three brothers—Mel, Herb, and Fred Simon—who were all self-described "deal makers." Their deal-making orientation was aptly captured in the saying at Simon that "The best place in the world to have a heart attack is in our board room, *because no deal ever died on our table!*" The Simons rode the wave of inflation in the United States, not just for years, but for several decades. Even if a shopping center was built at a cost over budget (which most were), inflation would "bail the Simons out" by increasing the value of their property.

Finally, as inflation ended, Melvin Simon & Associates began to experience the accumulated difficulties resulting from their failure to develop the managerial capabilities and infrastructure appropriate for the firm's size and complexity. This was symbolized by an ironic poster on the wall of Herb Simon's office showing the "Manneken Pis" statue that resides in Brussels, along with the words: "Please, Lord, let there be one more real estate boom, and *I promise not to 'piss it away' this time!*"[10] Today, after an organizational development effort and the entry of Mel's son, David Simon, as CEO, Melvin Simon & Associates has become "Simon Property Group" (a NYSE-listed company) and a family business champion.

Feuding families are those in which the family is dysfunctional but the company has developed the business capabilities or infrastructure to support effective and efficient operations. These companies tend to be reasonably successful, but never reach their full business potential because of family dynamics, generally including family feuds. In some cases, the company's infrastructure can compensate for the problems that the family is working through in the context of the business. In other cases, family issues can bring the business to near ruin. The challenge facing these companies is to find ways to manage the dysfunctional aspects of the family and reduce the negative impact of family dynamics on the business.

In one feuding family business, ("Battling Brothers, Inc."), where we were engaged as consultants, the eldest son had served as CEO until the family board decided that his performance was inadequate and replaced him with his younger brother. The younger brother, to his credit, worked with the leadership team—of which his older brother was now a member—to improve the company's operational systems, to implement more formal and size-appropriate management systems, and to develop a formal approach to culture management. Unfortunately, sometimes the older brother undermined the organizational development efforts of his younger brother and the senior leadership team. So, although the company had built the appropriate infrastructure, family dynamics adversely affected its ability to use it.

Sinking ships represent the worst of all possible worlds. Like the proverbial situation in which the ship is sinking and the crew is arguing about the placement of deck chairs and who retains the rights to occupy each chair, these family businesses argue about the wrong things and neglect to build the business infrastructure. In sinking ships, the family is dysfunctional and the business infrastructure is inadequate to support effective operations and long-term development. In the absence of an intervention to decrease family dysfunctionality or to build the necessary infrastructure, or both, these companies are sold or they fail.

Sinking ship–type family businesses are usually small—with under $100 million in revenue—but it is possible for a sinking ship to grow quite large if the company has a unique product or service or some other advantage. For example, we were engaged as consultants to help build organizational infrastructure by a food-processing company that had been founded by a talented individual; in our work with the firm, we also encountered a highly dysfunctional family. The products offered by the firm were well received and money flowed into the business. Over time, the founder was joined in the firm by several other family members, including his father, mother, and siblings. The founder was a visionary, but not interested in organizational development. His brother, who appeared to us to be the only mature and possibly sane individual in the family, engaged us to help build organizational infrastructure and convince his brother of the need for change. Their father seemed to be a lunatic, who (perhaps worried about the possible loss of his meal ticket) actually threatened to "punch out" one of the authors in a consulting meeting, for no obvious reason other than our attempt to help the founder become a better manager. The author calmly responded: "Go ahead and do it and I will punch you back and then sue you!" The young founder and CEO sat there through this encounter with a bemused look on his face and said nothing, as though this was "normal" behavior.

Dysfunctional family dynamics were an ongoing issue in this firm, and family drama of a variety of kinds was played out almost daily. Although the continued success of the core product masked the internal strife and limitations of the infrastructure, the firm's internal problems contributed to its inability to grow beyond about $150 million in revenue; it was ultimately sold.

The Continuum of Family Business Types

Although Table 2.2 shows four pure types of family businesses, the reality is that family business development takes place on a continuum—ranging from low to high organizational development and low to high family functionality. This means, for example, that a family business with a moderate degree of organizational development and a high level of family functionality is somewhere between being a high-potential and a superstar. A family business with a low degree of family functionality and medium organizational development is between a sinking ship and a feuding family on the continuum.

It should be noted that, as a family business grows, it can transition from one type to another, in a positive or not-so-positive manner. This transition can be the result of many factors, including leadership change from one generation to the next or from family to nonfamily leadership; or the development of more effective systems and processes. The good news is that where a company stands now is not a verdict, but an indicator. No matter where a company falls on the continuum, there are steps that it can take to promote long-term success.

The strategy a company adopts to maximize success will depend on the type of family business it is. A superstar, for example, will focus on continuing to do what the company and family are already doing; a feuding family will need to improve family functionality. It is important to identify precisely where a family business is in order to determine what needs to be done to further develop the business and position it for success.

Identifying the Current Family Business Type

The results of the two short questionnaires presented in chapter 1—Organizational Development (Table 1.1) and Degree of Family Functionality (Table 1.3)—will identify the family business type of any company. For example, a company with an organizational development score of 4.0+ and a family functionality score of 4.0+ is a superstar. A company with an organizational development score lower than 3.0 and a family functionality score lower than 3.0 is a sinking ship (see Table 2.3).

Knowing how effective it currently is as a company allows the family and nonfamily members of the management team to begin focusing on the areas that need improvement. This information also provides the basis for developing a strategic plan for the enterprise (as we discuss in chapter 3).

Table 2.3. Identifying the Family Business Type

Family Functionality	Degree of Organizational Development	
	Low	High
Functional	High-Potentials Organizational development score = < 3.0 Family functionality score = > 4.0	Superstars Organizational development score = > 4.0 Family functionality score = > 4.0
Dysfunctional	Sinking Ships Organizational development score = < 3.0 Family functionality score = < 3.0	Feuding Families Organizational development score = > 4.0 Family functionality score = < 3.0

The Conditional Stages of Family Business Development

By bringing together the family business type and the stages of organizational growth, we create a model that identifies "conditional stages" of family business development. At each stage of organizational growth identified earlier in this chapter, the family business can be a superstar, a high-potential, a feuding family, or a sinking ship (see Figure 2.1).

Identifying the conditional stage of the family business can help leaders understand what they should address in order to become more effective; one can think of this as the overarching mission of the family business at that conditional stage. Leaders can then develop a plan to meet the challenges at the next stage. We discuss the conditional stages of growth and the overarching mission of each stage in the sections that follow.

New Venture Conditional Stages

All family businesses face the same challenges and have the same mission at the New Venture stage: they must prove that they should exist as a business. The key issues at this stage are finding a viable market and developing products and services that will meet the needs of the customers that make up this market. In 1986, Bryan Maxwell and his future wife, Jennifer, along with Mike McCollum, a colleague, found an unmet market—athletes who needed additional energy to compete at a high level—and developed a product, Power-Bar, to meet this need. In 1912, olive growers Arthur and Henry Bell provided olives to processers who needed them. In 1913, Will Rehrig, founder of Rehrig Pacific, identified a market for reusable wooden crates. Today, Rehrig Pacific is the industry and market share leader in North America making rotationally molded plastic containers for commercial waste, food waste, and recyclables.[11]

Stage of Organizational Growth:		Family Business Type:		Conditional Stage of Family Business Development
I. New Venture		Superstar		
II. Expansion		High-Potential		
III. Professionalization	+	Feuding Family	=	
IV. Consolidation		Sinking Ship		
V. Diversification				
VI. Institutionalization				
VII. Decline				

Figure 2.1. Identifying the Conditional Stage of a Family Business

At this stage, there are few true superstars or feuding families because most very small companies do not have the resources (including management time) to invest in formal market research (to understand customer needs) and product development and distribution systems. Most New Ventures are more likely to "fly by the seat of their pants" either as high-potentials or sinking ships. At this stage, superstars and high-potentials have family members with a high level of agreement about the family and business concept—that is, they agree about who they are and what they want to achieve. Family members also work together to demonstrate that their business concept is viable. In feuding families and sinking ships, family members sometimes have dramatically different views of what business they are in and might work at cross-purposes.

A New Venture that is a sinking ship may or may not survive beyond this stage. If the company finds a relatively open market—that is, one with limited or no competition—it may survive in spite of the battles between family members and the company's lack of infrastructure. The company may increase its revenues beyond the New Venture stage, but its negative family dynamics may prevent it from growing further. A company in this position needs to focus on significantly improving the family's functionality if it wants to survive.

One company we worked with that had difficulty as a New Venture because of dysfunctional family dynamics was a relatively small architectural consulting firm in a niche market, with a husband and wife as equal partners. Although both were intelligent and well trained, they frequently clashed over project designs. This, in turn, led to difficulties in the execution of designs and cost overruns. The company survived to the Expansion stage, but the same difficulties intensified and the partners eventually sold the company. We revisit this example in more depth in chapter 7.

The most significant determinants of whether a family business will successfully transition to the next stage of development are the market's (the customers') acceptance of and the family's agreement on the company's business concept. If customers are actively purchasing the company's products or services and the family has at least marginal agreement about what they want to achieve, the business will begin to grow and will need to transition to the Expansion stage.

Expansion Conditional Stages

At the Expansion stage, there needs to be a focus on acquiring additional resources and on developing operational systems to support the company's continued growth. The need for more human resources can lead to bringing additional family members into the business (although this can happen at any stage) and to the hiring of nonfamily members in higher-level management/leadership positions (where they participate in making decisions about the strategic development of the business).

Bell-Carter Foods entered the Expansion stage at around $1 million in revenue, when its resources—especially human resources—were being stretched thin. In fact, one reason Tim Carter (grandson of the founder) rejoined the business after pursuing other types of work was because he and his brother, Jud, had the expertise that the company needed to process fruit.

When Tim and Jud joined the business in 1964, the company was not failing, but according to Tim, "We weren't making any money. Our goal in the 1960s and 1970s was to stay in business and do what we do better." This included continuing the family's practice of investing in operational systems as a way of increasing efficiency and reducing costs. The company also continued acquiring the resources needed to support its growth.

In 1978, the company purchased an olive-packing plant in Corning, California, that it renovated and made fully operational in 1980. In 1979, it acquired new administrative offices in Lafayette, California, where it remains today. Jud moved to Corning to oversee the production and grower sides of the business; while Tim was based in the Lafayette office, where sales, marketing, finance, and other company administrative functions were housed. In 1990, Bell-Carter acquired the operating assets of Olives, Inc. This acquisition enabled the company to increase its annual production capacity by 10,000 tons. In addition, the company added state-of-the-art equipment and processes to its plant to continue its movement toward low-cost production—a key to success in a highly competitive market.

Bell-Carter is an example of an Expansion superstar family business—where the strategic mission is to scale up by acquiring resources (people, plant, equipment, and, in their case, raw product) and developing the operational systems needed to support the growing business (and, in their case, the strategic mission of becoming a low-cost producer). In Expansion superstars like Bell-Carter, the family is willing to make investments in the business to support its growth. They have a long-term focus on company development because they want their business to survive for many generations.

If new family members are added to the team in the Expansion superstar stage, existing family members will take care to help them understand how the family does business. If one or more nonfamily members are hired into key leadership positions, their roles, responsibilities, and performance expectations will be clearly spelled out. The willingness to change and learn—part of having a high level of family functionality—is an important asset at this stage as old and more informal ways of operating are replaced with more formal operational systems. Over the years at Bell-Carter, for example, family company leaders and the board have been willing to try new things and invest to support the growth of the business.

In Expansion high-potential family businesses, leadership should now be focused on acquiring resources (including people) and on developing day-to-day operational systems (because the company is growing); but their attention is being diverted by customer and product/service challenges and problems (because the systems needed to understand customer needs and to efficiently deliver products/services to meet these needs are underdeveloped). A high level of family functionality might help compensate for an underdeveloped infrastructure as family members work long hours and do whatever is necessary to sustain the business. Over time, however, family members may burn out, or the lack of infrastructure may contribute to a decline in family functionality.

Like Expansion superstars, Expansion feuding families have well-developed systems and processes to help them understand their market and deliver products and services to meet customer needs. They are focused on acquiring the resources and developing the day-to-day systems needed to support their growth. Unfortunately, conflict among family members over the family business concept, how they are treated, or who receives which rewards has a negative impact on the company's ability to scale up. Family members may not agree about which systems or resources are needed or may avoid using new systems because they have always done things a certain way. If new family members join the business at this stage, they may increase the family's functionality (because they bring with them new skills, ideas, and ways of working) or decrease it (because they help to reinforce the not-so-positive ways of operating).

A family firm of this type was a distribution company led by two brothers who could hardly agree on anything—except that each one had a brother who was "stupid and foolish." The primary source of conflict was their different tolerance for risk: one brother wanted to invest in aggressive expansion and the other wanted to move more slowly. Their different approaches ultimately led one brother (the one with an aggressive risk-taking orientation) to buy out the other. After the buyout, the risk-taking brother was able to build the business to a very large and successful level.

Expansion sinking ships have a double problem: their infrastructure is underdeveloped for their size, and their family dynamics are dysfunctional. The company has grown in spite of itself. Although the leadership should be focusing on acquiring resources and developing operational systems to support company growth, they are dealing instead with family, customer, and product or service issues. Existing resources are being strained by growth and new resources (including new family members) that are acquired informally. Any new operational systems that are put in place may be ignored by family members who want to continue doing things "the old way."

A summary of the overarching missions for family businesses of each type in the Expansion stage is presented below.

Superstar: Scale up the family business.

High-Potential: Solve customer- and product/service-related problems and begin to scale up.

Feuding Family: Minimize the negative impact that family functionality is having on the company's ability to scale up.

Sinking Ship: Solve customer- and product/service-related problems and improve family functionality.

If a family business continues to grow, it will reach a point where it needs more sophisticated systems to support its continued long-term development; that is, it will need to transition to the Professionalization stage.

Professionalization Conditional Stages

The need to professionalize can occur slowly over many years or very quickly, through growth of the existing business or through acquisitions—as happened at Bell-Carter in the early 1990s.

In September 1992, Lindsay Olive Company, a well-known brand in the United States, came up for sale. At one time, Lindsay had a 40 percent share of the branded olive market. However, since the early 1980s, that share had been dropping, partly attributable to a lack of advertising. By 1992 Lindsay was essentially bankrupt. The company was in negotiations with one of Bell-Carter's competitors, but at the last minute those negotiations fell through. The processing facility owned by Lindsay was not what interested the Carters because they had capacity at their existing plant; they wanted Lindsay's olive inventory and grower base to help meet market demand. The Carters made an offer and within a week became the owners of not only additional inventory, but also the Lindsay brand.

The acquisition of Lindsay nearly doubled Bell-Carter's annual revenue in the period of about a year: According to Tim Carter, the firm's revenues at the time of the Lindsay acquisition in 1992 were $53 million; a year later they had grown to $85 million. Tim says, "We now needed to put processes in place and not just come to work and do things. We needed to move from activity-focused to results-focused." Bell-Carter had entered the professionalization stage and had done so as a superstar.

The overarching mission of a Professionalization superstar is to fully "professionalize" the business by implementing the management systems and developing the managerial capabilities needed to support longer-term growth and development. The planning process for both the business and the family needs to become formal and systematic. Roles, responsibilities, and reporting relationships for both family and nonfamily members need to be formalized, effectively communicated, and reinforced. A formal performance management system needs to be put in place, and the family may need to revisit and refine the structure of its own and the company's reward and recognition systems.

At this stage, there may be nonfamily members in key leadership roles. It will be important to focus on ensuring that both family and nonfamily managers/leaders have the capabilities to effectively execute their roles. Depending upon the growth rate of the company, the founder may be planning for or executing his or her succession as the company's leader.[12]

For Professionalization high-potentials, the overall mission can be stated simply as "get our house in order." The lack or underdevelopment of critical systems is putting the company at risk. The focus at this stage is on working to better align the company's infrastructure with its size. Even though the family—whose membership in the business may have grown since the company's founding—is highly functional, the positive impact of their ability to work effectively together is no longer sufficient to compensate for the lack of formal systems to manage the business. In the face of these challenges, the family may also be dealing with leadership succession (both family and nonfamily), as well as, in some cases, exploring the possibility of selling the company (even though a sale at this point might not be best, given the current state of the company's operations).

The leaders of Professionalization feuding families face the challenge of "managing" the impact of dysfunctional family dynamics on the company's ability to: (1) effectively use the formal systems, processes, and structure that have been put in place to manage day-to-day operations; and (2) build the management systems needed for continued growth. Sometimes, the well-developed infrastructure of this stage can be used to overcome problems with family dynamics. For example, if the family and leadership team (which is likely to comprise both family and nonfamily members) can agree that they will adopt and use formal strategic planning and performance management systems and hold each other accountable for doing so, the impact of family dynamics on the business can be minimized.

Additional problems can emerge as the family begins considering who should succeed the founder—especially if there is unhealthy competition between younger family members who consider themselves (and want to be perceived as) the "heir apparent." If family dynamics are extremely dysfunctional, some or all of the family might consider selling the firm to an outsider, selling to a subset of the family, or bringing in a team of professional managers to run the business.

Professionalization sinking ships must simultaneously focus on getting their house in order (from an infrastructure perspective) and managing negative family dynamics. Companies at this stage experience a variety of problems—both externally and internally—including delays in deliveries to customers, understaffing, ineffective operational systems, and family fighting over the company's business concept, strategic mission, and succession. An underdeveloped infrastructure and a dysfunctional family put a company at this stage at significant risk. Sometimes, the only resolution is the exit of all or a portion of the family through the sale of the business or the entrance of strong professional managers to run the business without family involvement.

In our consulting practice, we have worked with several dysfunctional families that were unable to achieve the required degree of professionalization because of internal family strife. The solution arrived at by the family, in some cases, was typically to sell the firm to avoid further damage to family relationships. However, we have also served as facilitators (or peacemakers) to help the family reach a more functional state, without the need for a sale of the company For example, in one distribution business, we proposed that the company be reorganized into separate divisions to give each of two brothers his own "playground." This recommendation was accepted, and solved most of the problems.

The overarching missions for family businesses of each type at the Professionalization stage are listed here:

Superstar: Transition to a professionally managed company—that is, one with formal management systems.

High-Potential: Build the infrastructure—including systems to acquire needed resources, manage day-to-day operations, and support the company's long-term development.

Feuding Family: Minimize the negative impact that family functionality is having on the company's ability to develop and implement the management systems needed to support continued growth.

Sinking Ship: Build the operational and management infrastructure needed support the current business, while improving family functionality.

It took about three years for Bell-Carter to develop and fully implement the management systems needed to support the company's continued growth (that is, to meet the challenges of the Professionalization stage). By 1997, the leadership team was holding quarterly meetings to review progress against strategic planning goals and the company was moving to implement departmental plans. The individual performance management system was redesigned to better focus all employees on working to achieve company goals. Managers at all levels had participated in Bell-Carter's formal in-house leadership development program (which we designed and delivered) to improve their skills. Formal role descriptions for all positions in the company had been developed, and the leadership team regularly assessed and made structural changes to better support the achievement of goals.

If a family business successfully meets the challenges of the Professionalization stage (as Bell-Carter did), it will be positioned to move into the Consolidation stage.

Consolidation Conditional Stages

From a business perspective, the focus for Consolidation superstars is on developing formal mechanisms to help all employees understand, embrace, and behave in ways consistent with company values (because the company has become so large that this can no longer be done informally through interactions with family and nonfamily company leaders). At this stage, a high level of family functionality becomes a tremendous asset because the family members serve as positive role models of the company culture: they model how employees are treated, what people are held accountable for, what people are rewarded for, and openness to change. There may already have been at least one leadership transition (as there was in 1996 at Bell-Carter when the third generation was leading the company). For Consolidation superstars, these leadership transitions tend to be well managed and completed with little conflict.

Bell-Carter's culture, which strongly reflects the family's culture, has always been a key strength and continued to be an asset well into the third decade of Tim and Jud Carter's tenure as leaders. The company did not have a formal statement of its culture, but it was clear that everyone understood what the culture should be and that most people operated in ways that were consistent with the family's core values. Beginning in 1996, however, the company's leadership decided that it was time to begin communicating and managing Bell-Carter's culture more formally, so that it would continue to be an asset. The culture management process Bell-Carter adopted is described in chapter 6.

Consolidation high-potentials have not yet developed the systems needed to effectively support day-to-day operations or the company's long-term development, or both. They have grown to a size that requires them to create systems to manage the company's culture—a much more complex infrastructure issue. The overarching mission of family businesses at this stage is to close any infrastructure gaps, while devoting at least some attention to managing the company's culture. The family's high level of functionality helps foster a positive culture and work environment—that is, it has a positive impact on the company's culture. However, the company has become so large that it is no longer possible for leaders to communicate and reinforce the company culture to each employee through face-to-face interaction. And the underdevelopment of other aspects of the company's infrastructure is putting it at risk.

Consolidation feuding family businesses have developed the infrastructure to support current and anticipated company operations, but the lack of family functionality may be adversely affecting their ability to use those systems effectively. For example, even if a company has well-developed planning and performance management systems in place, family members may ignore them. The overarching mission at this stage is to minimize the negative impact of family dynamics on the company's culture, which involves changing (sometimes dramatically) the company's existing culture. The "new" culture then needs to be communicated to all employees, reinforced (through, among other mechanisms, role modeling by family members), and managed. (Culture management in family businesses is examined in chapter 6.)

For Consolidation sinking ships, there is both good and bad news. The bad news is that the lack of infrastructure undermines the company's ability to compete effectively, given its size. The good news is that the business has become large enough that certain family and nonfamily members can act as buffers to protect parts of the organization from the negative impact of the family's dysfunctionality. The overarching mission of businesses at this stage is threefold: (1) close infrastructure gaps (typically at the operational and management systems levels); (2) change the existing culture—which is a reflection of the family's not-so-positive dynamics—so that it supports effective current operations and continued growth; and (3) develop formal processes to manage the company's culture. The family, which may have grown in number of members employed in the business and may have experienced one or more leadership successions, will need to be fully engaged in this effort. If they are not, the business will be at significant risk. In chapter 7 we describe one company that failed at this stage of development when it experienced "The King or Queen of the Hill Syndrome."

The overarching missions for family businesses at the Consolidation stage are listed here:

Superstar:	"Stay the course." Effectively manage all levels in the Pyramid of Organizational Development, while maintaining family functionality.
High-Potential:	Build the organizational infrastructure—including culture management systems—needed to support the company's current and anticipated future size.
Feuding Family:	Minimize the negative impact of family functionality on the company's culture.
Sinking Ship:	Build the organizational infrastructure needed to support the company's current and anticipated future size, while improving family functionality.

The Consolidation stage is the last stage in building a successful single product/service-line business. The move into the next stage of growth involves entering a new market (targeting new customers) or developing and offering new products and/or services. While the move to the Diversification stage typically occurs at around $500 million in revenue for manufacturing companies and $167 million for service companies, it can occur much earlier—even when a company has not yet completed the infrastructure development needed to support its original business.

Diversification Conditional Stages

Diversification superstars are effectively and efficiently providing target customers with products/services that meet their needs based on the initial concept of the business. However, for the family business to continue grow-ing, it needs to identify and successfully enter new markets or develop and offer new products or services, or both. The need to transition to this stage began for Bell-Carter in the late 1990s.

By 1997, the olive industry had consolidated to two companies—Musco and Bell-Carter. In order to continue growing, Bell-Carter would need to diversify. The company had already done so in 1985 by purchasing a small packaging business in Modesto, California, with the intent of using it to, as Tim Carter puts it, "deliver our olives." With the help of one of the com-pany's outside advisors, Bell-Carter identified a pickle company in Spring-field, Missouri, as a possible acquisition. According to Tim, the deal "looked good," and so in 2002, Bell-Carter entered the pickle business.

The overarching mission of Diversification superstars is to identify and successfully pursue new product and/or market opportunities. The high level of family functionality present in Diversification superstars—particularly the willingness to change—is a significant asset in meeting the challenges of this stage.

There are two parts to the overarching mission for Diversification high-potentials: (1) close the gaps between the infrastructure that the company has and the infrastructure that the company needs to support its existing business; and (2) identify and pursue one or more new business oppor-tunities. High-potentials at this stage are not serving their customers as effectively or efficiently as they should be and are faced with the need to diversify because the market for existing products or services is becoming saturated. The high level of family functionality is an asset in addressing these challenges, but in the absence of an intense focus on infrastructure development, the business is at serious risk. Implementing a formal stra-tegic planning process (described in chapter 3)—including a systematic assessment of current market conditions and the company's internal capa-bilities—will increase the probability that the company will meet its chal-lenges at this stage.

Like Diversification superstars, Diversification feuding families have built the infrastructure they need to support current operations, have been suc-cessful in their existing markets, and are now facing the need to diversify be-cause their market is becoming saturated. The company has a well-established infrastructure but is experiencing problems because of the family's low level of functionality. Family dysfunctionality reduces the effectiveness of specific internal systems and processes. In addition, the company may experience difficulty and delays in its efforts to diversify because the family cannot agree on which opportunities to pursue. The overarching mission of Diversification feuding families, then, is to address family functionality issues as the company works to identify new business opportunities. One valuable tool in this effort is strategic planning, which includes an assessment of possible new markets as well as a family business plan that incorporates the family's "new business concept" and strategic mission.

As is true for Consolidation sinking ships, there is both good news and bad news for Diversification sinking ships. The bad news is that the company's infrastructure is significantly underdeveloped, making it difficult to meet customers' needs and take advantage of new business opportunities. The good news is that the company is now large enough (in most cases) that at least some of the dysfunctional family dynamics can be "hidden" from many company employees (although dysfunctionality still has a negative impact on the company's performance).

The overarching mission for Diversification sinking ships is a challenging one because it involves undertaking three different, yet related tasks at the same time: (1) developing appropriate internal systems and processes to support the existing business; (2) identifying new markets and/or new products and services to promote the company's continued growth; and (3) managing the impact of family dynamics on the business. Implementing effective business and family planning are the keys to success at this stage. However, the classic solution for organizations of this type is a sale because the problems are usually too difficult to resolve.

The overarching missions for family businesses at the Diversification stage are listed here:

Superstar: Identify and successfully pursue new business opportunities (beyond the original business).

High-Potential: Build the organizational infrastructure needed to support the existing business, while identifying and pursuing new business opportunities.

Feuding Family: Minimize the negative impact of family functionality on the company's ability to pursue new business opportunities.

Sinking Ship: Build the organizational infrastructure needed to support the original business and address family functionality issues that are adversely affecting the company's ability to pursue new business opportunities.

If a company successfully expands beyond its original market and/or products and services, as Bell-Carter did by acquiring both a packaging and a pickle company, the next challenge is to build the infrastructure needed to support the operations and development of a multi-market and/ or multi-product/service business.

Institutionalization Conditional Stages

Even when a company has successfully expanded into new products or markets, the challenges at the Institutionalization stage can be significant, as they were for Bell-Carter (which entered this stage as a superstar).[13]

Bell-Carter's acquisition of the pickle company in Springfield, Missouri, in 2002 proved to be a distraction for its senior leadership team. Among the biggest challenges was finding the right person—someone who fit with Bell-Carter's culture and who would embrace how they did things—to run the pickle company (which was a completely different business). When problems arose at the pickle plant, a member of Bell-Carter's senior leadership team would intervene; for example, Ken Wienholz, Bell-Carter's COO, would travel to Springfield to work with pickle company employees in addressing sales, production, and marketing issues. According to Tim, the pickle business was taking too much of the executive team's time. From Tim: "[When] we lost a significant opportunity in the olive business . . . we decided that the pickle business needed to stand on its own."

The pickle business, while not failing, was also not growing, and the business was putting a strain on Bell-Carter's leadership team. Tim says of this time, "I said that I'd stay in the business until I was no longer having fun. Well, I [was] not having fun." The manager of the pickle business was asked to develop a plan to improve the company's performance. After the plan was presented, according to Tim, he and Jud walked out of the room and said to each other, "We should sell it," which they did in 2007.

Although Bell-Carter left the pickle business, its packaging business (acquired in 1985) has continued to grow profitably—at first very slowly, and then more rapidly. The packaging company now provides services to several other companies, not just Bell-Carter.

The development of Bell-Carter's packaging company is an example of an Institutionalization superstar, while Bell-Carter's entrance and then exit from the pickle business is an example of an Institutionalization high-potential. Based on the lessons learned from these diversification efforts, Bell-Carter is continuing its entrance into new products—through both acquisitions and internal development—now under the leadership of Tim T. Carter, Arthur's great-grandson.

The Institutionalization superstar is a well-established, successful family business that operates in several different markets and/or provides several different types of products or services (in Bell-Carter's case, private-label and branded olives and packaging). At this point in the company's life, it has probably adopted some type of divisional structure—that is, the company has several separate business units (at Bell-Carter, there is the olive company and the packaging company). Family members might lead or work in specific business units or be in corporate leadership positions, or both. The overarching mission of family businesses at this stage is to create the infrastructure—resource acquisition/management systems, operational systems, management systems, and culture management systems—needed to support the continued development and integration of all business units within the company. The high level of family functionality will be an asset as the company's leadership works to implement the new systems and processes of this more complex enterprise.

Although an Institutionalization high-potential firm has at least nominally diversified beyond its original business, the company does not yet have the infrastructure needed to support its original business and may be struggling to execute its diversification plan. The overarching mission of a family business at this stage is to build and manage systems and processes to support: (1) the operations of the original business; (2) diversification efforts; and (3) the management and integration of the new "businesses" created through the company's diversification efforts. As is true for businesses at the other high-potential conditional stage, the ability to achieve this mission will be enhanced by the family's high level of functionality.

Bell-Carter struggled to find the right person to manage the pickle business, and that business was also hampered by an underdeveloped infrastructure. Company leaders were spending so much time on the pickle business that the original business began to suffer. When this happened, the family decided that the pickle company acquisition was not going to work and sold it before it could harm the core business. That strategy is an option for high-potentials if the development of the systems needed to manage the new business is proving to be too costly.

For Institutionalization feuding families the challenge is to manage the negative impact that family dynamics is having on the company's ability to use the systems and processes that are in place to support the operations of the original business and continued diversification efforts; and build the infrastructure needed to manage and integrate the "old" and "new" businesses. If, for example, family members occupy key leadership positions in different business units (created as a part of the company's diversification), they may overtly or covertly compete for resources instead of working together to identify the best resource allocation strategies for the company as a whole. The overarching mission at this stage is to raise the level of family functionality. One option for achieving this goal is for all or part of the family to exit the business because the company has reached a size where the return to the family from such a sale could be quite high (particularly because the company has a strong infrastructure).

The challenges facing an Institutionalization sinking ship are daunting, to say the least. The company has moved beyond its original concept into new businesses, but has not yet solved all of the infrastructure problems of the original business. The company now faces the need to build a more complex infrastructure that can support the diversified (typically multi-divisional) business that it has become. In addition, dysfunctional family dynamics are adversely affecting the company's ability to develop and implement the needed infrastructure. Survival as a family business will depend on the family's willingness to fully support organizational development efforts and find ways to deal with family dynamics outside the business environment. Although one alternative is to sell all or part of the business, unless the company operates as a relative monopoly, the return to the family from such a sale may not be very high because there will be a lot of "deferred" maintenance needed to build the company's infrastructure.

The overarching missions for family businesses at the Institutionalization stage are listed here:

Superstar: Integrate "old" and "new" businesses and build the infrastructure needed to support a multi-market/product/service business.

High-Potential: Close "gaps" between the infrastructure that supports the existing business and the infrastructure needed for the new business.

Feuding Family: Minimize the negative impact of family dysfunctionality on the company's ability to integrate the "old" and "new" businesses.

Sinking Ship: Build the organizational infrastructure needed to support effective current and future operations of both the "old" and "new" businesses; address family dysfunctionality issues that are affecting the ability to fully integrate the entire company's operations.

When a company reaches this stage of development, it has (as the name of the stage implies) become an "institution." This does not mean that it is immune to failure. Even very large family businesses like Melvin Simon & Associates (now Simon Property Group), Westfield, and Bank Santander can experience decline and risk failure if they do not stay focused on managing both the development of their businesses and their family dynamics.

Decline Conditional Stages

A business can enter the stage of Decline directly from any other stage. The contributing factors differ by family business type. *Superstars* are more likely than other family businesses to enter the stage of Decline when markets (customer preferences) change or a competitor introduces a product or service that makes theirs obsolete; in contrast, *feuding family businesses* are more likely to go into decline when continuing family dysfunctionalities remain unaddressed. *High-potentials'* entrance into the stage of Decline is frequently due to their underdeveloped infrastructure, which reduces productivity and undermines the company's ability to compete effectively in its chosen market. *Sinking ships* are well positioned to go into decline from any of the other stages because they have both underdeveloped infrastructures and a low level of family functionality.

Regardless of the factors that lead a company into decline, once there, family businesses of all types face the same challenge and have the same overarching mission: the need to revitalize their operations so that they can survive. Every aspect of the company's infrastructure and every aspect of how the family works together needs to be examined and potentially refined. These include refining the family business concept, the strategic mission, and the core strategy.

Steps in the Transition from One Conditional Stage to the Next

Athough there is a progression to how all businesses evolve—from one stage of organizational growth to the next—there is no one pattern for how family businesses progress through the conditional stages. The overarching mission of a family business depends on the conditional stage that it occupies, but the ultimate goal is to make the "transition" to family business superstar—either within the current stage or as the company transitions to the next stage of development. What are the steps in this transition process?

Step one is to conduct a family business assessment. The purpose of this assessment is to identify the current status of the family business: its strengths and limitations at each level of the Pyramid of Organizational Development, as well as its strengths and opportunities to improve the family's functionality. The two surveys we presented in chapter 1 are useful tools in this process, with the "deliverable" being the identification of the company's current conditional stage.

All family members engaged in the business need to be willing to openly and honestly evaluate the company's operations—including how they work together within the business. In addition, they must be willing to change company systems and processes, as well as the family's ways of working together—if the assessment suggests that change is needed. The family leaders at Bell-Carter have devoted their energies to these issues throughout the company's history and continue to do so today.

The second step is to create a family business development plan. This plan should identify the family's long-term vision for the company and the infrastructure that will support the achievement of this vision. The plan should include specific, measurable, time-dated goals so that progress can be easily measured. In some cases, a company may have two plans: one that is used to manage the family's goals and expectations and one that is used to manage and grow the business. We discuss the creation and implementation of the family business development (strategic) plan in depth in chapter 3.

Step three is to implement and monitor progress against the family business development plan. The family and other members of the company's leadership team should evaluate progress no less frequently than once a quarter. This evaluation should focus on both the company goals and infrastructure and the family (specifically, family dynamics). Regular monitoring of progress against the plan will give leadership the opportunity to make changes, if necessary, to promote the achievement of the company's long-term goals.

Summary

The life-cycle model of the stages of family business growth, and the conditional stages of family business development described in this chapter help the leaders of family businesses take the next steps in their evolution. Next we explain the tools that family businesses can use to become superstars. These include strategic planning, structure design, performance management, and culture management

Part II

Tools for Building
Family Business Champions

3 Strategic Planning

In 1992, eighty years after the founding of Bell-Carter Foods, the company acquired the Lindsay brand of olives and virtually doubled its revenues in a single year. The acquisition created new opportunities, but the company was not yet fully prepared to take advantage of them. Bell-Carter needed to develop an infrastructure that would support the growth of its existing business (private-label olives), while building the Lindsay branded business. To support this effort, brothers Tim and Jud Carter realized they needed a more sophisticated approach to planning that dealt with all of the building blocks of organizational success. Utilizing the planning process described in this chapter, the Carters and their team defined a new vision to "become a successful private-label company and build a brand" and developed a formal plan to achieve it.

This chapter describes a process for developing a strategic plan for a family business from both the family and business perspectives. An effective planning process and strategic plan will increase the probability of a company's becoming a family business champion. As John Ward states, "Most family-owned businesses struggle to survive beyond a single generation. Strategic planning—for both business and family—can help strengthen the family enterprise and expand its lifespan."[1] This chapter deals with both the "technical" issues of strategic planning and the family issues. First, we address planning for the family in the context of the family business and the development of a "family business plan."[2] Then we address technical issues and present a method for developing a "strategic family business plan." The appendix offers a set of questions (based on the concepts presented in this chapter) that can be used to evaluate the company's family business strategic plan and planning process.

The methodology for strategic planning described here will help family businesses of *all sizes* (not just large companies) become champions. Initially, the approach might seem more complicated than is necessary for a smaller organization. But we have a great deal of experience with the application of this methodology in family businesses that range in size from very small ($2 million in revenue) to very large. All have found it to be a useful, even indispensable, managerial tool.

The Goal of Planning in a Family Business: Creating Equilibrium

For organizations of any size, strategic planning for a family business is more complex than for a nonfamily business because it involves balancing the needs of the family with the needs of the business. We term this finding the right "equilibrium." Finding the right equilibrium should take into account how the family views the current business and its vision for the company's future development. For example, the family business can be viewed as the de facto employer for nuclear and extended family members. Since the family owns the business, it is reasonable for the family to view it as a principal source of income for family members. However, this perspective can lead to a dysfunctional burden on the business to "take care" of the family; in extreme cases, it can lead to the demise of the business.

As Ward observes, "Strategic planning for family-owned businesses differs from planning for other types of companies largely because the family firm must incorporate family issues into its thinking."[3] This requires careful, systematic planning (rather than a series of ad hoc decisions) that optimizes family needs and business needs. Research by Ward found that one important feature among family businesses that lasted and prospered was continued strategic planning.[4] Ward's view, and we concur, is that sound strategic planning is a key to success in family businesses.[5]

Planning for the Family in the Context of the Business

Effective strategic planning in a family business involves creating both a "family business plan" and a plan for the long-term development of the business—thus ensuring that there is a focus on promoting equilibrium. The family business plan identifies the vision and the results the family expects from the business. Ideally, the family business plan operates in conjunction with a set of defined family business values (as explained in chapter 6). It should address strategic issues and provide a context for managing the family business.

Family Business Strategic Issues and the Creation of the Family Business Foundation

In creating a family business plan (whether formal or informal), some of the questions that need to be asked are:

- Should the business exist separately and independently of the family per se, even though some members of the family are employed by the business?
- What is the family's time horizon for the business? As Ward puts it, "Is the family committed to perpetuating the family business?"[6] Is it "unlimited" in the sense that there are no plans to exit the family business for the foreseeable future? Is there a defined time for some sort of exit or "liquidity event"?
- How will family business issues and conflicts be resolved in the context of their involvement in the business?
- Will all family members have special rights and privileges to work for the business and to have it support them?
- To what extent will personal needs of family members influence family business strategy and policies?
- What are the career paths for family members?

Although there are numerous issues that need to be resolved in creating family business plans (including those above), three issues are key because their resolution forms the family business foundation—the family business concept, strategic mission, and core strategy (as described in chapter 1)—and the foundation of the family business plan. These issues can be summarized by one question: "How does the family see itself and the business (today) and in the coming years?"[7]

What Is the Role of the Business for the Family?   The *purpose or function* of the business as defined by the family becomes the family business concept. At one extreme, the family business can be viewed as a kind of family charitable organization to support family members, regardless of the effects on or consequences for the business. In one family business we are familiar with, for example, anyone who was a member of the family or a friend of the founder could find a well-paying managerial job within the company, regardless of skill. As a result, other employees needed to "work around" managers who were not qualified for their role in the business. At another extreme, the business can be viewed as an asset of the family, but separate and distinct from the family members themselves. In such businesses, family members do not have special rights and privileges to work for the business and have it support them. Decisions made by company leadership are based on "what is best for the business." These two extremes can be viewed as end points on a continuum of views of the role of the business for the family.

What Do We Want the Family Business to Become over the Long Term?
Developing a long-term vision entails clearly identifying and reaching agreement on the overarching or "big picture" family goals for the business—that is, the family business strategic mission. Typically, the answer to this second question depends on the answer to the first. If the business is viewed as a vehicle to support family members, then the focus for the longer term will be on maximizing the return to family members—regardless of how this affects the ability of the business to grow. If the business is viewed as distinct from the family, the focus will be on growing the business, regardless of the return to family members. At Bell-Carter, for example, the answer to this question is clearly defined in the company's strategic plan, with the focus on growing and maximizing the company's success. To paraphrase one member of Bell-Carter's family board, "There is no expectation that we [the family members] will become rich as a result of our role as advisors."

What Is the Family's Core Strategy for Achieving the Long-Term Goals of the Business?   Some families adopt the principle "Business First." This means that in all decisions concerning the business, what is good for the business is the primary criterion. Others adopt the principle "Family First," meaning that the primary criterion is what is good for the family, regardless of whether it supports the successful development of the business. A third approach is to strive for "family–business equilibrium," which is defined as "optimizing the business and the family needs" and not letting one dominate the other. At Bell-Carter the focus has been and continues to be on growing a successful business for the long term, regardless of the return to family members. At the same time, according to Tim Carter, the company's now retired CEO, the strategy adopted by the family board continues to be to "keep the family together."

Resolving Strategic Issues and Creating the Family Business Foundation. In some family businesses, strategic issues are resolved and the family business foundation is created very formally in the context of strategic discussions and strategic plans. In others—typically those with low family functionality—the issues are addressed informally, if at all. In the latter case, both family and nonfamily members can have very different perceptions about the nature of the business (the concept), its long-term goals (the strategic mission), and how the long-term goals will be achieved (the core strategy). The resulting inefficiencies can lead to conflict that undermines the ability of the family business to grow successfully.

Steps in Developing the Family Business Strategic Plan

Once the family business foundation has been created—by addressing the key issues described above—a plan needs to be developed that focuses simultaneously on managing "family issues" and on building the Pyramid of Organizational Development needed to support the achievement of the company's and the family's strategic mission. Some families develop and use a distinct (though not always formal or written) plan as a basis for managing the family within the business. This plan could include such things as financial goals and how profit will be distributed to family members, goals for developing family members as future leaders, and exit plans. Other families incorporate the family's goals into the strategic plan for the company—that is, they have one family business plan.

Although we do not believe that one family business strategic planning process fits all, the methodology for strategic planning that we have developed can be adapted for use by all family business leaders. It has been used successfully by hundreds of family businesses ranging in size from very small to very large—including Bell-Carter Foods, Simon Property Group, and nearly one hundred International Truck Dealerships in the United States, Canada, and Latin America. The steps in this process are shown in Figure 3.1 and described in the following sections.

Step 1: Complete the SWOT Analysis

SWOT is the acronym for a four-dimensional analysis of the "strengths, weaknesses, opportunities, and threats" facing a business. In a family business, the SWOT analysis is *or should be* somewhat different from the classic SWOT analysis because it should focus on the business and the family as it operates within the business. Completing the family business SWOT analysis involves: (1) assessing the level of family functionality and the impact that it has or might have on the business; (2) identifying the threats and opportunities presented by the current and anticipated future environment in which the business operates; (3) identifying the strengths and weaknesses of the company's internal operations at each level of the Pyramid of Organizational Development.

Assessing Family Functionality

This involves identifying the strengths and weaknesses of the business with respect to each of the six dimensions of family functionality:

1. Treatment of family members
2. Treatment of nonfamily members
3. Expectations of performance and accountability within the family
4. Family rewards and recognition
5. Willingness of the family to learn and to change
6. Family and company leadership

```
┌─────────────────────────────────────────┐
│ Step 1: Complete the SWOT analysis*      │
│ • Assess family functionality            │
│ • Environmental scan: identify           │
│   opportunities and threats              │
│ • Organizational assessment: identify    │
│   internal strengths and weaknesses      │
│   (at each level in the Pyramid of       │
│   Organizational Development)            │
└─────────────────────────────────────────┘
                    │
                    ▼
┌─────────────────────────┬───────────────────────┐
│ Step 2A: Create the     │ Step 2B: Align the    │
│ business foundation     │ family business and   │
│ • Business concept      │ company business      │
│ • Strategic mission     │ foundations and       │
│ • Core strategy         │ manage family         │
│                         │ functionality issues  │
└─────────────────────────┴───────────────────────┘
                    │
                    ▼
┌─────────────────────────────────────────┐
│ Step 3: Design each level in the         │
│ Pyramid of Organizational                │
│ Development (to support the              │
│ company business foundation)             │
│ and manage family functionality issues   │
└─────────────────────────────────────────┘
                    │
                    ▼
┌─────────────────────────────────────────┐
│ Step 4: Develop objectives and goals     │
│ to move the Pyramid of Organizational    │
│ Development from its current to its       │
│ future state and manage family           │
│ functionality issues                     │
└─────────────────────────────────────────┘
                    │
                    ▼
┌─────────────────────────────────────────┐
│ Step 5: Create a budget to support       │
│ the achievement of company goals         │
│ and manage family functionality issues   │
└─────────────────────────────────────────┘
                    │
                    ▼
┌─────────────────────────────────────────┐
│ Step 6: Review performance against       │
│ the plan and manage family               │
│ functionality issues                     │
└─────────────────────────────────────────┘
```

* SWOT = Strengths, Weaknesses, Opportunities, and Threats.

Figure 3.1. Steps in the Family Business Strategic Planning Process

This assessment of family functionality is what makes a family SWOT analysis different from the traditional analysis.

One tool for completing this assessment was presented and described in chapter 1. The deliverable from this assessment is a clear identification of specific family functionality issues that need to be addressed to promote the development of the business. These could include: the growing number of family members who look to the business for their financial resources; concern about placing family members in positions without proper qualifications; growing conflicts within the family that are being played out in the business.

Environmental Scan: Identifying Opportunities and Threats

The environmental scan involves collecting and analyzing information about: (1) the market in which the business operates (the customers the company targets); (2) the company's competition; and (3) environmental trends that may affect the business (positively or negatively) in the future. Key questions to be addressed in completing the environmental scan include:

- Who are our target customers—present and potential?
- What are the threats and opportunities presented by our ability to meet current and anticipated customer needs?
- Who are our key competitors and what are their strengths and weaknesses?
- What are the threats and opportunities presented to our business by our competition?
- What environmental trends (demographic, economic, regulatory, socio-psychological) could affect our business over the next five years?
- What threats and opportunities do these trends present for our business?

The information collection process can be as simple as asking members of the company's leadership team for their insights; or can involve conducting more formal and systematic market assessments (these tend to be more appropriate and affordable for family businesses beyond the Professionalization stage). The goal is to collect and use the "best" available information (given time and other resources) as the basis for identifying opportunities and threats.

The output of the environmental scan analysis should be a very clear picture of the company's current market (that is, who its customers are), its competition, and trends. In addition, the information collected about the market, competition, and trends should be used as the basis for identifying the threats and opportunities that exist within the company's present and potential environment.

Organizational Assessment: Identifying Internal Strengths and Weaknesses

The framework we use to identify internal strengths and weaknesses is the Pyramid of Organizational Development because it incorporates the key building blocks of long-term success. Completing this part of the SWOT analysis entails identifying the company's strengths and weaknesses with respect to:

- Identifying and meeting target customers' needs;
- Effectively developing and delivering products or services to target customers that meet their needs;
- Having enough of the "right" human, technological, and physical (including space) resources to meet current and anticipated future needs;
- Developing and implementing systems that support current and will support future daily operations;
- Developing and implementing planning, structure management, performance management, and management/leadership development systems (i.e., management systems);
- Clearly defining, managing, and reinforcing a corporate culture that supports the achievement of long-term goals.

The process for collecting data about the company's internal strengths and weaknesses can range from an assessment by the family leadership team, to asking all or a sample of company employees for their input on key strengths and weaknesses, to having independent outsiders complete all or part of the assessment. The process can also include a quantitative assessment of organizational effectiveness (using a questionnaire like that presented in chapter 1).

The deliverable of the organizational assessment is the identification of the company's most significant strengths and weaknesses at each level in the Pyramid of Organizational Development.

Key Deliverables of Step 1

The output of Step 1—identification of family functionality strengths and weaknesses, identification of environmental opportunities and threats, and identification of organizational strengths and weaknesses—serves as the input for plan development. This information should be used to create the company's business foundation and the steps that will be taken to maximize the strengths and opportunities identified and minimize the threats and weaknesses.

Step 2: Create the Business Foundation, Align the Family and Company Business Foundations, and Manage Family Functionality Issues

This step involves creating a business foundation that is aligned with the family business foundation. During this step, the company should also address any family functionality issues that were identified in Step 1.

Creating and Aligning the Company Business Foundation with the Family Business Foundation

As discussed in chapter 1, the business foundation has three components:

- *Business concept*: Answers the question, What business are we in?
- *Strategic mission*: Answers the question, What do we want to achieve as a business over the next three to five years?
- *Core strategy*: Answers the question, How will we compete to "win" in our chosen markets and achieve our strategic mission?

In developing these three components, it is important to: (1) use the information collected in Step 1; and (2) focus on aligning each component with the family business foundation.

Creating the Business Concept.   The business concept is a one- or two-sentence statement that identifies the purpose of the business—that is, what the organization is in business to do. Effective business concept statements clearly identify the company's target customers and what the company will do for them. The broader purpose of the business concept is to provide focus for company employees. It helps them understand what the company does and, conversely, does not (or should not) do. If the business concept is too broad or too narrow, it is of no real strategic value. For example, it is technically correct to say that AT&T is in the telecommunications business, but that statement is of little or no strategic value.

While creating a business concept seems simple on the surface, in many cases it requires time and careful thought. For example, in 1994, when Bell-Carter's leadership team began developing a more formal strategic plan, they spent nearly an entire afternoon working to reach agreement on what business the company should be in. At the end of the day, the team had decided that the company should be in the business of "processing and selling ripe olives, green olives, and olive-related products to our customers." The next morning, CEO Tim Carter came in and said, in effect, "We can't do everything . . . We need to focus, so I am recommending that we limit our business definition to 'focusing on ripe olives, while working to build our presence in green olives.'" The team had the opportunity to discuss and challenge his thinking, but in the end, everyone agreed that the narrower business concept made sense. Tim has since said that this decision—to adopt a more limited business definition—contributed greatly to the company's success.

Sometimes, the level of family functionality can adversely impact the ability of a leadership team to develop an effective business concept, and this, in turn, can limit a company's success. For example, in a $150 million family-owned distribution company, the family board and the two brothers who (like the Carters) served respectively as CEO and COO disagreed about the business concept. The stated business concept (which the CEO supported) stated that the focus was on distributing products to resellers, but his brother (the COO) was focused on creating new businesses that did not "fit" with this definition. Because he was a family member, the COO was able to divert company resources from the core business to support his new ventures. The lack of focus and agreement on the business concept contributed to the company missing significant opportunities to expand. As a result, a new competitor was able to enter and take away a share of the company's core market.

Developing the Strategic Mission. The strategic mission should identify what the company wants to achieve in the long term (which we define as three to five years from the current time). The "big picture goals" contained in the strategic mission should be aspirational, but realistic; they should be grounded in the analysis of environmental scan and organizational assessment data. The purpose of the strategic mission is to help employees understand where the company is headed.

We believe that a strategic mission must include two components: (1) a qualitative statement of what the organization wants to achieve; and (2) a quantitative statement of the same thing. The strategic mission must be "measurable," at least in a broad sense. For example, the five-year strategic mission that was developed at Bell-Carter's 1994 strategic planning meeting was, "To develop into a $100 million company (from $85 million in 1993) and become the leader in the ripe olive category (defined as the company that is able to set prices, have the best cost production, and move toward a dominant share in the branded business), and have a strong regional presence in green olives."

By including the date by which the mission will be achieved, as well as measurable big-picture targets to aim for, the company gives employees a sense of direction, which is important for motivating people. The company's leadership team and family owners will be able to measure whether they accomplish the strategic mission—that is, they will be able measure company success. Mission statements that are vague, by their very nature, are not as motivational.

When family members (or family and nonfamily members) do not agree on the company's long-term goals, people may actually work at cross purposes, and the effectiveness of the company will suffer. We examine one such company in chapter 7, in our discussion of the Gladiator Syndrome.

Developing the Core Strategy. The third component of the business foundation should identify how the company will compete to maximize its success in its chosen market (specified in the business concept) and achieve the long-term results identified in the strategic mission. In developing this core strategy, the company's leadership team again needs to consider the results of its environmental scan and organizational assessment. They should identify the company's true competitive advantages (the things the company does better than any present or potential competitor) and how they will use those advantages to respond to the opportunities and threats presented by the environment.

In 1994, Bell-Carter's leadership team identified the company's competitive advantages, some of which continue to influence their core strategy well into the second century of the company's existence: (1) the company's culture (which fostered employee retention and their support of the company goals); (2) the strong relationships the company had built with its customers (as a result of the service it provides and the quality of its product); (3) the ability to acquire the fruit needed to support its growth (through strong relationships with its growers); (4) the scale of its plant and the willingness of Tim, Jud, and the other family board members to continue to invest in making the plant state-of-the art; (5) the company's knowledge of the olive industry.

While Bell-Carter's leadership team did not initially develop a formal statement of the company's core strategy—which is typically presented in one or two sentences—they had an *implicit* core strategy, which was to be "the low-cost producer of black olives" by building on their competitive advantages. Today Bell-Carter has a well-articulated core strategy that clearly identifies how they will use their current advantages to maximize their ongoing success.

At 99 Cents Only Stores, a family business founded by David and Sherry Gold, the original core strategy was to sell everything for $0.99, in order to provide the buyer with "great values." Their prices were much lower than those of their competitors.

When a core strategy is unique, it can be sufficiently powerful not only to fuel a company's growth, but also to force competitors to change the way they do business. But many companies do not have a core strategy, or at least cannot clearly identify one. These organizations' reactions to the challenges of their competition tend to be chaotic, rather than proactive in determining how they will defend or attack. Because they have not developed a clear strategy for competing, they may miss major opportunities and risk losing market share to a rival firm. In one family-run $75 million consumer products company, for example, senior management spent years trying to determine not only what business the company should be in, but also what its strategy should be. Even though this firm saw a major competitor rising within its market and major opportunities being created within its existing market, senior management developed no concrete strategy to "attack" the rival firm or defend its position. Over a period of five years, the competitor grew to national dominance of its market, while the other company continued to lose market share and argue about whether they could or should take advantage of new market opportunities.

Aligning the Company and Family Business Foundations

In high-performing (superstar) family businesses, there is a high degree of alignment between family and company business foundations. Typically, these companies emphasize maximizing the success of the business rather than simply maximizing the value of the company (financial return, secure employment, etc.) to family members. If the alignment between company and family business foundations is poor or there is disagreement between family members about what the family and/or business foundations should be, performance will suffer. (See discussion of the Family Business Civil War Syndrome in chapter 7.)

Some families do agree about what they want the business to be and what they want to accomplish, but do not share this information with nonfamily managers and leaders. When the company business foundation differs somewhat or dramatically from the family business foundation, nonfamily company leaders may be caught off guard by decisions that are made. In one $250 million family-owned manufacturing business, the founder-CEO seldom participated in formal strategic planning meetings of his senior leadership team (which included two of his siblings and seven nonfamily members). He would "approve" the strategic plan and then proceed to make decisions to pursue business opportunities that offered a potentially high return, but were not aligned with the business concept. Understandably, the leadership team came to view the strategic planning process as a somewhat useless exercise.

Resolving Family Functionality Issues

This final component of Step 2 is typically accomplished in a family business planning meeting or retreat. One output should include an agreed-upon set of norms that will guide the behavior of family members as they work to develop, implement, and manage performance against their company's strategic plan. Another output might be a separate formal plan for the family aspects of the business (such as a family succession plan or a plan for exiting the business) that is distinct from that of the business plan per se.

For example, the family owners of GOJO™—the inventors and manufacturers of Purell™—decided to create what Marcella Kanfer Rolnick (the great-niece of co-founders Jerry and Goldie Lippman) calls a "family business foundation" that details the vision, purpose, and values for what has become the Kanfer Family Enterprise. This plan establishes how the family will manage its portfolio of businesses and activities that includes GOJO™, early-stage ventures, nonprofit entities, and resources that facilitate what Marcella calls "family member competency development and growth." GOJO™ as a business has a strategic plan that is managed by its leadership team, subject to the approval of the board, which includes both family and nonfamily directors. Each year, the entire family is invited to an annual meeting where the performance of its overall portfolio—including GOJO™—is reviewed. We return to the Kanfer Family Enterprise in the conclusion of this book.

Key Deliverables of Step 2

There are two key deliverables from Step 2: (1) a clear statement (usually in writing) of the company's business concept, strategic mission, and core strategy that is aligned with the family business foundation; and (2) the resolution of any family functionality issues identified in Step 1. The first deliverable is the input to Step 3 of the plan development process, which is to design the Pyramid of Organizational Development needed to support the achievement of the company's strategic mission consistent with the core strategy. The second deliverable supports the implementation of the plan and, in turn, the continued successful growth of the company.

Step 3: Designing the Pyramid of Organizational Development

Once the company business foundation has been created, the next step is to decide what each level in the Pyramid of Organizational Development should "look like" to be consistent with the business concept, to support the achievement of the strategic mission, and to reflect and support the core strategy. When completing this step, the leadership team should decide what is needed at each level and avoid being influenced by what currently exists. Specific questions that might be used to help develop this "future" pyramid include:

- What processes or systems need to be in place to help us understand and monitor our target customers' needs?
- What products and services should we offer to best meet our target customers' needs, and through what mechanisms should these products and services be delivered?
- What resources—human, technological, physical, and financial—will we need to support effective operations and product or service delivery?
- What key operational systems should we have in place, and how should each be designed and implemented to promote efficient and effective day-to-day operations?
- What should our planning and performance management processes look like?
- How should we be structured?
- What process will we use to ensure that we have the management and leadership capabilities needed to support our continued growth?
- What will be the key elements of our corporate culture, and how will we ensure that all employees understand and embrace it?

If family functionality issues arise, they will need to be dealt with. There can be hidden agendas that masquerade as strategic issues, but that are really personal family issues. For example, family members with a vested interest in "the way we've always done things" may resist any proposals for change in systems or processes. There may also be a need to manage family members whose real agenda is what their future role will be in the business. Some family members may resist the implementation of sophisticated planning and performance management systems because they do not want to be held accountable for their own performance. When family functionality issues are present, they need to be dealt with (for example, in a family-only meeting) because they can undermine everyone else's ability to think creatively and strategically about what the company needs to do to promote business success.

Key Deliverables from Step 3

The deliverable from Step 3 is a picture of the future Pyramid of Organizational Development (three to five years out). Figure 3.2 presents the output of this step from Bell-Carter's 1994 strategic planning process. This pyramid identifies what the company will be working to put in place over the course of implementing the five-year strategic plan.

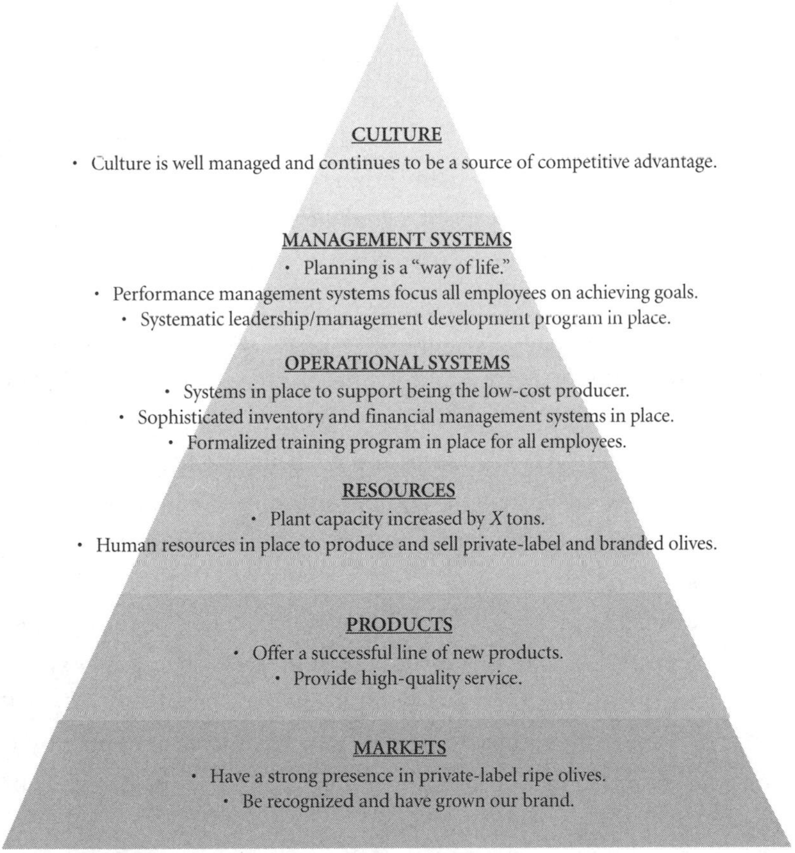

CULTURE
- Culture is well managed and continues to be a source of competitive advantage.

MANAGEMENT SYSTEMS
- Planning is a "way of life."
- Performance management systems focus all employees on achieving goals.
- Systematic leadership/management development program in place.

OPERATIONAL SYSTEMS
- Systems in place to support being the low-cost producer.
- Sophisticated inventory and financial management systems in place.
- Formalized training program in place for all employees.

RESOURCES
- Plant capacity increased by X tons.
- Human resources in place to produce and sell private-label and branded olives.

PRODUCTS
- Offer a successful line of new products.
- Provide high-quality service.

MARKETS
- Have a strong presence in private-label ripe olives.
- Be recognized and have grown our brand.

Figure 3.2. Bell-Carter Pyramid Design: Developed for the Period 1994–1998 during the 1994 Planning Meeting
SOURCE: Created by the authors, based on input from Bell-Carter.

Step 4: Develop Objectives and Goals

Once the company's leadership has developed the business foundation and designed the pyramid to support it, the next step is to identify objectives and goals for moving from where the company is today to where it wants to or needs to be in three to five years. Objectives are broad statements of what the company wants to or needs to achieve over the next three to five years; goals are specific, measurable, time-dated results to be achieved within the next twelve to eighteen months to support the achievement of a specific objective. Each goal should have an owner—typically a member of the senior leadership team—who is responsible for ensuring that progress is being made. Objectives can be viewed as a strategic component of the plan, while goals are the tactics for helping the company make progress in achieving its broader strategic mission.

For example, a medium-sized manufacturer of electronic components might set the objective "To increase our annual sales volume"; and a specific goal might be "Achieve $180 million in the year 20xx." An objective in the area of facilities and equipment might be "To increase our capability for inventory storage"; and a specific goal would be "To increase inventory capacity by 150 percent by the year 20xx."

In our approach to strategic planning, objectives and goals are established for each level of the Pyramid of Organizational Development, and for financial results or performance. The purpose is to create a plan—consisting of objectives and goals—for moving from the current pyramid to the future pyramid. The objectives and goals should also specify how the company will maximize strengths and opportunities and minimize threats and weaknesses as it builds the pyramid of the future. The output of Step 1 is an important input to this step.

In the context of preparing the written strategic plan, we refer to the six levels of the pyramid (markets, products, resources, operational systems, management systems, and culture), along with financial results, as "Key Result Areas." Objectives and goals are organized in the written plan by Key Result Area so that there is a plan for building and maximizing the effectiveness of each level in the pyramid.

Family functionality issues that can undermine the effectiveness of the output from this step include disagreement over objectives and goals and an unwillingness to commit to or be held accountable for objectives and goals. Endless planning (and arguing) can ensue. The planning process becomes an end in itself instead of the means to identify, implement, and achieve goals for the long-term development of the company. When family functionality is low and the leadership team defers to the most senior leader or family member, there is unlikely to be full team buy-in and support for the goals because the plan has become the leader's. At every step in the planning process, these issues need to be addressed so that they do not interfere with the development and implementation of the plan for promoting long-term success.

Step 5: Create a Budget

Once the nonfinancial plan has been completed (Steps 1 through 4), the next step is budgeting. Budgeting involves translating the strategic plan (focusing on goals) into financial terms. It should be noted that the development of a strategic plan and budget is an iterative process; the company's leadership team will need to adjust its strategic plan if it finds that there are inadequate financial resources to support it. Similarly, if there are more financial resources than anticipated, it may be able to accelerate the plan or adjust the goals. Once developed, the budget then creates standards against which actual performance can be assessed. Budgeting includes capital expenditures as well as operating costs.

Managing the expectations of family members with respect to how "their money" will be invested and distributed to them is critical. At Bell-Carter, for example, the family has always agreed to invest in the business rather than try to maximize their financial return. Within the Kanfer Family Enterprise there is agreement that the return from the family business portfolio will be used to fund both new external and family ventures, with the decisions about the nature of these distributions being made as a family. In contrast, some companies fight about what should and should not be done with "the family's money."

Minimizing family functionality issues at this step begins with clearly defining and reaching agreement on the family business concept and strategic mission. If it is clear what the family wants the business to be and what they want to accomplish, issues related to how financial resources will be used can be minimized. When these issues do arise, they should be dealt with "offline" (away from nonfamily members).

Step 6: Manage Performance against the Plan and Manage Family Functionality Issues

The final step in the strategic planning process is "management review," the process by which company leadership evaluates performance against goals and makes adjustments as required. To implement this step. we recommend that the senior leadership team hold quarterly plan implementation and review meetings. The purpose is twofold: (1) to review and discuss progress toward goals; and (2) to discuss and resolve specific strategic issues as they arise. Each goal owner (the person responsible for managing the achievement of a specific goal) should be asked to provide a progress report. If problems with respect to achieving a specific goal are identified, the entire team might be asked for their ideas about how to resolve them. Quarterly meetings reinforce the idea that strategic planning is a way of life in a company and part of the organization's culture. They also help hold individual managers accountable for results that will support the achievement of the company's strategic mission.

The quarterly review process can include the presentation of results to the board, if it is separate from the company's leadership team. This practice is used effectively at Bell-Carter, where the role of the board is to provide input and advice rather than make decisions. In other companies, the board (which sometimes includes both family and nonfamily members) may be asked to approve the plan. The purpose of the board is to help the leadership team make the best business decisions possible.

Family functionality issues that arise during this step tend to center on accountability. Common problems are lack of accountability for goal achievement, different standards of accountability for family and nonfamily members, and family members who do not disclose problems until it is too late to fix them. Strategies for addressing these issues by developing and implementing effective performance management systems are discussed in chapter 5.

If family business norms have been developed in Step 2, they can be used as the basis for minimizing problems that occur during the implementation and monitoring process. These norms should include how the family wants to operate within the business and the standards that they want to hold family members to. Again, if problems arise, they should be taken off-line in a family meeting, where they can be discussed and resolved.

Strategies for Implementing the Strategic Planning Process

There are a variety of methods that can be used to implement the six steps described in the preceding text, and this implementation should become more formalized as the company moves from the New Venture to the Consolidation stage of growth. The approach taken by Bell-Carter's leadership team during the period 1994–1998 and that is still being used today by CEO Tim T. Carter and his leadership team, provides one example of how to implement these steps.

In 1994, our firm was brought in to assist Bell-Carter in designing and implementing a more formal strategic planning process. At the time, Bell-Carter had approximately $85 million in annual revenues. According to Tim Carter, then CEO, they hired an outside consultant because, "Once we determined what we needed to do, we realized we needed someone to help. The process . . . is a lot more complex than meets the eye, and you can't afford to make mistakes."

We began the planning process at Bell-Carter with the administration of a planning survey to all members of the company's senior management team. The survey collected information about Bell-Carter's environment and its internal capabilities (using the Pyramid of Organizational Development as the lens for this assessment). The survey results, along with competitive and industry studies, served as the basis for developing the company's plan.

Once the information had been collected, Bell-Carter's planning team—consisting of Tim, his brother Jud (then president), the company's CFO, the vice president of sales, and six other key managers—met with us for two days to begin developing the company's five-year strategic plan. The tone of this meeting was highly collaborative, with neither Tim nor Jud dominating the discussion or the decision-making.

Meeting time was devoted to developing the business concept and strategic mission; and identifying the firm's significant competitive advantages, objectives, and goals. The company's strengths, as well as "opportunities to improve" that were identified by the environmental scan and organizational assessment were used to develop objectives and specific, measurable, time-dated goals. The team developed objectives and goals to achieve the targets included in the company's strategic mission (including growing revenues to $100 million in five years) and promote the development of a company infrastructure (including resources, operational systems, management systems, and culture) that would support the size and type of business that the company was going to become.

Every quarter since this first meeting (with a few exceptions), the leadership team has met to review progress against the plan, update the plan, and discuss and work to resolve specific problems related to achieving the plan. If problems are identified, the team works together to resolve them. The strategic plan for Bell-Carter is owned by senior leadership, not just the CEO and the family.

The leadership team devotes one to two days every year to setting the strategic direction for the company for the coming five years; they are always planning and managing for the longer term. Before they finalize the plan, it is presented to the family board for input and advice. In 1998, the Carters created a Director Team (DT) that included both family members and outside advisors. This team met quarterly with members of the company's executive team—Tim, Jud, the company's CFO, and the VP of sales—to provide input on company plans and strategic issues. The DT (which now includes Tim and Jud) continues to this day to be advisors rather than decision makers.

After Tim and Jud retired (in 2007 and 2008, respectively), the new leadership team made some changes to the planning process. When the "new" process didn't seem to be working as effectively as it should, Tim asked one of the senior executives, "How are you doing on the strategic plan?" and received the response, "We were too busy to do it." Tim understandably became concerned.

In 2010, a committee was formed consisting of CEO Ken Wienholz, Tim, Tim T. Carter (Tim's son, who was working his way through various roles in the company), Jud, and the company's CFO to refresh the company's strategic planning process. Tim says, "We needed to get back to basics." The leadership team, with support from Tim and Jud, revived the strategic planning process that had been put in place in 1994 and began meeting quarterly to discuss and resolve both strategic and operational issues. Tim describes what happened when the original planning process was abandoned: "When we got away from it, it started hurting the firm. We went from results-oriented [back to] activity-oriented, and we just weren't getting anything done. Activities didn't make a difference to the bottom line."

Summary

The six-step strategic planning process described in this chapter is a proven approach to helping both family-owned and nonfamily-owned businesses grow successfully because it focuses leadership teams on all the key drivers of long-term success. It requires patience and discipline to implement, but as suggested by Tim Carter, the return on investment will be significant. It is more formal than some processes, but its implementation leads to positive results, as experienced by Bell-Carter. And in small family businesses, the process is less complicated than in larger companies.

Family business-related issues need to be resolved before the family business takes on the development of a strategic plan for the business as a whole. These issues are separate from the strategic business plan per se. Treating them as such enables a view of the business as its own entity and does not force the business to deal with what are in reality family issues. This is an ideal that might or might not be able to be achieved in an actual family business situation, but it is necessary to attempt to do so. Given the complexity of these issues, the implementation of the process may require the use of an outside facilitator who can bring the family and nonfamily members of the leadership team together to identify and address both company and family-related issues.

Once the family business strategy has been defined and the strategic plan has been developed, the next step is to structure the business to support the strategy.

4 Organizational Structure and Roles

Over the first seventy years of its existence, as Bell-Carter grew from a small entrepreneurship to a company with over $50 million in annual revenue, its leadership structure evolved from the two brothers who founded the company to, by 1992, what might be described as a senior leadership team (although it wasn't called that). The company also grew from a few people in one location to several hundred at two locations in California. But as in many family business entrepreneurships, the overall structure of the company and individual roles remained fairly informal. According to Tim, "We had titles, but they didn't mean anything." People knew what they needed to do and did it.

In 1993, as Bell-Carter's leadership team began to implement the approach to strategic planning described in chapter 3, they recognized the need to formalize and more explicitly manage the company's structure so that it would more effectively support the achievement of company goals. This included developing formal (written) role descriptions for each position within the company and restructuring specific functions to maximize efficiency.

This chapter provides a framework for the design and use of organizational structures in family business. Like the planning process in family businesses, the organizational structure needs to strike the right balance between family needs and business needs—that is, achieve the "right" equilibrium. We begin by examining some basics of and tools for designing and managing structure. We then discuss some of the family issues that can undermine effective structure design. Part 2 of the appendix contains a set of questions that can be used to assess the extent to which family business leaders have developed and are effectively managing their company's structure.

Designing Organizational Structure and Roles: The Basics

We define structure as the patterned arrangement of specified roles to be performed by people within an organization. How a business is structured and how its structure is managed can have a significant positive or negative impact on organizational success. In the early stages of growth, roles are typically defined fairly informally, as they were at Bell-Carter. However, once a business reaches the Professionalization stage of development, a more formal structure is needed. Without it, people will spend time on activities that add no value; there will be duplication of effort, "role conflict," and ultimately, an inability to achieve important goals.

There is no one best structure for all organizations, or even for all organizations of a specific size or type; every organization has a unique culture, staff, and history. There are, however, four design principles that all leadership teams need to understand and use as they work to create and manage their company's structure.

Principle #1: Align Strategy and Structure

Frank Lloyd Wright, the iconic architect of the twentieth century, based his work on the principle that form must follow function. This means that the form of a building or structure must be determined by its function or intended use. We believe that this same principle applies to the design of organizational structures—that is, the various roles (individual and functional) that constitute a structure should be designed to maximize the likelihood of effectively and efficiently achieving the company's goals. For example, if a business offers several different products to several different customers, its structure should be different from that of a business that sells a single product to a single customer.

The starting point for designing any structure, then, is the clear identification of the company's purpose (business concept) and goals, which should be included in the strategic plan. As the leadership team plans for the company's growth and development, it needs to identify the structural changes that should be made to support it. As discussed in chapter 3, building the strategic plan around the levels in the Pyramid of Organizational Development increases the probability that during the annual plan development meeting, the leadership team will discuss structure (a key management system) and identify short- and longer-term changes that need to be made to ensure that it is aligned with the company's strategy.

Principle #2: Consider the Advantages and Disadvantages of Different Structural Forms in Designing the "Macro Structure"

There are three basic forms of structure to choose from in developing what we call the macro structure of an organization (that is, the functions and organization of functions typically included in an organizational chart), and each has strengths and limitations. Each is also most likely to be effective under certain conditions. It should be noted that for some companies a "hybrid" or blend of these three basic forms is appropriate. It is important that leaders understand the structural forms they have to choose from and under which conditions they are most likely to be effective.

The three basic forms of organizational structure are: (1) the functional structure; (2) the divisional structure; and (3) the matrix structure. In what follows, we discuss their strengths and weaknesses, as well as the circumstances in which each structure tends to be the best fit. However, each basic form must always be customized to the specific situation, including any relevant family considerations.

Functional Structure.   In a functional organizational structure, roles are organized according to the various "functions" that have to be performed to achieve the company's overall mission. All functions report to the CEO or president, who is responsible for coordinating all operations and for maximizing the company's overall profitability. For example, at Bell-Carter Foods in 1995, the major functions (each led by a member of the senior leadership team)—sales/marketing, production (olive processing and packing), olive acquisition/grower relations, and finance—were organized as shown in Figure 4.1. Tim and Jud Carter shared the role of CEO. Jud also had a functional role as the manager of grower relations.

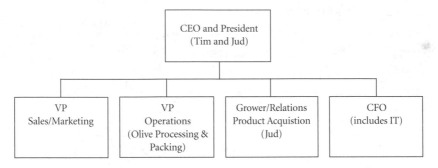

Figure 4.1. Example of a Functional Organizational Structure: Bell-Carter Olive Company, 1995
SOURCE: Created by the authors, based on input from Bell-Carter.

A variation of the functional structure—what we call a prefunctional structure—is typically used at the birth of a business and during its initial stages of growth.[1] When an organization is very small and has only its founder or a pair of family founders and a small number of "helpers," it is a bit of an overstatement to call it a functional structure. This is the type of structure that Henry and Arthur Bell used at the founding of Bell-Carter and that the company used up until the 1980s.

The primary strength of a functional structure is that it provides for specialization of function, allowing people to develop specialized skills in one area and allowing each area of the company to focus on developing specific capabilities.

One disadvantage of a functional structure is that the strong focus on maximizing functional expertise can minimize the extent to which the company as a whole is able to identify and capitalize on new market or product opportunities. Another disadvantage is that, as the organization increases in size, senior leadership time is spread thin because they are focused on ensuring that the various functions work effectively together in achieving goals. This structure also tends to promote "business as usual," and may lead to a situation in which new products or services do not receive the attention they need to become successful.

The functional structure is usually the first structure created for a business during its startup phase and early development. Typically, it is used until a second (different) product line is either developed or acquired, or the organization reaches between $100 million and $1 billion in revenue.

Often, meeting the needs of a new market or offering new products or services is the catalyst for a transition to a divisional form of structure.

Divisional Structure.   The divisional structure was created to take advantage of key aspects of the functional form, while also addressing the problems of reduced focus and lack of in-depth concern for a particular product or customer grouping. In this structure, the larger organization is divided into smaller units each of which offers unique products or services to a specific market (set of customers) and controls its operations and the development of its infrastructure (the Pyramid of Organizational Development). Divisions can also be structured around products, technologies, and even geographic locations.

A division is essentially a mini-company within a company, with each divisional leadership team having responsibility for managing the division's profitability; except that certain functions are still performed at the corporate level. The concept for this structure is to create separate divisions with a defined focus and then provide a common set of services to these divisions at the corporate level. The common services can include capital allocation, finance, legal, human resource management, and administrative services, among others. The functions that are performed at the corporate level can differ depending on the size of the divisions, and they can differ from company to company.

The divisional approach is widely used in large well-known companies like Johnson & Johnson and GE, as well as in many smaller businesses. For example, in 2002, with the acquisition of a pickle company located in Springfield, Missouri, Bell-Carter moved to a divisional structure and formally adopted the name Bell-Carter Foods, Inc. They also owned and were beginning to grow a small (around $1 million in annual revenue at the time) co-packing company (Bell-Carter Packaging) in Modesto, California. Bell-Carter Packaging was led by a general manager who happened to be Tim and Jud Carter's nephew; the pickle company would eventually have its own president who had been a member of the Bell-Carter production team. The general manager of Bell-Carter Packaging and the president of the pickle company reported to Tim and Jud (see Figure 4.2), and each had responsibility for managing the operations and profitability of their respec-

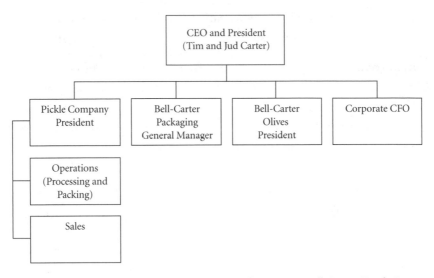

Figure 4.2. Example of a Divisional Organizational Structure: Bell-Carter Foods, Inc., 2002–2007
SOURCE: Created by the authors, based on input from Bell-Carter.

tive businesses. Tim, Jud, and their leadership team continued to oversee the operations and profit of the olive company.

The primary strength of the divisional structure is that it creates a focus on specific market or product segments. The primary disadvantage is that it results in the duplication of functions in each division. The divisional structure can also lead to intense competition for corporate resources among the general managers of each division. Therefore it is important for the organization that decides to adopt a divisional structure to invest in training true general managers who understand not only how to run a "business within a business," but also how to be an effective member of the broader corporate management team.

The divisional structure is very robust. It can be found at most of the later stages of growth—from Professionalization to Institutionalization. Because of its robustness, many very large family businesses use it. For example, a family business owned by three brothers, Simon Property Group (owners of Mall of America) had a development and a property management division.

Matrix Structure.   In principle, the classic matrix structure is intended to achieve the best of both the functional and divisional forms. As in the divisional structure, in a matrix, managers are responsible for all aspects of a particular program, project, or client. The matrix also includes specific functions headed by senior managers who typically report directly to the most senior executive (the CEO or president).

In a matrix, each program, project, or client manager forms a team of functional specialists (drawn from the various functions) who work together to achieve program-, project-, or client-related goals. These functional specialists thus have "dual reporting relationships": to the project, program, or client manager and to their functional manager. Functional and program/project/client managers must coordinate frequently on the deployment and management of human resources, and those allocated to specific teams can move onto and off of these teams as needed to support the achievement of overall company goals.

The matrix structure is appropriate in businesses where there are reasons for different business units to focus on customer groups or "projects" and where there is a need for a common set of support services. It was first developed in the aerospace industry, but it has been applied in many other industries, including publishing, real estate, and professional services. Figure 4.3 shows a matrix structure for a publishing company, which was a family business before its sale to a much larger company, Condé Nast, in 1993. The family company was Knapp Communications Corporation, publisher of *Architectural Digest*, *Bon Appétit*, and *Geo* magazines, as well as other periodicals.

Each of the company's products (magazines) has a general manager who is responsible for maximizing the success of the specific product. Each functional area—graphics, marketing, sales, and manufacturing—is headed by an executive who is responsible managing and maximizing the effectiveness of a team of functional specialists.

The strength of the matrix structure is that it permits a focus on the customer and the product, and also allows for functional specialization. It adds to the organization's flexibility because human resources can be moved from one project, program, or product to another so as to maximize return. The major limitation of the matrix structure is that it requires a high degree of coordination to be effective. The keys to successfully operating a matrix structure are conducting regularly scheduled meetings to review the status of work

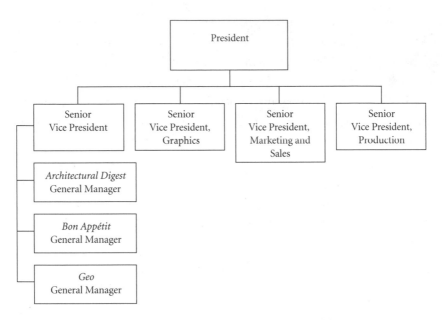

Figure 4.3. Example of a Matrix Organizational Structure: Knapp Communications Corporation, Early 1990s

and having the ability to deal with the inevitable conflict that arises when employees are accountable to more than one supervisor (a program, project, or product manager and a functional manager) and possibly involved in more than one program or project (and therefore responsible to multiple supervisors). Accordingly, the matrix structure requires a considerable amount of training in work-related interpersonal skills to ensure its smooth operation.

Principle #3: Define and Communicate Roles and Responsibilities

A "role" is a set of responsibilities to be performed by the person occupying it. Roles are basic units and building blocks of an organizational structure. If properly designed, each role provides a unique contribution to the achievement of the organization's goals. Further, effective *role descriptions* help people understand their own responsibilities, other positions' responsibilities, and the relationship between positions. This minimizes duplication of effort and the possibility that important decisions, tasks, projects, etc., will "fall through the cracks" because they are no one's responsibility.

Formal (written) role descriptions should provide those occupying a particular position with the information they need to understand what is expected of them. In a sense, the role description should be a "playbook"—that is, a guide for individual behavior—and it should be used as the foundation of the individual performance management system (discussed in chapter 5). As organizations grow and consider changing their structures, they need to identify how the roles themselves should change and may, at times, need to create new roles. For example, in the late 1990s, the executive team at Bell-Carter (consisting of Tim, Jud, the VP of sales, and the CFO) found that they did not have the time to focus on both the strategic development of the business and day-to-day operations. To solve this problem, they created the position of chief operating officer (COO) to manage day-to-day operations; the VP of sales was given this position, and his former position was filled by one of his direct reports.

While there are several ways to create these playbooks, we have developed and successfully worked with hundreds of both family and nonfamily businesses to implement an approach we call Key Result Area (KRA)–based role descriptions. A KRA-based role description consists of:

- A mission: A one- or two-sentence statement that identifies the purpose or reason the position exists. The mission of the CEO might be stated simply as, "To profitably and effectively lead the organization."

- Five to nine KRAs: Categories of activities that the position holder needs to focus on to be successful in his or her role. KRAs should be stated in a few words (as if they were labels on tabs in a binder), and each should specify "results" that the position holder should be focused on achieving. The rationale for having five to nine KRAs is that people can remember only five to nine things at any one time.[2] It follows that if people can remember the things that they need to do, there is a higher probability that they will actually do them. A CEO's KRAs might include:
  - Strategic Plan Development and Implementation
  - Corporate Financial Results Management
  - Senior Leadership Team Development and Management
  - Corporate Culture Management
  - Board and External Relations
- The amount of time (as a percentage), on average, that should be allocated to each Key Result Area. This provides guidance for the position

holder about how time should be invested to best support the organization's goals. It also creates standards for performance.

- For each KRA, a list of on-going responsibilities that identify what the individual should be doing when focused on that Key Result Area. Stated in another way, the purpose of this element of the role description (what we refer to as "objectives/activities") is to define for the position holder what each KRA means.

Typically, the process of developing KRA-based role descriptions begins with a workshop for managers—starting with the most senior leadership team—during which they are introduced to the methodology and terminology. During the workshop, participants are asked to use what they are learning to create, share, and solicit feedback on draft components of the KRA-based role description for their position. One purpose of these workshops is to help managers at all levels understand how to create role descriptions that support the effective implementation of the structure and, in turn, the achievement of company goals. A second purpose is to help minimize duplication between roles and ensure that everything that is important to an organization's success is "owned" by someone on the team.

Key Principle #4: Align the Informal with the Formal Structure

The "formal" or defined structure is documented in the organizational chart and in the written role descriptions. The informal structure is how the organization actually works or functions, which might or might not be aligned with the formal structure. The distinction between the formal and informal structures is particularly important in family businesses because of the possibility that family members can occupy roles due to their membership in the family regardless of their competence. Recognizing that family membership may have been a factor in assigning roles is important to both family and nonfamily members employed in the business. It helps everyone understand "why we do things the way that we do." One nonfamily senior manager of a family business said this upon being introduced to the firm: "It would be nice if each box on the organizational chart of a family business would 'blink' or 'twinkle,' showing that a family member occupied the box, so you could know the terrain." He also suggested that maybe the organizational chart could be color coded so that "core family members" were one color, the "secondary" family was a second color, and nonfamily was a third!

In all companies, two key strategies for maximizing the alignment between the formal and informal structure are to: (1) effectively and frequently communicate the formal structure; and (2) reinforce the formal structure by embedding it in the performance evaluation process.

An overview of the company's organizational chart—including information about who is responsible for what—should be included in the new-employee orientation process. In addition, the senior leadership team should periodically review the structure and communicate to the staff any changes that will or have been made. Finally, each manager should, as a part of each direct report's annual performance evaluation meeting, review and discuss the individual's role description.

Role descriptions should be used as one component of the individual performance management process (discussed in chapter 5). Managers should periodically discuss with each direct report how he or she is performing with respect to each Key Result Area and time utilization targets.

The level of family functionality will affect a leadership team's ability to reinforce, manage, and align the structure with the strategy, as described next.

Aligning Family and Business Needs: Key Structural Challenges

The overall challenge faced by family businesses in creating and managing structure is to find the right balance, or equilibrium, between meeting family member and business needs. In many family businesses, structures are designed to reduce the potential for family conflict rather than to optimize the functioning and long-term development of the organization. This is far less likely to happen in highly functional families like the one that owns Bell-Carter.

It is only natural for family membership and needs (including opportunities for employment) to play some role in how the business is structured. For example, at Bell-Carter, a decision was made in 1973 to have Tim and Jud Carter jointly lead the company upon their father's retirement, with each directly managing specific organizational functions, while working together to make strategic decisions about the company's development. This structural option would probably not have been considered if they were not family members and if they did not work well together.

While this example suggests that creative structures can be developed that meet both family and business needs, some companies create structures that only meet one or more family members' needs. Sibling competition can influence the design of organizational structure, as illustrated in the following example.

Several years ago, we were asked to assist a family business in creating a new organizational structure as the business transitioned from the founder to his two sons, Dave and Jim. The idea was that they were to "share leadership of the business" to avoid family conflicts and take advantage of their complementary skills. After studying the business and proposing an organizational structure (in this case, the details of the structure do not matter), we held a meeting to discuss the structure with the two young men, both in their mid-thirties. Dave said that there was something he did not like about the proposed structure, but he was unable to articulate what exactly was troubling him. The meeting dragged on for hours, because Dave kept saying, "This won't work."

After trying to examine each aspect of the structure component by component, we said, in exasperation, "We understand that there is something that is bothering you about this structure, but we have examined virtually everything. We are not sure where to go from here. Is there something specific that is a problem?" Dave replied, "Yes, he has more people reporting to him than I do." We suggested that one of Jim's direct reports move to Dave, and he quickly agreed. This simple compromise structure dealt with dysfunctional family sibling rivalry, rather than with any business requirements per se.

Sometimes the consequences of structuring around the family are minimal; at other times they can be quite significant. For example, when a role is created only to provide income to a family member, regardless of competency, we call this the Albatross Syndrome (see chapter 7). Other structural issues caused by family dysfunctionality include:

- family members occupying roles they are not qualified for;
- family members occupying "artificial roles";
- family roles interfering or conflicting with business roles;

- special reporting relationships based on family membership rather than what is best for the business;
- organizational silos that result from family dynamics being played out in the business.

Family Members in Roles They Are not Qualified For

Companies sometimes place family members in roles they are not qualified to perform in the belief that a family member is more trustworthy than an outsider. This might be true, but the consequences of placing an underqualified individual in an important role can be quite significant—including failure to effectively perform the role and damage to organizational climate and morale.

In one family distribution company, the owner had decided to retire and appointed his son, a longtime employee of the business, to replace him as CEO. The son, who had some management experience, was ill-equipped to lead what was by that time a $50 million business, but did his best. When his father asked how things were going, the son assured him that results were "great." In reality, the company was beginning to lose market share to a competitor, the senior executive team was becoming demoralized by the son's lack of leadership, and profits were beginning to decline. When financial results were reviewed at year-end, it was clear that the son was in over his head, and his sister, who had a strong financial management background and was an experienced manager, was brought in as CEO. Her brother returned to his role as operations manager.

In some businesses, a family member may have the skills to be effective in his or her role, but not be accepted by nonfamily members of the team. We worked with one business in the financial industry, in which the CEO's son was not originally employed by the business because his expertise was in a different industry, video software development. After the son's company was purchased by a competitor, his father offered him a job as CEO in the financial services firm, and the father moved to the role of chairman. Some of the senior executives with several years of service were irate and disheartened by what they termed "a total incompetent" being brought in over them, simply because he was the son of the founder. In their eyes, the message was clear that family membership meant more than competence and experience.

Sometimes family members fail because they are put in roles where they are not provided with appropriate support, given their qualifications. In one medium-sized family business, the founder, whom we will call Robert, acquired a small business (related to the core of his existing business) and installed his son, Robert Jr. (known as "Junior"), as manager. Not surprisingly, Junior, who was inexperienced, failed badly. The business was sold and Junior was brought back into the core family business. Since everyone in the business knew about Junior's failure, he was labeled and treated as a loser. Junior lived down to that reputation by becoming a dilettante who cared more about his car than he did about the business. In reality, however, Junior was a talented individual who was untrained. He had been set up for failure.

We were working with this company doing strategic planning and management development, and Robert asked if we could coach Junior. We agreed and through the coaching process, in a relatively short time (less than one year), he showed great aptitude as a manager. Junior soon became perhaps *the best, and maybe the only true manager* in the family business. Eventually, his father recognized this, as did others in the family business, who had grown to perceive him as a threat. When Junior was seen as a total loser, he was not perceived as a factor in the "political" system of the firm. Specifically, he was not seen as a candidate for succession to the position of CEO. Once he became competent, it was a different ball game entirely. Instead of being pleased that he was in a position to become the next CEO, other managers were now uncomfortable.

Artificial Roles for Family Members

When the concept of a family member's role is not clear or well defined, it is usually a sign that the role is artificial and has been created to satisfy a family need, not a business need. Sometimes this is done to take care of a family member whom the business leaders believe can't make it in another business. The family member is given a position that nominally makes a contribution to the company, but the real reason is to provide him or her with a means of support and source of self-esteem. The job title "vice president of special projects" is often a sign that the position is artificial, especially when occupied by a family member. Artificial titles can lead to the creation of artificial units to support them, which can be quite costly.

If the organization can afford the cost of the artificial position and the occupant of the position is relatively isolated from other positions, it may create few problems. As the company grows, though, people will start to question why the individual is there, what he or she actually does, and why he or she is rewarded for sometimes doing relatively little. The presence of these positions can, in fact, have a negative impact on the morale of the entire team. We provide more details in chapter 7 in our discussion of the Albatross Syndrome.

The Family Role Interferes with the Business Role

A lack of separation or conflict between the business role of family members and their role in the family can affect the overall functioning of any structure. One typical problem of this type is the elevation of a younger sibling over an older brother or sister. This type of family and business role conflict was aptly illustrated in the film *Godfather 2*, when Fredo explains his betrayal of Michael by saying, "I'm your older brother, Mike, and I was stepped over!" Michael replies, "That's the way Pop wanted it." Fredo then raises his voice and says, "That's not the way I wanted it! I can handle things. I'm smart, not dumb like everyone says. I'm smart, and I want respect!" See also chapter 7, where we discuss the Family Business Civil War Syndrome.

Reporting Relationships Based on Family Relationships

Family dynamics can play a role in both the formal structure (what is on the organizational chart) and the informal structure (how the structure really works). In the formal structure, family dynamics can create organizational structure anomalies. For example, in a divisional structure all divisions should report to the COO or CEO. In some family businesses, however, a division reports to a family member, not to a nonfamily COO or CEO. For example, in one family-owned truck dealership, both the nonfamily president of the firm and the family-member head of the parts department reported directly to the head of the family and chairman. This was a clear organizational anomaly. It did not make structural sense and was a result of family "dynamics." While the structure worked for this business, creating reporting relationships based on family relationships frequently contributes to morale and other problems.

Even when a structure seems to be logically arranged "on paper," when family members report to nonfamily members problems can arise. Although a nonfamily member is nominally in charge of his or her direct reports, a family member may feel entitled as "family royalty" and, therefore, able to ignore the directives of his or her supervisor. In one medium-sized retail company, a nonfamily member serving as COO had two senior family members reporting to him. One was the founder's son and the other was his son-in-law. Both family members seemed to resent the "intrusion" of the nonfamily interloper, and both seemed to believe they were better qualified than the nonfamily COO for his job.

When a family member imposes the "family trump card," the problem of dual reporting can ensue. Examples are when a junior member of the family who is supposed to report to a nonfamily member chooses, instead, to report to a senior member of the family (regardless of the structure that appears on the formal organization chart); or when a senior member of the family ignores the formal reporting structure and requires an individual to report informally to him or her. Such dual reporting relationships create confusion, reduce efficiency, and undermine the authority of the nonfamily manager. The key point is that the structure is the result of family politics rather than business considerations—a classic symptom of low family functionality.

Organizational Silos Caused by Family Issues

Another structural problem in family businesses occurs when family members create "fiefdoms" or "silos"—business units that do not work effectively together. Sometimes they do this simply as a way of "marking their territory," as animals do in the wild. At other times, divisive family feuds are the catalyst.

Silos cannot be identified by examining a formal organizational chart, but they do reflect how an organization really works. Obviously, when different parts of the organization are not working effectively together toward common goals, overall organizational performance suffers. In chapter 7, we describe one company, Healthco, in which the presence of organizational silos created by dysfunctional family dynamics eventually contributed to the company's demise.

Designing and Implementing
Effective Family Business Structures

The fundamental question to be addressed in designing the structure for a family business is, "How should we organize the company to most effectively and efficiently achieve our long-term goals?" As described in this chapter, the answer involves selecting the macro-structural form (functional, divisional, matrix, or a blend) that best fits the strategy adopted, defining the roles of each function and position within the structure, and clearly defining reporting relationships. The detailed design of an actual organizational structure is a complex and company-specific process that is beyond the scope of this book, and might well require the assistance of outside experts.[3]

It is only after this process is complete and the best structure has been identified that the focus should shift to identifying the people (both family and nonfamily members) who should occupy each role. When designing the structure, business leaders must consider the skills and capabilities of all existing personnel, family and nonfamily. The challenge is to avoid emphasizing the family over the business needs.

Once the best structure has been identified and designed (including clearly defining individual roles and responsibilities), it needs to be implemented and reinforced. One key is to separate and reinforce the separation of the "business roles" (the formal roles that people occupy in the business) from the "family roles" (the role people occupy in the family). Developing and using formal, written role descriptions can help clarify business roles. At the same time, family members need to work to minimize the extent to which family dynamics undermine the ability of people to fulfill their defined roles. One solution is to distinguish between working roles and family roles at home. We discuss this in more depth in chapter 8.

Summary

Designing and managing organizational structure is about more than just boxes on a chart and roles described in written documents. It is always also about people and their perceptions and feelings, especially in family businesses. Roles in any structure are not just about work; they also relate to organizational status. Designing and managing structure in a family business involves both understanding the technical side of structure management and being willing to address family issues that could undermine choosing and implementing the best design for the business. Where there is a high degree of family functionality, there is a higher probability that structure will be managed effectively. The greater the degree of family dysfunctionality, the more we can expect to see a number of family-related organizational problems.

5 Performance Management

As Bell-Carter Foods grew, and as its environment became more competitive, more formal systems needed to be put in place to focus people on achieving the company's goals. As retired CEO Tim Carter stated, "We needed to demand that people start making changes. If they are not performing, we needed to find another place for them."

In 1997, Bell-Carter began the process of taking its performance management systems to the next level. In addition to regularly reviewing progress and taking steps to enhance performance toward goals at the company level (which were included in the strategic plan), Bell-Carter's leadership team worked to ensure that performance-based goals were used as the basis for individual evaluations. The foundation of the individual performance management system were the Key Result Area–based" role descriptions (discussed in chapter 4), which were first created by participants in the company's leadership development program (see chapter 9). Each individual worked with his or her manager to create specific, measurable, time-dated goals for the Key Result Areas (KRAs) in his or her position's role description; these, in turn, supported the achievement of the company's (or department's) annual goals. The goals were used as the basis for evaluating performance. The company has refined this process the over the years and continues to use it today.

This chapter examines performance management in family businesses from the perspective of creating family–business equilibrium. We discuss both the technical aspects of performance management and the special challenges and issues related to performance management in family business. Part 3 of the appendix provides a set of questions (based on the concepts presented in this chapter) that can be used to assess the extent to which a family business has effectively designed and implemented its performance management systems.

Performance Management and the Purpose of Performance Management Systems

Bell-Carter's experience with performance management is typical of family businesses. All organizations, not just family businesses, require people to achieve organizational goals. The process of motivating people (including family members) to achieve those goals is defined as "performance management."[1] During the early stages of family business development, the performance management process can be very informal. However, as a company grows in size and complexity and the number of nonfamily employees increases, there is a corresponding need for a more systematic, formalized system for performance management.

A performance management system is a set of mechanisms designed to increase the probability that people will behave in ways that lead to the attainment of organizational goals." This system is intended to replace personal control over performance that occurs through supervision and leadership with a more comprehensive process that permits decentralized decision making with a degree of "control."

A performance management system has several related objectives or functions. First, it is intended to motivate people to pursue organizational goals. Without a performance management system, people might take actions or make decisions that meet their own needs rather than those of the organization. Next, a performance management system can help to coordinate and align the efforts of several parts of the business. Even though people might be trying to act in the organization's best interest, in the absence of a well-designed and implemented performance management system, they sometimes work at cross purposes. A third objective of a performance management system is to provide information about the results of operations that can be used by decision makers (company, department, and individual managers) to monitor performance and make adjustments as required. A fourth objective is to promote the effective and efficient implementation of the strategic plan.

There are some key things to note about performance management system development and implementation that are significant for supporting successful family businesses. First, there is a moment when an organization must inevitably transition from using an informal performance management process to using a more formal system. This is a function of the company's stage of growth or size (defined in chapter 2) and is independent of whether it is or is not a family business.

Second, the effectiveness of the performance management process depends to a great extent on the degree of family functionality. In a functional family like the Carters, performance management will be effective; in a dysfunctional family, it will be the source of problems.

Third, there is a need to develop and implement performance management systems that promote family–business equilibrium—that is, the optimum balance between the needs of the business and the needs of the family. When there is a lack of equilibrium, there can be dual performance standards—one for family members and another for "everyone else." A dual standard sends a powerful message through the organization about expectations for performance.

The way that performance management is handled drives many other aspects of organizational functioning. When done effectively, performance management is a powerful tool for shaping an organization's culture.[2] When done ineffectively, it can create a form of "organizational cancer" in the organization.

The Evolution of Performance Management Systems in Family Businesses

When an organization is relatively small, performance management normally occurs informally via supervision and day-to-day observation of activities. Management has a "sense" of what is happening, what the problems are, and what needs to be done; and this is enough to manage performance. In brief, the performance management "system" in the early stages of organizational growth can be described as informal and personal.

As a business increases in size and complexity (typically beyond the Expansion stage), management's ability to maintain control over all aspects of its operations using informal systems will inevitably begin to attenuate. Senior leadership will no longer be able to directly influence employee behavior because they can no longer "touch" all employees on a regular basis. In the absence of more formal performance management systems, the business may begin to experience symptoms of "generic performance management problems":

- Although plans are made and goals set, desired results are not achieved.

- People are not sure what is expected of them—what their roles are and what goals they should be working to achieve—and so they just do what seems appropriate.

- Managers do not take the time to provide feedback to direct reports on their performance during the year, resulting in some people receiving performance evaluations that are a "complete surprise."

- People complain that their performance is not appreciated.

- People feel that rewards are not administered in relation to their performance, and this, in turn, leads to questions about the fairness or equity of the performance management process.

In addition to these problems—which can occur in any business—there are also family specific performance management challenges that result from a low level of family functionality. These include:

- Having different standards of performance for all (or some) family versus nonfamily members. At the extreme, all (or some) family members may be allowed to do whatever they want to do—which may or may not be aligned with the best interests of the company.

- Inability or unwillingness to hold all (or some) family members accountable for performance. This can include nonfamily members who are reluctant or unwilling to provide feedback to family members who are not meeting performance expectations.

- Regardless of performance, providing family members with greater rewards than nonfamily members because it is a family business. All or some family members might expect "perks" such as longer vacations or flying first class as a "divine right" of family membership.

The solution for many of these problems is to create a performance management system that applies to all employees, family and nonfamily alike. A formal rather than ad hoc system should resolve at least some of the family-specific issues. These problems or dilemmas ought to be resolved in the context of the overall performance management system and not as a series of ad hoc decisions. As organizations grow, their leadership teams will need to develop and implement performance management systems at the company level (to promote the achievement of company goals), at the functional or departmental level (to promote achievement of functional or departmental goals), and at the individual level (to focus individuals on achieving their goals, which in turn support the achievement of functional/department and company goals). In family businesses, the effective implementation of these systems can be positively or not-so-positively influenced by family dynamics.

Components of an Effective Performance Management System

There are six primary components of a performance management system: (1) planning, (2) operations, (3) results, (4) performance measurement, (5) performance evaluation, and (6) rewards. Each one can be thought of as a tool to influence people to focus on goal achievement. When these six tools are brought together into an integrated performance management *system*, the probability of achieving desired results rises dramatically. We first examine each tool individually and then describe how to combine them into an integrated system that supports effective family business operations and continued growth.

Planning

Planning, which can occur at the company or department level (as described in chapter 3) or at the individual level (in the context of the individual goal-setting process that serves as the basis for annual performance evaluations), has a dual function in the context of influencing people's behavior. First, objectives and goals contained in a plan help people understand what is expected of them. A second function of planning is to establish standards for performance and accountability.

Three subcomponents of the planning process are: (1) Key Result Areas; (2) objectives; and (3) goals (see chapter 3). In chapter 3 we examined the use of each of these constructs in planning. Here we review their role in performance management.

Key Result Areas. The first step in designing a performance management system is to identify the Key Result Areas for each target level: the organization as a whole, sub-units such as divisions or departments, and individuals.

At the corporate level, KRAs consist of the six strategic building blocks of the Pyramid of Organizational Development, as well as financial results (as explained in chapter 3). Each department and each individual will also have KRAs that identify results the department team and individuals should be focused on achieving. For a manufacturing plant, KRAs might include production volume, quality, scrap, safety, and technical training. At the individual level, the KRAs that are included in the role description (described in chapter 4), serve as the basis for the performance management system.

In designing the performance management system, it is important to keep in mind that KRAs are *categories* of activities, not the activities themselves. They tend to be stated in one, two, or three words. Further, there should be between five and nine KRAs for the company as a whole, for individual departments or divisions, and for individual position holders.

Objectives. Objectives reflect results to be achieved over the longer term (defined as three to five years out) in a given KRA to make progress in achieving the mission. Examples of objectives:

- Achieve a satisfactory return on assets.
- Develop a new market for a product line.
- Expand the scope of the business to meet a competitive threat.

In the context of performance management system development, objectives help to channel the efforts of people in an organization toward achieving certain results. At the company and functional unit levels, objectives are contained in the strategic or departmental plan and are organized by

Key Result Area. At the individual level, objectives (ongoing responsibilities) identify what the position holder should be doing when he or she is focused on a specific KRA (contained in the position's role description).

Goals. Goals are specific, measurable, and time-dated. A goal states what performance is necessary in order to achieve a given objective. The objective of a salesperson may be to generate revenue for the firm, while the goal for the revenue may be last month's (or last year's) sales plus 5 percent. Goals may be based on management judgment, expectations, or historical data.

Goals are used to establish desired performance levels, to motivate performance, and to serve as a benchmark against which performance can be assessed. For example, "standard costs" can be used in a manufacturing plant as a goal to motivate employees to control production costs and also as a way to evaluate their performance.

Family Issues in Planning. Family dynamics can have an impact on all three aspects of planning at the company level. Problems include lack of agreement or actual conflict over what company goals should be and an inability to hold individuals accountable for goals. These same two issues can also arise at the individual level. Family members may work at cross purposes with each other or with nonfamily members because they do not agree with the goals or choose to ignore the goals that they are responsible for achieving. When goals are not met, family members who are responsible may be given a "pass." A third problem at the individual level occurs when ineffective communication of goals, or changes to goals, sets family or nonfamily members up for failure. In one family business, for example,, the son of the owner, who was the designated successor, constantly felt that he was not meeting his father's expectations. The underlying problem, however, was that his father—a brilliant entrepreneur—frequently changed his mind about what the company's team should be working to accomplish. Unfortunately, he often failed to share his thinking with his son, who understandably continued pursuing the goals they had previously agreed to.

In working with individuals to set their personal goals, the focus should be on the role they occupy within the business and on the company's or unit's goals, not on who they are in the family. Goals should be documented in writing, discussed, and agreed to by the manager and each of his or her direct reports. With respect to holding people accountable for performance against goals, the same standards for performance need to be applied to all family and nonfamily employees in order to avoid creating family–business disequilibrium.

Operations and Results

Operations refers to the daily decisions and actions that constitute the "work" of the business and are performed in the service of supporting and achieving the goals that are part of the planning component. Results are the outcomes created by the work (operations) of the company as a whole, individual departments or functions, and individuals. They include financial outcomes such as sales and profit, and nonfinancial outcomes such as innovation and product or service delivery to customers or clients.

Family Issues in Operations and Results.   Family dynamics can positively or negatively affect the decisions that are made and the work that is performed. Conflict between family members can lead to delays in making and implementing important decisions, which in turn can undermine the ability to achieve important goals by their due dates. Disagreements among family members about how things should be done can create confusion among nonfamily members and lead to inefficiencies in operations. Unwillingness of all or some family members to change can hinder the implementation of new systems that support overall goal achievement and company efficiency.

Sometimes these problems arise because family members disagree about what the goals should be. In other instances, family members have agreed to the goals, but then do not agree on the activities that should be engaged in to achieve the goals. In all cases, minimizing operational problems involves ensuring that family members agree on the goals (at the company, unit, or individual level), that there is an agreed-upon action (step-by-step) plan to achieve important goals, and that there is a regular process to evaluate and provide feedback on performance achieved against goals. Needless to say, achieving these results is easier in functional than in dysfunctional families.

Performance Measurement

Measurement is the process of representing the properties or qualities of objects in numerical terms. Performance measurement is the process of measuring organizational performance in quantitative terms.

Performance measurement has a dual function. One purpose is to provide information that can be used for evaluating performance and making corrections in goal-directed behavior. This is the information function of measurement. The accounting system, with its measures of financial and managerial performance, is a part of the overall measurement system that contributes to the informational function. The informational function also draws on nonfinancial measures of performance such as market share, production indices, and measures of product quality.

The second purpose of measurement is to help people focus on what is most important. The very act of measuring something has an effect on people's behavior because people tend to pay more attention to the aspects of jobs or goals that are measured. For example, in one small family quick-copy business in Santa Monica, California, employees tended not to pay attention to scrap losses until a measurement system to monitor them was put in place. This aspect of measurement may be termed the *process function*. It is related to Marshall McLuhan's notion that the medium is the message.[3] The "medium of measurement" is itself a stimulus. As the managing partner of a medium-sized national CPA firm once said to us, "What gets measured gets counted."

An effective performance management system ought to have systems in place to measure progress toward all major goals because of the process function of measurement; otherwise, some goals may be ignored. For example, if a store uses an incentive pay plan that compensates employees on the basis of sales volume, employees will tend to compete for sales and ignore unmeasured functions such as stock work.

It is also important that the information produced by the system be used by decision makers to assess progress, and that they then use this assessment as the basis for adjusting "operations" (whether company, department, or individual behavior), if needed, to increase the probability that the goal will be achieved. Ignoring the output of measurement can lead to suboptimal performance. In one $150 million manufacturing company, for example, senior leadership made a practice of collecting customer feedback on products and services. But the leadership seldom looked at or acted on customers' compliments or complaints, some of which could have been easily addressed. Over time, the company began to lose market share to one of its competitors.

There has been a great deal of theoretical work on the criteria of effective performance measures.[4] It is sufficient to point out here that the process of measuring performance in actual organizations can be very complicated, and the failure to do it well can lead to dysfunctional behaviors and unintended outcomes.

Family Issues in Performance Measurement.   As is true of other components of performance management, family conflict or disagreement can have an impact on measurement. Specifically, family members may overtly or covertly disagree about the system that should be used to measure performance and may interpret the system's output differently. This occurs most often when goals are vague—that is, the units of measurement (dollars, the number of X) are not clearly specified in the goal. For example, the objective to "improve performance" is very general. It does not indicate what specific aspects of performance need to be improved. Similarly, "improve quality" is of no value for the same reason.

One way to manage this component is to discuss how performance will be measured while goals are being developed. This is important at all levels, but especially at the individual level, when the focus is very personal. Each individual and the manager that he or she reports to should have a very clear understanding of and be in agreement about, what excellent, average, and below average performance look like.

Performance Evaluation

Performance evaluation is a systematic process by which organizations, departments, and individuals receive information about their effectiveness in achieving their goals over a specific period of time. While measurement and feedback (progress reviews) are occurring on a regular basis, performance evaluation typically occurs at the end of the planning period (i.e., after the due date for the goals that have been established).

Evaluations include both positive feedback (to reinforce behavior consistent with the achievement of goals) and constructive criticism (which helps individuals understand what needs to be done to improve performance). Evaluative reports generated by the measurement system—containing such items as net income, budgets compared with actual expenditures, and return on investment—are used in performance evaluation at the organizational and departmental levels. At the individual level, an organization typically uses performance appraisal forms to provide feedback on individuals' performance against their goals. Through evaluation, management decides how individuals and groups will be rewarded.

Family Issues in Performance Evaluation.   Serious and special family dynamics issues can affect the evaluation of performance, and at least some of these issues can relate to the goals that were established for individuals during the planning process. In brief, the use of different standards as the basis for evaluating some or all family and nonfamily members can undermine the effectiveness of the team or the organization as a whole.

In one $150 million distribution company, the two daughters of the entrepreneur were members of the senior leadership team. One daughter, "Helen," was the vice president of operations; the other daughter, "Mary," was the director of marketing. Helen's father held her to very high standards of performance and blamed her when the company did not achieve its goals (even though he nominally still managed the senior leadership team). Mary, in contrast, was given a great deal of freedom with respect to how she spent her time and what she was expected to deliver. She seldom received any feedback—positive or negative—from her father or other members of the team, even when her area did not perform as expected. The sometimes harsh and what Helen perceived to be unfair feedback she received from her father eventually contributed to her leaving the family business.

The underlying reason for this disparity in treatment was that the father believed Helen was far more capable than Mary and therefore held her to a higher standard of performance. Unfortunately, he never communicated this to Helen, out of concern that he would damage Mary's sense of self-worth and his belief that "she was doing the best she could with limited capabilities." Although his motives were understandable (perhaps even admirable), it led to a dysfunctional result both for Helen and for the business.

How feedback is given is another issue that can emerge with respect to evaluation. When there is a lack of separation between the family and the business, business feedback is sometimes given in a form that would be more appropriate in the family home. We have seen, for example, emails in which brothers called each other pejorative names, parents scolding their adult children in front of their senior leadership teams, and spouses yelling at each other loud enough for the entire office to overhear. None of these behaviors promote effective performance and may cause nonfamily members to work hard at staying out of the "line of fire."

The foundation for effective performance evaluation is twofold: (1) the creation of measurable goals; and (2) the development and utilization of information produced by a measurement system to assess performance against each goal. It is also important that all managers—both family and nonfamily—understand and are able to use strategies for providing effective feedback (both positive feedback and constructive criticism). Finally, while it can sometimes be difficult, family members need to control the tendency to provide feedback to each other as if they were in their own living room.

Rewards

Although all components of a performance management system are important, rewards are perhaps the most powerful in motivating behavior. Rewards are defined as desirable or valued outcomes for behavior required by organizations. Organizations offer a wide variety of rewards, ranging from compensation and bonuses to recognition and promotion. Rewards can be extrinsic or intrinsic. When people perform tasks because the work is interesting or challenging, their rewards are intrinsic. When people perform tasks because of the rewards they expect to receive from others—such as praise or pay—rewards are extrinsic.

Whatever the nature of rewards, they should reinforce good performance and promote modification of poor performance relative to the goals that the individual or team is working to achieve. Stated in another way, the rewards received need to be clearly linked to performance achieved in order to be effective as motivators.

For something to be considered a reward, it must be valued by the individual receiving it. For example, if a person values being "in charge," he or she might view the opportunity to chair an important committee or a promotion to a management role as a reward. If, however, the person values being part of a team, then chairing a committee might not necessarily be viewed as a reward.

Sometimes organizations fail to offer rewards that motivate people to behave in desired ways, or they offer rewards for one type of behavior while actually trying to motivate another. This has been described as "the folly of rewarding A, while hoping for B."[5] For example, a business manager may be rewarded only for not exceeding his budget, even though the firm hopes that he will also pay attention to personnel development. Similarly, an organization that wants to motivate people to be good planners, but rewards only "firefighters" may soon find that some managers have become "arsonists."

Rewards can be useful in motivating employees before behavior occurs because of the expectation of receiving a reward in the future. Once employees are performing well, rewards reinforce the positive behavior and lead to a greater probability that the behavior will continue. Good behavior that is not followed by a reward is less likely to happen in the future. Financial compensation is one of the primary rewards that organizations use to motivate employees to achieve goals. Incentive compensation methods can be very technical, and have legal aspects as well. These issues are beyond the scope of this book. But undoubtedly, the family business that wants to structure a rewards system will require outside assistance from compensation and benefit specialists.

Family Issues in Managing Rewards.   A core issue with respect to rewards in family businesses is what might be termed "differential" rewards: rewards that are different for some or all family and rewards that are different for family and nonfamily members. When different standards are used to reward different members of the family, when family members perceive that reward distribution is unfair, or when they believe their compensation is less than they deserve, both the family and the business can suffer. In chapter 7, we present several case studies of companies in which problems with the reward system for family members contributed to significant problems for the business.

While it may be appropriate to provide family members with differential rewards (because, after all, it is their business), this practice can create problems for the family members involved and for the business if it is not carefully managed. One relatively atypical but impressive solution to this problem was adopted by the family that founded and managed 99 Cents Only Stores—a company that went private in 2012, but that was previously listed on the NYSE for about twenty-five years. The Gold and Schiffer families owned a significant portion of the stock and were involved in the management of the company as well. Several members of the family were employed by the company, including CEO Eric Schiffer (son-in-law of the founder and chairman of the board, the late David Gold), COO Jeff Gold, and VP of Special Projects Howard Gold. All three of these family members were in executive positions, and all took modest salaries of $150,000 or less.[6] They all owned significant stock in the company, which aligned them with other shareholder interests. Given their relatively modest salaries, no one ever criticized the family for taking too much from the company.[7]

One strategy for effectively managing rewards in family businesses is for the family to agree—as the family did at 99 Cents Only Stores—what the reward system and structure will be. This should include (1) rewarding family (and nonfamily) members based on performance rather than other factors; (2) how profits will be shared by those who actually work in the business and those who are "silent partners" (that is, those who don't work in the business); and (3) how changes to the reward structure will be proposed, discussed, and approved.

Creating Performance Management Systems That Link the Six Components

Ideally, the six components discussed above must be connected and function as an integrated whole, as shown in Figure 5.1. The foundational component of the system is the "plan," which is the output of the planning

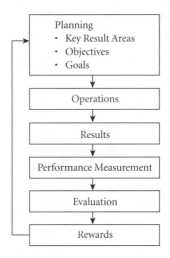

Figure 5.1. Performance Management Process

process. The plan affects performance management through the process of operations, because it identifies the "areas of focus" (KRAs) and the standards of performance (objectives and goals). "Operations" produces results that are then measured in either financial or nonfinancial terms. These measurements provide data for two kinds of feedback: (1) corrective feedback, which involves using the output of the measurement process on an ongoing basis to make adjustments in operations that improve the probability that goals will be achieved; and (2) evaluative feedback, which is used to assess overall performance at each goal's due date and which, in turn, is the basis for the administration of rewards. Rewards can be financial or nonfinancial, or a combination of both. Rewards are not only the final step in the process; they also link back to the planning component because knowledge of rewards helps incentivize people to achieve the plans that have been created.

To maximize the extent to which the system promotes desired behavior (that is, influences people to achieve goals) each component needs to be effectively designed and linked appropriately to all other components; and family issues that might undermine the performance of the system need to be identified and managed.[8]

Special Performance Management Issues in Family Businesses

As described in this chapter, the level of family functionality can have a significant impact on performance management in family businesses. Three of the most common problems are:

- perceived favoritism toward family members when establishing performance standards, evaluating performance, and providing rewards that can sometimes result in creating a feeling of second-class citizenship among nonfamily members;

- the presence of an "entitlement mentality" among members of the family;

- killing the "Goose that Laid the Golden Eggs."

Perceived Favoritism toward Family

Nonfamily members who work in family businesses expect and are willing to accept that family "investors" should receive an appropriate return. However, when nonfamily employees perceive that performance standards are different for family members or that there is not equitable compensation in relation to performance, they can become demoralized and care less about performing well themselves. If, for example, in a period of financial difficulty, like the so-called Great Recession of 2007–2009, all employees except family members are asked to take pay cuts, widespread resentment is likely to occur.

Nonfamily members respond to inequitable treatment in a variety of ways: with humor, by making sarcastic comments about the family, with open hostility, and by acting out in ways such as (at an extreme) stealing from the business. An example of the consequences of this is presented in the next section.

The most fundamental problem with "treating family differently" is that it can conflict with the stated culture of the business concerning performance and accountability. Assuming that the business has a stated cultural value that "rewards will be based on performance" (which is consistent with effective performance management system design), "family exceptions" to this practice suggest that the real culture is that "rewards are based more on family membership than on performance." This exception to the stated culture can undermine management's overall credibility, and nonfamily employees may come to believe that performance no longer matters. Treating family members differently with respect to performance standards and accountability can poison the culture and climate of the business. It can lead nonfamily members to believe that one must be a member of the family to get ahead and create a loss of accountability in the corporate culture.

An "Entitlement Mentality" among Family Members

In some family businesses, family members feel entitled to do whatever they want to do. They may have very few performance standards that they need to meet or they may simply choose to ignore them. They may also expect to be paid what they "need," regardless of their performance. When nonfamily members become aware of these circumstances, their morale and motivation can decline. This situation can create special problems for the leader of the family business who is caught between the expectations of the family and the needs of the business. What happened at Wainwright Automotive is a good example.

Charles ("Chuck") Wainwright, founder and CEO of Wainwright Automotive Company, a successful truck dealership and family business, often found that the most complicated aspect of his role was balancing family expectations and a family sense of entitlement with what was appropriate for his business as a whole. Family members frequently took whatever vacation time they wanted, regardless of company policy, sometimes without even informing Chuck or their managers that they would be absent. Two of his children, who occupied middle management roles in the company, were regularly granted permission to fly first class when company policy was for middle managers to fly coach. Chuck's wife put pressure on him to increase the salary of their eldest son, Edward (who was being groomed to take over the company), because she said he needed a larger house closer to the business. His sister, whose husband had been laid off from his job elsewhere, nudged Chuck to hire him in a leadership role, even though his skill set did not meet the needs of Chuck's company. Even his parents hinted to him that they needed money for a new car, a new TV, and a trip to Florida.

The behavior of Chuck's family members and their "requests" were evidence of the entitlement mentality often observed in family businesses. The implicit syllogism is: Family members in a family-owned business are special. Our family owns this business. Therefore, we are entitled to the "perks" of family ownership.

As the de facto leader of the family as well as the business, Chuck was continuously torn between family loyalty and the need to avoid demoralizing the nonfamily employees of his business. He also silently resented his family members' assumption that he would assist them simply because they were family.

This family leadership dilemma is inherent in all family businesses. The need to create equilibrium needs to be considered and managed when designing and implementing performance management systems in family businesses.

Killing the Goose That Laid the Golden Eggs

The parable of the golden goose is well known. A family has a magical goose that lays golden eggs. At first, everyone is happy. One day, greed causes the family to kill the goose to get all of its golden eggs at once (on the assumption that all the eggs are inside her). Alas, once the goose is dead, there are no more golden eggs to be had. This parable is often cited in family businesses by family members themselves. It is invoked when the burden of family expectations on the business is more than the business can handle and endangers its existence. What happened at Hosta Construction (the disguised name of a real company) is a good example.

Performance Management in a Dysfunctional Family Business: A Case Study

The consequences of several of the family performance management problems just described were experienced by Hosta Construction, a family business that did not survive beyond the third generation. A relatively small family business located in Los Angeles, California, Hosta Construction specialized in remodeling residential homes, but occasionally did some commercial work as well. Over four decades it had grown from a startup to a company with average annual revenue of $2 to $3 million.

By the early 2000s, the firm employed three generations of family members: the founder, Calvin Hosta (in his eighties); his son, Leonard; and two of Leonard's sons. Although he made a six-figure salary, Calvin did not really have a defined role, but still went into work each day and in his own words "puttered around." The salary Calvin received could be thought of as a payment for all the years he spent building the business. Leonard (known as Len) basically ran the company, building on the foundation created by Calvin. Leonard's two sons, Mike and Todd, did construction work under the supervision of more experienced project managers: Tobey ("Buddy") Burnett, Walter Halverson, and Sam Fisher. Len's wife, Sally, also worked in the business, taking care of billings and "the books." Sally also prepared all checks for Len's signature.

The family typically withdrew about $500,000 per year from the business in salaries. In early 2009, after the financial crisis hit the U.S. economy, the construction business slowed and company revenue declined sharply. When the company projected that revenue would fall from $2.8 million in 2008 to $1.8 million in 2009, all employees, except family, were asked to take a 15 percent cut in salary and hourly wages. In addition, the company, which had historically paid for employees' gas, rescinded that practice. For the firm's salaried and hourly workers, these cutbacks were severe. Virtually all lived paycheck to paycheck.

Initially there was no grumbling, until it became apparent that the cuts were not being applied to family. Then an undercurrent of resentment rose to the surface. In April 2009, Sam Fisher left Hosta Construction after eight years and joined a competitor. Since Sam had relationships with two of the firm's longtime commercial clients, Len expected Hosta to lose future business from those clients. He was not pleased, and he now knew that both Buddy Burnett and Walt Halverson were not happy campers.

Len faced a dilemma: His family was "bitching at him" to maintain their standard of living, and he realized that he might well be killing the golden goose that provided all of them their income. In an expansive moment before the financial crisis hit, Todd had been promised a new car for his thirty-fifth birthday. Sally expected a trip to Mexico for her and her husband's fortieth anniversary, and Calvin needed hip surgery. Len felt he had no choice but to squeeze costs wherever he could, and that meant salary and benefits reductions for nonfamily employees.

When Todd drove up to Hosta with a new BMW in May 2009, it was the final straw for Buddy. He knew he could not leave Hosta at that point because the job market in construction was dismal. But the seed for his ultimate departure had been planted. He vowed to his wife that he would leave as soon as the market recovered. In the meantime, he felt justified in not being as "responsible" an employee as he had been. Walt responded differently. He too bore resentment and secretly was seething, and he expressed it in subtle ways. Always humorous, his comments took on an edge. While he had frequently ignored the work-related foibles of the two youngest Hostas, he began to talk about their errors in front of them. The implication of his remarks was that they were incompetent. He referred to them jokingly as the two knuckleheads. When they worked for him on a project, he would sometimes call them by their new nicknames: "Knuckle 1" and "Knuckle 2."

Len was aware of this, but simply could not deal with it. Walt was too experienced and too valuable to alienate. So he let it go. He admonished Todd and Mike to get better, so "Walt won't have reason to refer to you that way." Todd and Mike were not happy about it, but were powerless to do anything. In addition, Walt's comments seemed to lead to a self-fulfilling prophecy: the more he referred to Todd and Mike as knuckleheads, the more they seemed to mess up! Privately, Bill Campbell, who replaced Sam Fisher as project manager, referred to Mike and Todd as "the two jokes." There was poison in the atmosphere at Hosta Construction—not a fast-acting poison, but one that was nevertheless corrosive.

All of this drama did not help business. When the company made mistakes, customers complained and employees pointed fingers at each other. The atmosphere changed from one in which everyone in the small company worked as a team to one in which it was every man for himself.

Len, who knew construction from a technical perspective, was not an effective leader and did not know what to do to deal with this situation. It continued getting worse until in 2011 there was a major error on a $750,000 construction project followed by a lawsuit. Hosta was forced to declare bankruptcy. The goose was dead, killed by a failure to manage the expectations of the family, which in turn led to a downward spiral in performance. Calvin and Len "retired" and Mike and Todd tried to find jobs with other construction firms, but their reputation prevented that. Todd took a job as a "bag boy" at a nearby Wal-Mart and Mike went on unemployment until his benefits ran out. He moved back home and Len supported him with a monthly allowance, just as he had as a teenager.

How Did It Happen?

There were several contributing factors to what happened at Hosta. First, there was an entitlement mentality in the family that was totally unrealistic, especially given the changing economic conditions. Second, there was a leadership failure by Len Hosta. He accepted family expectations as a given and avoided short-term conflict in the family by conceding to unreasonable demands. This put increased pressure on the business and led to turnover and resentment among nonfamily employees. It damaged the culture and climate of the firm, led to performance problems, and ultimately contributed to the firm's demise.

Often in his free moments, Len wondered how it all happened, and what, if anything, he might have done differently. The company needed a performance management system that included a culture of performance-based compensation. A more well developed (rather than ad hoc) performance management system would have provided the basis for evaluation (in the form of measurable goals) and feedback. This, combined with performance-based compensation, would have led to lower compensation for family and maintained compensation for key nonfamily employees, which in turn would have reduced the probability of costly turnover. The company also needed a systematic approach to compensation rather than a series of ad hoc decisions. A performance management system is not a panacea, but it might have made some of the problems more manageable. It would have given Len a rationale for adjusting the salaries of Todd, Mike, and even Calvin, as well as his own, rather than just those of nonfamily employees.

The family also could have sent the message that "we are all in this together" by making some sacrifices and deferring some of their personal expenditures. Did Todd really need a new BMW at that time? Did Len and Sally really need to take the trip to the Mexican Riviera? These expenditures sent a bad signal to other employees, especially at a time when their income was being reduced. Although it is not possible to know for sure, the demoralization caused by the different treatment of family and nonfamily employees appears to have been a significant factor in the firm's declining performance and the eventual bankruptcy.

The example of Hosta Construction is a classic case of family–business "disequilibrium" as it relates to performance management. The failure to achieve family–business equilibrium in the performance management process is the key underlying cause of the failure of this family business. If this were an isolated case, it would not be noteworthy. However, our experiences in working with family businesses for several decades show that similar problems and circumstances are pervasive.

Summary

Like other tools that can be used to support a company's successful growth and development, performance management tools in a family business play a dual role: one is technical; the other is social-psychological. The technical aspect refers to the performance management process *itself*—that is, the design and management of the six components of the system and of the performance management system as a whole. The social-psychological dimension involves the family and its expectations of the business—what we have referred to as "family functionality." Family functionality can have a significant impact on the ability to focus people's efforts on the achievement of company goals, which is the overall purpose of a performance management system.

In highly functional families such as Bell-Carter Foods, where the business is to a very great extent, separate and distinct from the family, the process for developing and implementing performance management systems is largely a technical process. In dysfunctional families such as Hosta Construction, where family decisions are inextricably tied to performance and compensation-benefit decisions, problems can create family conflict and lead (in extreme cases) to the destruction of the family business.

6 Culture Management

As is true of all family businesses, the culture of Bell-Carter Foods has been and (after 100 years) continues to be influenced by the family's culture. At Bell-Carter, the focus has always been on both working hard and having fun. The company has a highly functional culture that helps it attract and retain good people.

Although Bell-Carter had completed several assessments of its culture before the early 2000s, when CEO Tim Carter and his brother Jud, then president, decided to retire, there was no formal (written) statement of the company's culture; everyone understood it and, for the most part, "lived it." The primary way of communicating and managing the company's culture was through the interactions that Tim, Jud, and other members of their senior leadership had with employees. The company also tried to hire people that "fit" the Bell-Carter culture (using an industrial psychologist to assist in the process). Company events tended to reflect the sense of family that employees valued, including the annual Halloween party in Corning, California, where employees would "dress like Jud" in khaki pants, blue work shirt, and red wigs.

Tim, Jud, and other leaders at Bell-Carter were not consciously managing the culture; it was just how they did things. Bell-Carter's culture reflected the way the family operated outside of the business. For employees, Bell-Carter was simply a great place to work.

As Tim and Jud approached full retirement in 2007, they and the executive team decided that there was a need to articulate the company's culture more formally. The team began to focus on creating a written document that would convey the positive aspects of the culture that was first created by Arthur and Henry Bell and that had been passed down to and nurtured by Tim, Jud, and the other members of their leadership team. They also began discussing ways that the culture could be more formally managed. As Tim T. Carter moved into his role as CEO in 2012, he and his leadership team continued the culture management process by focusing on how it would support changes in the company's market and employee base (for example, meeting the needs of millennials).

Most companies manage their cultures very informally as they grow. When family functionality is high, the corporate culture tends to be positive and tends to contribute, as it did at Bell-Carter, to organizational effectiveness and success. In fact, a positive or functional corporate culture in a family business can be a significant asset.[1] As John Ward and Craig Aronoff have stated, "An enduring commitment to values is the greatest strength a family can bring to a business."[2] When family functionality is low, the resulting business culture can detract from organizational success and can be a significant liability or even toxic to the business.

Regardless of the level of family functionality, all family businesses will reach a point when the company's culture will need to be more formally articulated, communicated, managed, and reinforced. Sometimes this is brought about by the departure of long-term family leaders or by the growth of the company.

This chapter describes a framework for the management of corporate culture in a family business. Our overarching objective is to provide the concepts and tools required to help create and manage a functional family business culture. We discuss the concept of organizational culture, the key dimensions of culture, the critical role of culture in business and family business, the tools of culture management, and the special problems of managing culture in a family business. We also examine real cases of corporate culture and culture management—both functional and dysfunctional—in family business. We include in Part 4 of the appendix a set of questions that can be used to assess the effectiveness of your company's culture and culture management process.

The Concept of Corporate Culture

Over the past several decades, the concept of corporate culture has become embedded in management vocabulary and thought.[3] As defined here, corporate culture consists of values, beliefs, and norms that influence the thoughts and actions (behaviors) of people in organizations. This definition is consistent with Ward and Aronoff's: "Corporate culture is the buildup of beliefs and values that drive the business, and the day-to-day assumptions and behaviors that reflect those values."[4]

Values are the things an organization considers most important with respect to its operations, its employees, and its customers. These are the things an organization holds dear, the things it strives for and wants to protect at all costs. Beliefs are assumptions individuals hold about themselves, their customers, and their organization. Norms are unwritten rules of behavior that address such issues as how employees dress and interact. Norms help "operationalize" actions that are consistent with values and beliefs.

Values, beliefs, and norms constitute the overall mosaic of culture in an organization. As Kelin Gersick and his co-authors state, "A company's *culture* (like the culture of any social group) is its strongly held values and assumptions about correct behavior in a number of areas.[5]" In a family business, the company culture is very much a reflection of family dynamics and family functionality—in other words, the culture of the family infuses the culture of the company.

All organizations have cultures or sets of values that influence the way people behave in a variety of areas, such as treatment of customers, standards of performance, and innovation—even if the values are not captured in some type of written statement.

There are actually several layers of culture in an organization.[6] There is the surface layer, which is what we see and observe—the "norms" of everyday behavior. Then there are the core values and related beliefs or assumptions that drive or underlie the behavioral norms. Below that is what might be termed a set of "cultural attributes," which are the "DNA" of the company's "corporate personality" (that is, its culture). These are things such as attitudes toward risk, ethics, planning, systems, processes, professionalism, entrepreneurialism, and even bureaucracy. These cultural attributes drive the core beliefs, values, and norms that constitute the most observable level of culture.

It is important to note that there can be significant differences between what a company says its culture is (as written in a formal values or culture statement) and what it really is (the messages that influence employees' daily behavior). Culture management efforts need to focus on both, but the most important factor is what drives employee behavior.

Creation and Evolution of Corporate Culture in Family Businesses

A company's culture reflects the personal and professional values of the founder(s). Stated in another way, the founders' values are the "DNA" of the culture of the company during its initial stages of development. As Gersick and co-authors state, "The founder also symbolizes, through words and behavior, these underlying values and basic beliefs."[7] If the founder is a perfectionist, then the performance standards for the company will be all about perfection. If the founder is hypercritical, then the culture will take on a critical character.

In a family business, the culture is defined and influenced not just by the founder, but also by how the family interacts in the business. If the family values learning, the company's culture and ways of operating will do so as well. If the family uses humor as a way of diffusing conflict, this will become a corporate norm. If there is conflict among family members who occupy senior leadership roles, the culture may evolve to include the practice "staying out of the way."

Most early-stage entrepreneurial companies do not have formal systems (including formal statements) of culture management. Instead, the culture is transmitted by the daily personal interactions of people with the entrepreneur or founding group. As the entrepreneur makes decisions, his or her values are communicated in the form of behavior. As a business grows, there is a corresponding need for a greater degree of formal culture management. People must understand what the culture is in order to be able to practice it and this can no longer be accomplished solely through personal interaction. By the time a company reaches $100 million in revenue (the

Consolidation stage), it will need to develop a more formal approach for communicating, managing, and reinforcing its culture.

Conventional Statements of Corporate Culture

Edward Hess has proposed the need for a "statement of family values," but this is different from a family business culture statement.[8] Family values include things such as "honesty," "respect," and "the golden rule." These are values for interpersonal relations among family members, rather than values for management of the family business itself.

Most attempts (almost all that we have seen) to define and manage a company's culture are based on ad hoc statements of core values that have "face validity" (intuitively they "make sense") to organizations and entrepreneurs. Formal definitions of culture typically consist of lists of key words or phrases that seem reasonable or meaningful. One company we worked with stated, "Our core values are 'professionalism,' 'integrity,' 'hard work,' 'teamwork,' and 'results.'" Another used phrases such as "every penny counts," "doing more with less," "the best idea wins," and "working managers."

Although generating a list of key words or phrases that reflect the culture of the company might seem to be a reasonable approach, this "method" has two problems. First, it is lacking in empirical (predictive) validity. How do we know that these asserted values are meaningful or relevant to performance and organizational success? Second, how do we know that these are what the key core values ought to be?

The Key Dimensions of Corporate Culture

While many aspects of culture are important, some are demonstrably more important than others.[9] Based on our own original research and experience working with organizations, we have identified five key aspects of culture that *have a statistically significant relationship to financial performance.*[10] These are: (1) customer orientation; (2) people (employee) orientation; (3) performance standards and accountability; (4) innovation or commitment to change; and (5) company process orientation.[11] Each of these dimensions, described briefly in the following text, can be positively or negatively influenced by the level of family functionality.

Customer Orientation

The importance attached to how the company views its customers or clients, as well as the assumptions employees hold about their customers and clients has a profound impact on how the company operates and thus on its success. Views of the customer can range from "the customer is the #1 priority" to the "customer is a nuisance," and can include everything in between.

Some companies clearly develop and communicate to their employees their values with respect to customers. For example, at one family manufacturing company that we will call Regent, the formal values statement contained the following: "The customers' perspective of the relationship they have with our company is the key to our success. . . . Therefore, each associate has total authority and with it the obligation to make every effort to satisfy our customers." The value placed on customer service excellence was important to the founder, and it included not just day-to-day service, but a strong emphasis on research and development. The goal was to continue refining existing products and creating new ones that would meet changing customer needs. This aspect of the culture helped Regent grow very rapidly over a decade and contributed to the premium price the family received when they eventually sold Regent to a larger company.

People (Employee) Orientation

This value reflects how people view themselves and others within the organization. Again it has two components: (1) how people are viewed with respect to their roles within the company, and (2) how important people feel. Some companies devote a great deal of effort to satisfying employee needs and making them feel valued. At the other end of the spectrum are companies in which employees are viewed as replaceable. Somewhere in between are companies where some employees are considered valuable assets and others are viewed as second-class citizens.

The level of family functionality can have a significant impact on this dimension. During the early stages of company growth, employees frequently describe themselves as a family, regardless of whether they are related to the family that owns the business. As Bell-Carter was working toward developing a formal statement of its values in 2007, for example, it developed the following wording:

> Throughout the years, Bell-Carter employees have worked together like a well-functioning family. We do what we need to do to be successful, regardless of what our formal job is. We support one another. . . . We believe that when you treat people like family, you foster the kind of intimacy and informality that builds strong relationships and makes work more fun. Strong relationships build strong teams, and strong teams breed success.

This statement provides a comprehensive definition of what it means to be a part of the "Bell-Carter family" and says a great deal about how people should be treated.

When the people orientation value is managed effectively, it leads to employees having a high commitment to the business—both in their work and in their willingness to remain with and contribute to the business as it grows. When, however, there are different standards of performance for family and nonfamily members, or when family members receive special treatment or benefits, nonfamily members can come to feel that they are second-class citizens and that their contributions are not valued. This can result in a lack of employee commitment, high turnover, and ultimately poor business performance.

Performance Standards and Accountability

Performance standards include what and how much employees are held accountable for, the level of quality expected in products, and the expected level of customer satisfaction. Whether the standards of performance embedded in an organization's culture are high or low, they can have a profound impact on people's behavior. Performance standards identified in Bell-Carter's 2007 formal values statement included "use common sense and good judgment every moment of the day," "measure what matters and take action with that information to continually improve the business," and "show up with passion." At Regent, performance standards included "commitment to timeliness and a sense of urgency," "doing the best job at all times and going the extra mile," and "ethical behavior." Both companies reinforced the standards daily and, as a result, they contributed to the company's success.

Accountability is the extent to which people are willing to accept responsibility for goals or actions and the extent to which leaders reinforce this. At Bell-Carter, the formal culture statement focused explicitly on this aspect of culture: "Creating value . . . means fostering accountability and ownership in all facets of the business." At Regent, associates were held accountable for "using resources wisely and efficiently," "proactively utilizing training programs," and "following up on every commitment made to customers."

Unfortunately, there are many companies in which accountability is not explicitly part of the culture. In these companies, people perceive that they can do whatever they want, even if it is not in the best interests of the company. We call this a "country club mentality."

Performance standards and accountability is not only a key dimension of culture; it is also a factor that influences family functionality. When family functionality is high, the expectations for family and nonfamily members with respect to performance and accountability are the same. When family functionality is low, nonfamily members may perceive that family members are held to different standards and that they are not held accountable for their performance. Family members "doing whatever they want" can undermine morale and negatively impact overall company performance.

Commitment to Change and Innovation

This dimension of culture relates to how a company views and reacts to change, including innovation. Growing organizations that embrace change as a way of life tend to experience less difficulty in making the required transitions that have been discussed throughout this book. Organizations that view change as threatening are likely to experience significant problems.

A family's willingness to learn and to embrace change—one of the six determinants of family functionality—directly affects this value within a family business. The strong focus on learning, innovation, and change management at Bell-Carter was captured succinctly in their formal 2007 values statement as, "Creating value means innovating." The family board and company leadership are willing to invest in employee development and in making the operational changes needed to enhance the organization's effectiveness. Tim T. Carter, who became CEO in 2012, has a very strong focus on innovation in both products and strategy.

Dysfunctional family dynamics can negatively impact the company's ability to define and manage this dimension of culture. Problems in this area include disagreements among family members about what "change" means, resistance by some family members to making specific changes, an unwillingness to accept proposed changes from anyone other than a family member, and an unwillingness to learn from the lessons of others. When these types of family issues are present, even if the company's formal culture statement contains something about the importance of change and continuous improvement, it will not be reflected in how people behave and in how the company operates.

Company Process Orientation

This final dimension of culture consists of the view that people hold about "organizational processes." Some organizations are process oriented, while others are not. Some organizations neglect processes, and others go so far as to reject the need for defined processes. These "meta views" of processes have an important impact on the extent to which planning, decision making, and even operations are systematized or ad hoc.

The view held about the role of processes is a cultural value and is typically based on a belief that processes either add economic value or imply "bureaucracy." This, in turn, influences the extent to which an organization is focused on developing formal processes or not. For example, at GOJO™, a highly successful family business, there is a strong belief in the value of processes that infuses everything the company does. Leaders at all levels of the company use sophisticated research to determine many aspects of the organization's functioning, including the layout of the facilities—not just the manufacturing plant, but all facilities.

Other organizations that are not process oriented tend to do things in an ad hoc way. Our experience working with organizations in China suggests that there is a cultural bias against processes in most Chinese entrepreneurial organizations (there are a few notable exceptions, such as Huawei). Many, perhaps most, Chinese entrepreneurships are family businesses that tend to be run by a single strong leader who gives directives to "helpers." Defined processes for planning, decision making, performance management, and communication are lacking. Our research indicates that the existence of a process orientation has an impact on bottom-line financial performance.[12]

The Five Dimensions of Culture
as Represented in Company Culture Statements

Most attempts to formulate culture statements are based on ad hoc statements of core values that make sense to the owners of the business. As a result, they typically reflect about 50 percent of what our research has shown a culture statement should focus on. The key dimensions of culture most frequently included in corporate culture statements are: customer orientation, orientation toward employees, and performance standards. Those that are *not* typically included are: accountability, innovation and commitment to change, and "process orientation." We are not suggesting that all formal statements of culture should include a specific value related to each dimension. But we do believe that these dimensions should be included in some way in the formal culture statement. For example, in Bell-Carter's 2007 statement of values, the company lists six "themes" that it refers to as "the roots of our olive tree." These are: (1) Family "Feel"'; (2) Trust and Respect for Individuals; (3) Common Sense and Good Judgment; (4) Create Value; (5) Show Up with Passion; and (6) Enjoy the Journey. The definition of each value or theme reflects Bell-Carter's culture with respect to one or more of the five cultural dimensions; that is, the document as a whole incorporates all five dimensions.

Each dimension has an empirical relationship to financial performance. Unless all are clearly identified and managed, a company is not likely to achieve optimal financial performance. One family business that created a set of values that closely corresponds to the five key dimensions is Taylor-Dunn.

Corporate Values at Taylor-Dunn

Taylor-Dunn was founded in 1949 by Davis Taylor Sr., who built an electric-powered cart to use in his wholesale poultry business. According to a history of the firm, "Mr. Taylor built his first vehicle exclusively for use on his own ranch; however, it wasn't long before the young company began producing trucks for other ranchers and nursery owners. Later that same year, Fred A. Dunn joined Mr. Taylor in the business and four years later the company's name was changed to Taylor-Dunn Manufacturing Company."[13] Taylor and Dunn decided to sell the poultry supply business and specialize strictly in the production of electric utility vehicles.

In 1990, the company was acquired by World Class Management, Inc., a holding company owned by Jim Goodwin and Milt Sneller. Jim served as the company's chairman and CEO, and Milt served as vice chairman and COO. In late 1996, the WCM-affiliated group changed the holding company's name from World Class Management, Inc., to Taylor-Dunn Corporation. In 2000, Jim acquired the ownership interest of his partner, Milt Sneller, and became the sole owner of Taylor-Dunn Corporation.

In 1981, Jim formulated a statement of values for Taylor-Dunn (see Table 6.1). and we have identified (in parentheses) how specific aspects of this statement correspond to the five key dimensions of culture. It comes very close to capturing all of the dimensions that affect financial performance. The only missing dimension is "accountability." This is not to sug-

Table 6.1. Taylor-Dunn Corporation's Values Statement and Identification of How the Five Culture Dimensions Are Addressed

Taylor-Dunn Values	Culture Dimension Addressed
How we accomplish our mission is as important as the mission itself. Fundamental to the success of our company are these basic values:	Process orientation
Customers are the focus of everything we do. Our products and services must totally satisfy our customers' needs and provide better value than our competition.	Customer orientation; performance standards
Quality comes first. To achieve customer satisfaction, the quality of our products and services must be our first priority.	Performance standards; customer orientation
Our people are the source of our strength. They provide our company its vitality and determination. Involvement and teamwork are the cornerstones of our human values.	People orientation
It is our way of life. Our employees, suppliers, and customers are a team. We must treat each other with trust and respect while maintaining mutually beneficial relationships.	People orientation; customer orientation; performance standards
Our products are the result of our efforts; they should be the best in serving our customers worldwide. As our products are viewed, so are we viewed.	Performance standards
Continuous improvement is essential to our success. We must strive to excel in everything we do, in our products and services as well as our human relations and competitiveness.	Innovation and commitment to change; performance standards
Integrity is never compromised. The conduct of our company must be pursued in a manner that is socially responsible and commands respect for its integrity and for its positive contributions to society. We are composed of men and women alike without discrimination and without regard to ethnic origin or personal beliefs.	Performance standards; people orientation

gest that the statement is perfect or could not be improved. However, it is impressive that the CEO of a family business intuitively understood what was most important about corporate culture and was able to express this in his company's culture statement.

The Process of Managing Corporate Culture

In working with companies of all sizes, we have found that the process of managing corporate culture—which includes communicating and reinforcing it—is as important as its content. [14] A model of the culture management process we have developed and applied in many businesses is shown in Figure 6-1. Each phase in the process is described below, using

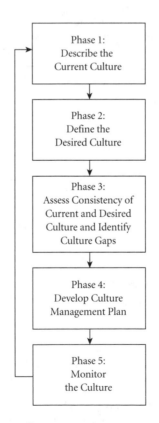

Figure 6.1. Culture Management Process

SOURCE: Eric G. Flamholtz, "Corporate Culture and the Bottom Line," *European Management Journal* 19, no. 3 (2001): 270.

Bell-Carter as the case study. In 1996, Bell-Carter's executive team (Tim, Jud, the VP of sales, and the CFO) decided that it was time to formally assess the extent to which Bell-Carter employees understood and behaved in ways consistent with the culture. They built on the output of this initial formal culture management effort over time to create the formal statement of values referred to earlier in this chapter.

Phase 1: Identification of the Current Culture

The culture management process begins with the identification of the existing corporate culture—that is, the culture that is currently influencing people's behavior. There are various ways to collect this information, including surveys, interviews, and workshops. At Bell-Carter in 1996, this information was collected through one-on-one interviews with a representative sample of employees at both company locations—the company's administrative and sales offices in Lafayette, California, and the plant in Corning, California—and through a workshop with the company's senior leadership team. Not surprisingly, the information collected suggested that, for the most part, the culture at Bell-Carter was positive and functional.

The goal of this data collection effort is to identify any differences in perception among family members regarding the current culture and its impact on organizational performance. The data collection effort will help identify family functionality issues that need to be addressed with respect to both what the culture currently is and what it will need to be to support the company's continued successful development.

Phase 2: Defining the Desired Culture

The next step is to formulate the ideal or desired culture of the organization. This "strategic culture" is what leadership believes the culture should be or become to support the overall strategic development of the enterprise.[15] The desired culture can be very consistent with or differ dramatically from the current culture.

Typically, the desired culture is defined by the senior leadership team working together. In a family business, it is also important to engage all family members in this effort. For the desired culture to become a reality, both company leaders and the family will need to embrace and support it. When there are family functionality issues, the process of reaching agreement on what the culture should be can be challenging. As in phase 1 of this process, there may be a need to work independently with the family to develop and reach agreement on what they believe the culture should be.

As Hess has cogently stated, "Family values should be the foundation, the bedrock, the basic building blocks upon which family decisions are made."[16] This implies that family members should reach consensus about the company's fundamental values. When family functionality is high, doing so will be easy. When family functionality is low, it will be difficult, and maybe impossible.

At Bell-Carter, one of us (Yvonne) worked with the company's leadership team to identify thirty-five statements that captured what they wanted their company's culture to be. We used the five dimensions of organizational culture—treatment of people (people orientation); treatment of customers (customer orientation); performance standards/accountability; openness to change; and company process orientation—as the basis for formulating these statements. It should be noted that at Bell-Carter, interviews conducted as a part of step 1 of this process revealed that many of these statements reflected Bell-Carter's already existing (current) culture.

Phase 3: Assessing Consistency of Current and Desired Cultures and Identifying "Gaps"

The third step in the culture management process is to assess the extent to which the current and desired cultures are consistent and identify any "cultural gaps"—that is, significant differences between them. The focus in this step is on identifying the extent to which the desired or strategic culture is actually being practiced in day-to-day behavior.

This step involves collecting information from employees about the extent to which they agree with the desired culture as defined by senior management, and the extent to which it is currently being practiced or realized. The information can be collected using interviews or surveys, or a combination of the two. When analyzing this information, it is important to keep in mind that employees' perceptions of the company's culture drive how they behave. Significant differences between groups of employees (e.g., in different departments or locations) will need to be considered when developing the culture management plan.

When family functionality is low, gaps between the current and desired cultures can be quite large. Family members may themselves see the current culture differently from one another. In these circumstances, the family may need to work together and separately from other members of the leadership team to identify and address specific family-related culture management issues.

At Bell-Carter, the thirty-five items developed as a part of step 2 (defining the desired culture) were incorporated into a culture survey that was designed to assess the extent to which Bell-Carter employees (1) believed that the culture—as defined by the items in the survey—represented what the company's culture *should* be (that is, the "desired" culture); and (2) saw people behaving in ways consistent with this desired culture.

The survey was administered to all employees. As expected, Bell-Carter's results were very positive. On all dimensions assessed, over 50 percent of the employees agreed that Bell-Carter employees were currently "living and breathing" the company's culture as reflected in the survey items. While the company at that time did not have a formal statement of its culture, it was clear that everyone understood what the culture should be and that most people were operating in ways consistent with this culture.

Phase 4: Developing a Culture Management Plan

The fourth step is to develop a plan to manage the company's culture, paying particular attention to closing any gaps between the current and desired cultures. Typically, this plan is included as part of the overall strategic plan for the business (described in chapter 3) and incorporates specific objectives and goals for making the desired culture a reality.

A challenge in this step may be the need for some or all of the family to change their behavior to better support the realization of the desired culture. Mechanisms that can be put in place to support this include providing the family members in question with coaches, providing regular feedback, and utilizing rewards to recognize behavior change. As with the other steps in this process, the family may need to take certain issues "off line" and develop its own internal culture management plan for changing their behavior.

Once the culture management plan has been developed, a typical first step in this process is to develop a formal statement of the desired corporate culture or core values (see Table 6.1) and communicate it to all employees. Effective communication of values should not be an "event"; instead, it should be an ongoing process of continual reinforcement. This can take place in employee meetings, in periodic written communication to all employees, and with rewards that recognize individual employees for behavior consistent with company values.

At Bell-Carter, specific objectives and goals for culture management were included in the company's strategic plan. In addition, a task force led by the company's CFO was formed to promote Bell-Carter's culture throughout the company. The task force included representatives from both of the company's locations. The task force—as a unit and at each location—was responsible for developing and implementing programs that would help make the desired culture real for all Bell-Carter employees.

Phase 5: Monitoring the Culture over Time

The fifth (and nominally the final) step in the culture management process is monitoring cultural changes to assess the effectiveness of the culture management program and identify any necessary future interventions. This step leads back to step 1, suggesting that culture management is an ongoing, iterative process. Culture management is not a five-steps-and-done process; it is, or must become, a way of life in an organization. At Bell-Carter, this monitoring process occurred in the context of the company's strategic plan quarterly review meetings.

Some Culture Management Challenges Facing Family Businesses

As companies grow, they will face numerous cultural problems. Some are common to all businesses, including increasing size and managing acquisitions; others are specific to family businesses.

As the number of employees increases, a company's culture tends to evolve or mutate. New people enter the organization, and some of the original founding group of employees leave. The resulting weakening of the culture becomes significant when a company reaches about 100 employees. Geographic dispersion of operations can accelerate the process. If a company operates in multiple locations, even within the same state or country, the culture can fragment into multiple cultures or subcultures. By the time a company reaches approximately 500 employees or five "generations" of employees, the need for formal culture management is critical.[17] With approximately 500 people, the cultural issues and conflicts that can emerge can be catastrophic for a company, if not managed correctly.

If a company is created through the process of corporate acquisitions, culture can become a critical variable earlier in its evolution. Each acquired company comes with its own culture, and the result can be a company with multiple-personality disorder.

It is widely accepted that approximately 90 percent of acquisitions fail and that the key to a successful acquisition is not strategic fit, but cultural fit. In chapter 7 we describe the failure of a large family-run business led by a husband and wife "team" to effectively manage the culture of its acquisitions.

Cultural Issues Specific to Family Businesses

In addition to the cultural issues that all business face, there are cultural issues that are specific to family businesses. These include the need to effectively manage all six factors that determine the level of family functionality (see chapter 1).

Favoritism.   The primary cultural problem that arises with respect to the "treatment of family members" functionality factor occurs when there is favoritism among family members. If some family members feel valued and others do not, significant conflict can arise. Favoritism can also exist between family and nonfamily employees (which relates to the family functionality factor of "treatment of nonfamily members"). This is the classic problem known as "nepotism," and it can include having different standards for family members and nonfamily members. In extreme cases, such as when family members are incompetent, the result can be a dysfunctional culture in which nonfamily employees become demoralized by their treatment as outsiders or second-class citizens. Hess has observed: "Family members can have a disruptive and devastating effect on a business's performance and employee morale if the family employee behaves in an arrogant manner or in a non-professional manner, flaunting rules, and/or treating employees with disrespect."[18]

Misuse of Rewards and Recognition.   Since rewards are powerful motivators, their misuse can lead to a dysfunctional climate and culture. The prescription for avoiding these problems is to create a reward system that is based on the principle of fairness and evenhandedness to all employees.

This issue is not only a problem between family members and nonfamily members; it can also be a problem *among* family members. There can be sibling rivalry and competition among family members as well as different perceptions of value to the business. Hess notes, and we agree, that hiring of family members should be "based upon merit, qualifications, and needs," that family members should be compensated "at arm's length" for a particular job, and that they should be evaluated, promoted, and demoted "based on consistent standards that are applied to all employees."[19]

Bell-Carter is one company that followed this prescription precisely: hiring family members who were qualified for their positions; compensating family members "fairly" in relation to their contributions; and evaluating them according to standards applied to all employees.

Resistance to Change.   Things change in business. The environment changes, people come and go, and the business changes in size and complexity. Families need to adjust to these forces. Some families are resistant to change, while others understand and embrace the need for change. The willingness to learn and adapt to change can be a powerful intangible asset in a family business. One company that has embraced the willingness to learn and change is GOJO™, whose owners and managers think of GOJO™ as a "purpose-driven learning organization." (We provide more details about GOJO™ in the final chapter.)

Transmission of Culture across Family Generations.   The inception of a culture typically comes from a business's founders. However, unless the culture is clear and measures are taken to ensure its transmission to different generations of family members, the culture can weaken.

To some extent, a company's culture is transmitted across generations through contact with the founding members of the organization. However, a formal culture management process or system will facilitate a more complete transmission of the culture. In addition, family members must be held accountable for behaving in ways consistent with the company's desired culture. This is not to suggest that the company's culture should remain unchanged from generation to generation of family members. The culture should change to support the company's goals, its growth, and changes in its environment. These changes should be managed using the process described earlier in this chapter.

Culture Conflict between Family Values and Business Values. Another culture-related problem in family businesses occurs when the family's culture (or values) and the business's culture are in conflict. Values-based conflict can arise for many reasons. Family members can differ in their willingness to assume business risk. Leaders may not share the same values. For example, a stated family value might well be that "all of the children are of equal importance to the family." But with respect to the business, all of a family's children might not be equal in capabilities, performance, or value to the enterprise.

When the family makes the distinction between people's treatment in the family and their treatment in the business, the result is a functional family business culture, like that at Bell-Carter. Where this distinction does not occur, problems inevitably follow.

Culture Management as a Way of Life

The leaders of successful companies and family business champions recognize the importance of culture and develop formal systems to manage this invaluable asset. When these systems are working effectively, they achieve a level of recognition that is embodied in phrases such as "the Hewlett-Packard Way," "the Wal-Mart Way, or "the Bell-Carter Way." At that point, culture management has been ingrained or institutionalized in the fabric of the firm's daily life.

Summary

The development, evolution, and management of corporate culture in a family business are elusive but critical processes. Corporate culture is an extraordinarily valuable intangible asset that can affect the financial performance of business organizations.[20] It can also become toxic and cause companies to experience distress or even fail. We examine dysfunctional and toxic cultures in the next chapter.

Part III

Special Issues
in Family Businesses

7 The Dark Side

In a family business owned by two brothers, one of the authors was asked to mediate a conflict between the brothers that threatened to paralyze, if not destroy, the company. In gathering background about this situation, we were shown a series of emails exchanged between the brothers. These emails consisted of little more than a series of insults, personal criticisms, and behavioral "suggestions" (i.e., "drop dead," "go —— yourself," etc.). These were the most vicious, demeaning, nasty, and bitter communications we have ever seen in a business or in any other context; and, it should be noted, several members of the company's leadership team were aware of and had seen some of these exchanges. During the first "mediation" session, we happened to ask, "Where were you both when this series of email was sent?" The answer was shocking and almost funny, but in a tragic way: "We were in our offices next door to each other!" The situation involving these brothers was ultimately unresolvable, and the brothers went through a "business divorce."

Family businesses like this one, which are particularly troubled, dysfunctional, and "toxic," represent "the dark side" of family business. On the basis of our experience working with and doing research on family business, we have identified ten family business "syndromes" that cause varying degrees of harm to the business and people within the business. These are listed below, from least to most dysfunctional.

- The Family Drama
- The Family Business Civil War

- The Family Albatross
- George Bailey
- The Money Tree
- King (or Queen) of the Hill
- Family Gladiator
- The Smiling Cobra
- I Deserve It
- Medea

Unfortunately, these syndromes are not rare. From our more than thirty-five years of professional experience working with family businesses of all types, we estimate that more than 50 percent of family businesses are dysfunctional in some way.

In this chapter we explain each syndrome and provide a framework for readers to use in assessing whether their family business has any of these problems. We suggest ways to overcome each syndrome using one or more of the tools presented earlier in the book.

The underlying causes of each syndrome relate to one or more of the six factors (described in chapter 1) that must be managed to promote a high degree of family functionality: treatment of family members, treatment of nonfamily members, expectations of performance and accountability within the family, family rewards and recognition, willingness of the family to learn and change, and family and company leadership. For each syndrome, we provide case examples to illustrate what it looks like in practice, based on our work with family businesses. Each example is real, but for obvious reasons we have changed the company names and the names of the individuals involved and have disguised the nature of their companies.

The Family Drama Syndrome

Garden-variety family dramas and family issues are often played out in the business arena. Family members behave as if the office is their own living room, rather than as they should in a business environment. We have observed many variations on this theme: conflicts between husbands and wives, brothers battling brothers, fathers battling sons, and mothers battling everyone!

Sometimes it seems as though the drama is not just inevitable in a family business, but is actually a form of entertainment for bored and jaded family members. At other times the family members seem so accustomed to the conflict that they are oblivious to its effects on the business.

One family drama occurred at MW Design. It was the result of an underlying conflict or power struggle between a husband and wife that manifested itself in the business arena. Walter Mathews and his wife, Deborah ("Debbie")Wilson, co-owned a graphic design firm. The firm had revenues of about $5 million and was located in Indianapolis, Indiana. Walter and Debbie were creative, talented individuals, with strong personalities who rarely saw eye-to-eye on anything. Walter, a Midwesterner, tended to be a bit conservative both in his design and in his ambitions for the business. Debbie, from Boston, tended to be more flamboyant and ambitious.

They had met at the Rhode Island School of Design in Providence, taken an instant liking to each other, married, and co-founded a firm. At that time, they perceived their differences as complementary. Walter was more of a traditionalist and used his background in the fine arts as a foundation for his work in applied arts such as graphic design. Debbie was more adventurous and tended to stretch the boundaries of whatever she was interested in. This included both design and the business concept. As their reputation for high-quality work grew, people began asking for work and products that they had not regularly produced before, such as logos and special pictures for advertising or financial reports. Debbie was very open to these projects, while Walter was reluctant to stray beyond the boundaries of his view of graphic design.

There was always some conflict in these situations between Walter and Debbie, but even more conflict erupted over the "design concepts" for various projects. The problem was that their conflicts usually ended in a stalemate because neither Debbie nor Walter would let the other have the final say. Nonfamily members employed in the business appreciated both owners' perspectives and chose to ignore the conflict between them. At the same time, however, they sometimes found it difficult to get their work done and meet client needs because they could not get answers to important questions. Over time, some customers grew tired of missed deadlines, and even though they viewed the work they received as "top notch," they began to consider using other firms to meet their needs.

This syndrome is driven by treatment of family members, where the family behaves in the business as it might at home. However, as was true of Walter and Debbie, there can also be issues related to family and business leaders—particularly if those in conflict are both in senior leadership roles.

Formal role descriptions are one tool that can be used to overcome or minimize the impact of this syndrome on the business. Family members must agree on "who is responsible for what" and then support the implementation of these roles with both performance management systems and effective decision-making processes. It might also be necessary for family members to develop a feedback process through which they can "alert" anyone who is not performing in a way consistent with the roles and decision-making processes that have been developed and agreed to.

The Family Business Civil War Syndrome

A few years ago during a business trip to Charleston, South Carolina, where the first shots of the U.S. Civil War were fired at Fort Sumter, we had a down day and took a tour by carriage around this beautiful Southern city. The tour guide, who recognized us as "Yankees," noted, with humor, that "there was nothing civil about it!" Similarly, there is nothing civil about a "Family Business Civil War." Like the real Civil War, it can be an intrafamily battle, with brother pitted against brother, father against son, mother against son or daughter, and all the other possible combinations of family members in conflict with other family members.

A company that experienced a classic family business civil war was Dixon International, a dealership for a large global truck manufacturer. The company, founded by Paul and Marcy Dixon in the early 1960s, had grown from a single dealership to three locations in southern Illinois and Missouri. In 1994, Paul Dixon suffered a stroke and needed to withdraw from the business. The family had to choose his successor. Since Paul was somewhat incapacitated by his illness, Marcy made the choice. Marcy chose Robert, the younger of their two sons, rather than Herbert, the eldest. Herbert was quietly livid. He considered himself smarter than Robert. Rather than accepting his role in the business, Herbert adopted a passive-aggressive strategy, opposing his younger brother in everything he did even if he would have agreed with the strategy or action under other circumstances.

This pattern soon became obvious to Robert and other managers in the company, who desperately tried not to get caught in the crossfire between the battling brothers. Robert felt betrayed by his brother, but did not confront the issue directly. Soon this internecine warfare led to a variety of problems. Some senior managers left for jobs with competitors. There were also operational problems in the business, customer dissatisfaction, and, finally, declining revenues and profits.

Herbert used these problems as ammunition at family meetings to try to convince his parents that he should be the leader of the company. Robert responded in kind, and the bickering became intense, personal, and vicious. It also led to conflict between the two brothers' immediate families and reached the point where Sally, Robert's wife, refused to come to events where Herbert and Cathy Dixon would be present, to the chagrin of Robert and his mother.

The problem was finally resolved when the global truck company, for which Dixon had been a longtime dealer, purchased the dealership. The brothers, Robert and Herbert, went their separate ways and never spoke to each other again.

The family civil war is an extreme version of the family drama and, as such, is driven primarily by the same underlying factor: treatment of family. However, there can also be issues with respect to how the family recognizes and rewards its members; in the case of the Dixon International, it was never clear to anyone but Marcy why one brother was chosen over the other to lead the company.

Having formal role descriptions for the positions that family members occupy in the business (and ensuring that family members agree to them) and promoting behavior consistent with the responsibilities of the role (by using effective performance management systems) can reduce some of the conflict. Using these role descriptions (which should include skills and competencies needed to perform the role) as the basis for promotion decisions can reinforce the idea that these decisions are being made in the best interest of the business, as well as the best interest of the family.

The Family Albatross Syndrome

Some family business owners use their businesses to take care of family members they believe "can't make it" in another business. These family members might be thought of as the family albatrosses, "constant, worrisome burdens" on their families and "barriers to success," as the dictionary defines the term.

The family albatross is given a position that may nominally make a contribution to the company, but the real reason for the person's involvement in the business is to provide him or her with a means of support and a source of self-esteem. Sometimes, especially when working in the family business is viewed as an entitlement, the albatross may not grow and may expect to be promoted or receive other perks (regardless of the contribution being made). When a family member makes no real contribution, everyone—both family and nonfamily members—knows it. If this situation is not carefully managed, it may become a source of resentment that, in turn, can affect overall company morale, as illustrated in the case of Lenny Fiske.

During high school and college, Lenny Fiske, the son of Eli Fiske, the founder of Fiske Marketing, spent his summers working in his father's company doing various jobs—proofreading reports, filing, and filling in for the receptionist when she was on vacation. According to other employees, all Lenny really did was receive a weekly allowance from his father. They never knew when he would show up. There was always a reason he was late or not in the office. Other employees suspected that he was at the beach (he was an avid surfer). Eli never questioned his son's absence and encouraged other employees to avoid giving Lenny anything that was too urgent or critical because there was a high probability that it wouldn't get done. This frustrated other employees, but they accepted it as "what the boss wanted to do."

After graduating from a private university with a degree in sociology, Lenny held sales positions in various companies and, though reasonably successful, never stayed in one place for very long. When things didn't work out, Lenny would ask his father, Eli, for assistance—including, at times, returning home to live. As Lenny approached his thirtieth birthday with still no clear career path, Eli decided that it might be "a good idea" to see if his son could do something of value in his business.

Lenny returned to the business as an assistant to one of the marketing directors, Pam. The goal, as Eli explained it, was for Lenny to learn the business so that he could eventually become a marketing director himself. Initially, Lenny appeared enthusiastic about his new position and talked with his father about the possibility of someday becoming Fiske's CEO. For the first three months, everything seemed to be going according to plan. Pam was reasonably happy with Lenny's performance and he seemed to be "getting the hang of things." But in the fourth month, Lenny went back to his old habits: coming to work late, not completing assignments, and sometimes not coming to work at all. Pam did her best to provide feedback to Lenny and to encourage him to "take the job more seriously." As she was a long-term employee at Fiske, she felt comfortable also telling Eli about his son's performance problems.

As performance continued to deteriorate, Pam told Eli that she could no longer work with Lenny and that he would have to find someplace else to "put his son." Eli accepted Pam's feedback, but believed that Lenny just needed some additional coaching. He decided to give Lenny a position that would report directly to him and take over the role of coach. Although he wasn't certain what he was going to have Lenny do, he was certain that he wanted his son employed in the family business. Lenny continued to use the business as his "home base," while pursuing activities like surfing, hiking, and snowboarding. His father continued to pay him, regardless of his performance and attendance. Other employees resented what they suspected was the relatively high salary that "Lenny the Loser" was receiving, but they accepted it because it was "Eli's business."

While it wasn't true of Lenny, sometimes the albatross evolves into a valued member of the company's team. In one family business we advised, the college-graduate son of the entrepreneur became the head of facilities management, which in the early years was really the head of janitorial services. The family and other employees believed that the son would never make a real contribution. Over the years, however, he learned the business and eventually became a member of the senior management team, respected for his in-depth knowledge and understanding of how the business worked.

The Albatross Syndrome results from bringing family roles and responsibilities into the business (treatment of family) combined with failing to clearly define expectations of performance and then holding people accountable for meeting those expectations. In Lenny's case, there was also confusion with respect to rewards and recognition. The albatross (supported by the behavior of the company and family leader) typically believes that family membership is enough to justify receiving rewards regardless of his or her actual performance.

The challenge for the family is to find ways to maximize the contribution the person makes and try to turn someone who is perceived as an albatross into a real contributor. This involves clearly defining the role that the individual will play, establishing clear goals for performance, providing feedback on performance, providing coaching to develop skills (which we discuss in chapters 8 and 9), and ensuring that whatever rewards are received are clearly linked to the results achieved. There may also be a need to help nonfamily members support the albatross's development, particularly if, as in the case of Lenny, they view the individual as a loser.

If the albatross won't or can't develop into a reasonably competent contributor, the family may need to find another way to take care of this individual without having him or her involved in the business. If the family can afford it, the individual could receive an allowance for living expenses. Another possibility is to set the individual up in a career that matches his or her interests, such as photography, an antique store, running a coffee shop—anything to keep him or her out of the business.

The George Bailey Syndrome

The classic film *It's a Wonderful Life* presents George Bailey (played by James Stewart) at a moment of crisis—contemplating suicide on Christmas Eve. As we learn later, he is facing possible disgrace and prison because his bumbling uncle has misplaced (lost) a great deal of money intended as a deposit from the family business, the Bailey Building and Loan, to the local bank.

As George contemplates suicide on a bridge, his "guardian angel," Clarence, jumps into the water. After George rescues him, Clarence helps George review his life. We learn that George grew up dreaming of travel to distant, exotic places, of a future as an architect, and of leaving the town of Bedford Falls far behind. We also learn that George has a finely honed sense of duty and responsibility and has continually sacrificed his dreams for the good of his family—including remaining in Bedford Falls and assuming leadership of the Bailey Building and Loan after his father's untimely death.

George never realizes any of his dreams. He never gets to leave Bedford Falls, never goes to college, and never becomes an architect. Instead, he remains the president of the family business, which to some extent he despises. The film shows us how different life for his family and his community would be had he never been born. Over the years, George has touched the lives of many people and has made many close friends. These friends ultimately come to George's rescue when asked by his wife to help replace the lost money. The film's message is that George really did have a "wonderful life," in spite of never realizing his dreams.

As we use the term here, the George Bailey Syndrome refers to anyone (male or female) who sacrifices his or her personal dreams out of a sense of duty and loyalty to the family or a parent and takes a role in the family business. In our consulting practice, we have observed many George and Georgina Baileys, men and women who are victims of this syndrome. One such victim was a woman, Kelly Roberts.

Kelly had graduated from a prestigious university and over about a decade had become very successful in her chosen profession. She, her husband, and their two children lived in Idaho, where they could fish in the summer, ski in the winter, and enjoy a fairly quiet life. Kelly's father, Gary, had a successful and growing distribution business in the San Francisco Bay Area and was looking to retire. Her younger sister had worked in the business for a number of years, but it was not really her "thing." In fact, everyone in the family knew that the younger sister was employed in the business only because Gary felt that he needed to take care of her (she was somewhat of an albatross).

As Gary looked toward retirement, he began to put pressure on Kelly to "move home and take over the business." Kelly was reluctant to give up her career and her lifestyle, but felt an obligation to her father and to the family. After a year of steady pressure from her father and mother, Kelly and her husband decided to sell their home and move back to the San Francisco Bay area.

Kelly, who had worked part-time in the business while she was in high school and college, assumed the role of COO, reporting directly to her father. She and her father developed a five-year plan, during which he would gradually move out of the business and Kelly would assume the CEO role. Several problems arose as they began to implement this plan. First, the other senior leaders of the company did not fully embrace Kelly as a peer or as their future leader. Nothing was said aloud, but their behavior spoke volumes. When Kelly asked them about progress in meeting goals or their unit's operations, she usually had to ask more than once or have her father intervene. While these leaders would never dare miss a meeting with her father, they would frequently blow off or "forget" meetings that Kelly had scheduled with them. Second, it became clear to Kelly in that first year that her father had very little intention of retiring. He continued to come to the office every day, and occasionally he overruled a decision that Kelly had made, thus further diminishing her credibility as a leader.

Kelly met regularly with her father to discuss business issues and used these opportunities to try to help him manage his behavior so that she could grow into her role and gain the respect of the other senior leaders. Although he agreed to avoid making decisions or doing things that would undermine her authority, he did not always follow through. Kelly's long hours were putting a strain on her marriage and she was upset with herself that she couldn't spend more time with her children. She grew to hate the business, but still felt an obligation to her family to try to make it work. The final straw for Kelly was when, after three years, her father one day announced that he no longer intended to retire at the appointed date and that his plan now was to continue working until he no longer could "make it out of the house." Flabbergasted, Kelly abruptly resigned and began to look for opportunities outside of the family business. On several occasions her father asked her to return to the business, to which she simply said no.

The factors underlying the George Bailey Syndrome are the confusion of family and business roles and, most importantly, how the family and company leadership role is viewed. The family creates expectations about the obligations of family members to the family through the business. In brief, it is expected that family members will place the family's and the business's best interests ahead of their own. Frequently, but not always, the syndrome occurs when the current generation of leadership is looking toward retirement and wants to name a successor who is a member of the family. If there is no family member working in the business who is qualified, pressure may be put on a family member from outside the business to take over because "the family needs you."

One useful tool to overcome, and even prevent, this syndrome is effective succession planning, which is the subject of chapter 9. This involves clearly defining the leadership role, specifying the skills needed to occupy the role, and identifying the candidates to fill it. Family members who are not already working in the business can be considered, but the family needs to be willing to let those individuals decline the offer when they feel it is in their best interest to do so. Once the successor is identified, the current leader needs to work to ensure that the transition is effective. While Kelly and her father had a plan for her succession, her father did not follow through, and this eventually led to her leaving the company for good.

The Money Tree Syndrome

As the label implies, the Money Tree Syndrome involves family members viewing the business as their personal source of financial assets to too great an extent—that is, they view the business as a reliable and endless source of income. Although the tree (business) provides nourishment and resources for the family, it requires maintenance and care. Yet the family seems unable to take the long-term view and places too much strain on the business to provide what its members think they need.

There are two underlying causes of this problem. One is the founders' belief that it is their responsibility to take care of family members. The other is family members' belief that they have a right to be taken care of. Family members who feel this way put an excessive financial burden on the business to meet their "needs." Generosity is a virtue, of course, but the financial burden of caring for a family can exceed the capabilities of the business. It can also damage the long-term viability of the business by siphoning off resources that are more appropriately devoted to its maintenance and growth. Carried to an extreme, the family can kill the tree (destroy the business).

One example of a family business that fell victim to the Money Tree Syndrome was Hosta Construction, as described in chapter 5. Another was McDonald Industrial Abrasives. Founded by Jim McDonald in the late 1940s, the company specialized in providing all kinds of abrasive products for industrial uses. Its products ranged from grinding wheels to sandpaper.

In the 1970s, Walter McDonald, Jim's son, joined the firm. He was energetic and talented, and through his efforts the firm attracted more business.

By 1990, Jim had moved from the sales to the administrative side of the business, playing a significant role in managing the company's back office. Walter's three sons, Brad, Steve, and Carl, had also started working in the business. None were particularly competent or motivated, but they very much liked the money they were being paid. Throughout the 1990s, business was good, and Walter kept increasing the amount of money he took as compensation. Jim, though not very active, also continued to receive his salary. Walter's sons received annual raises and bonuses. They were all used to a very comfortable lifestyle.

Everything went smoothly until the early 2000s, when there was a decline in the economy. Even though business had slowed, the McDonald family kept their salaries at the same levels. To provide for this same level of income, Walter laid off some employees. He also reduced expenses by "nickel-and-diming" customers.

As the economy continued to deteriorate, Walter eliminated or reduced certain reimbursements that the company had customarily made to its employees. He stopped paying a mileage reimbursement when employees used their personal autos for company business, and he cut the firm's contribution to their health care premiums. At the same time that these cuts were being made, employees saw the new cars being driven by the McDonald family and heard about their vacations. They began to feel taken advantage of and less loyal to the firm.

In January 2004, one longtime key employee, Mark Reed, left McDonald Industrial Abrasives to take a job with a competitor. Mark was good with customers and had frequently brought new business into the firm. His comment to a co-worker when he left was, "I am tired of busting my butt so that Brad, Steve, and Carl can drive new Mercedes and Porsches and go to Mexico for weekend holidays!" With his departure, McDonald Industrial Abrasives lost a valuable asset, and its performance continued to decline.

Family expectations about performance, accountability, treatment of nonfamily members, and rewards are the underlying factors that lead to this syndrome. Regardless of individual or business performance, family members believe that they are entitled to rewards above and beyond what might be available to nonfamily members. At the extreme, the family reduces the compensation of even high-performing nonfamily members in the interest of satisfying their own desires.

Developing, implementing, and utilizing effective performance management systems can minimize the impact of this syndrome on the business. As a part of this process, the family needs to reach agreement about how much money is and is not acceptable to take out of the business each year and how the funds should be distributed. Ideally, the distribution should be based on the contributions made by individual family members. Consideration should also be given to what the family will do to recognize and reward high-performing nonfamily members.

King (or Queen) of the Hill Syndrome

This syndrome is the result of intense competition among family members for dominance in the most senior leadership role: that is, to become king or queen of the hill. In family businesses that suffer from this syndrome, the degree of rivalry goes beyond healthy competition to become almost pathological. One might assume that this occurs most often among siblings, but we have also observed it between fathers and sons and husbands and wives.

Extreme competition among family members for leadership can cause havoc as people take sides in the battle or "run for cover" so as not to become collateral damage. The battle to be king or queen of the hill can be so intense as to cause a business to perish.

One tragic example of this occurred in a battle between a husband and wife for control over the business that they jointly founded. This business, which we shall call Healthco, was a prepaid medical insurance plan. George Harris was CEO, and his wife, Kathy Marshall, was COO. The company had been successful and had grown rapidly, but it was experiencing the classic growing pains of a business undergoing "hyper-growth"—growth more rapid than it can keep up with.[1] The two leaders, George and Kathy, disagreed sharply over virtually everything from strategy to staffing. Their marriage had deteriorated, and they were playing out their mutual anger in the business.

As a result of their conflict, the organization was extremely "siloed" and divided into "George's people" and "Kathy's people." Any idea, action, or program proposed by one faction was viewed with suspicion by the other faction. Some people within the firm were cautious about getting caught in the crossfire. Decision making slowed to a crawl, and problems accumulated without solutions.

Recognizing the problems facing Healthco, our firm was invited by two of "Kathy's people" to do an organizational assessment, including the administration of our proprietary organizational assessment surveys. After conducting interviews and analyzing the survey data, we presented our findings to Kathy and her senior team. George did not attend the session. We do not know whether he was invited or if he just elected not to attend.

Our conclusions were unusually negative, and our prognosis was clear. We stated that within twelve months the firm would be in a crisis if the current issues were not dealt with. We were then asked to propose an approach for assisting Healthco in addressing the problems. We proposed as a first step an "all leaders' retreat" to develop a plan of action. We stated that the meeting must include George and other key members of his team. Our proposal was not accepted. Offline, we were told by two members of Kathy's team that since she had brought us into the firm, we were viewed as Kathy's consultants and thus were unacceptable to George.

Approximately nine months after our presentation of the assessment's results, Healthco filed for bankruptcy, as we had predicted. The family business war was over, and both combatants lost.

Performance expectations, family rewards and recognition, and family leadership issues contribute to the battle to become king or queen of the hill. It is a battle for recognition or dominance within the family as well as in the business. Each person battling for the leadership role has a different set of expectations for themselves and for the company. They believe they should be rewarded for their investment in the company's success, which in their minds should be the assumption of the most senior leadership role.

If the participants in this battle are co-owners, the situation might be difficult to resolve. If, however, the participants recognize the impact their behavior is having on the company, creating a structure that allows each person to lead one portion of the company is one solution. Effectively implementing this structure involves clearly defining the roles of each senior leader, the reporting relationships, and how the two leaders will work together to make strategic decisions for the company as a whole.

If the participants in king or queen of the hill are the designated successors, developing and implementing a succession plan that the family agrees to can sometimes end the battle (see chapter 9). This plan needs to clearly define the roles and responsibilities of those involved, the performance standards that each needs to meet, each individual's development goals, and how each participant will be rewarded for achieving both performance and development goals.

The Family Gladiator Syndrome

In family businesses that suffer from the Family Gladiator Syndrome, family members are pitted against each other for the perverted amusement of a senior member of the family (usually the most senior leader in the company). Just as in the King of the Hill Syndrome, the degree of rivalry can be borderline pathological, as it was in the case of the Breitbart family.

Dietrich Breitbart's family immigrated from Germany to the midwestern United States in the early 1900s. In the "old country," Dietrich had been an apprentice to a chef, and so in this country in his later twenties he founded a restaurant called "Old Germany." The restaurant was successful, and it ultimately passed to his son, Samuel, in the 1940s. Samuel married in the early 1940s and had two sons, Henry and Karl. Henry was Karl's senior by four years. Under Samuel, the business grew from one restaurant to three, with Samuel managing one and his two sons managing the others.

Of the two sons, Henry was the more entrepreneurial, and he proposed creating a "store within a store" concept for the business, so that customers could take home some of the fine foods and bakery items (for which the restaurant was well known) sold on the regular menu.

Henry viewed the bakery as a specialty store that could be expanded or scaled up as a stand-alone concept. He convinced the family to open what he termed a bakery-café, where people could enjoy a pastry with a cup of coffee or tea. It was a successful venture. Karl, however, believed that the business should maintain its focus on traditional restaurants rather than diversify into what he saw as a "different business." Henry's and Karl's different perspectives about the future of the business became an ongoing source of conflict. Over time, the conflict became very personal and escalated to include old grudges and other unresolved issues.

There was another, less visible dimension to the situation and conflict. Rachel, Henry and Karl's mother, was seen by some observers in the business as the agent provocateur. People in the firm said she seemed to enjoy and even egg on the conflict between her sons. It was a classic case of pitting the brothers against each other. Within the firm, the family began to be called "the battling Breitbarts." It was widely believed that the family was spending much more time and effort battling among themselves than focusing on competition and building the business. In fact, a smaller competitor with the same idea as Henry created their own bakery-café and ultimately became a large national firm. The Breitbarts' restaurants stayed in business, but they never reached their potential as a business concept.

The Family Gladiator Syndrome is driven by how the family treats each other, by performance standards, and often by how the family leader views and executes his or her role. The family leader may even be unaware of the games that he or she oversees within the company and that the participants in these games may or may not enjoy them. The message, however, is that to be valued by family leadership, participation is mandatory. As in a family civil war, gladiators may enlist the support of nonfamily members. When this happens, it can be extremely disruptive and may ultimately undermine company success.

A formal family business planning process, clear role descriptions (that include identification of reporting relationships), and clear performance standards for all family members and nonfamily managers are tools that can be used to overcome or minimize the impact of this syndrome. A well-developed family business planning process (that includes a family business foundation that all family members have agreed to, measurable goals, and a process for monitoring performance against the plan) focuses family members on what each individual should be doing, how individuals should be working together to achieve company goals, and how performance is or is not aligned with company goals. If the plan has been approved by all family members, it can be used as the basis for eliminating gladiator games. Similarly, formal role descriptions and individual performance standards that have been shared with and approved by all family members can be used to reinforce what each team member should be doing, rather than what the leader wants people to be engaged in.

The Smiling Cobra Syndrome

Extremely intense competition among family members sometimes contributes to a desire for other family members to fail. It is *not* a battle to become the king or queen (the dominant leader of the business); instead, it occurs when the current dominant leader within the business wants the potential successor to *fail*. Often this syndrome plays out between a father and son, when the father (consciously or not) does not want his son to succeed.

Most of the time, the real agenda of the person in charge is not revealed. The parent *seems* to be supportive of the son or daughter but is secretly trying to sabotage him or her. It is *possible* for the parent to be unaware of this motive; however, when we have encountered this situation, we could easily see what was going on, though it might have been less obvious to others. That is why we have used the metaphor of "a smiling cobra" to describe this syndrome. A cobra is a deadly snake, but unlike a cobra, a person can be smiling but deadly. One egregious example of this syndrome is described in the case below.

James Wallingford Jr. was the second-generation owner of Wallingford Insurance, a successful insurance brokerage firm. His son "Trip" (James Wallingford III) had joined the family business after graduating as an accounting major from Cal State Northridge, located in the San Fernando Valley adjacent to Los Angeles. At the age of 33, Trip was running Wallingford Insurance on a day-to-day basis, though his father was still owner and chairman.

In an effort to become a true leader and manager of the business, the younger Wallingford hired us to coach him. As part of the process of helping him develop, we conducted a "360-degree assessment" that involved conducting interviews with his direct reports, peers, and with his father, James Jr., to collect information on his strengths and opportunities to improve as a leader. A number of Trip's direct reports suggested during the interviews that there was significant conflict between father and son. They felt Trip was trying to prove to his father that he was worthy of running the business, but that James Jr. always found something to criticize.

One longtime Wallingford employee told us he had a feeling that James Jr. was actually in competition with his son. He stated that, at some level, it seemed as though James Jr. did not want Trip to succeed. He told us that James Jr. had been raised by a domineering, almost abusive, father, and that he experienced a great deal of humiliation from his father. This employee stated that James Jr. was seen as someone who was passive-aggressive and as someone who harbored a great deal of anger. He went on to say this about James Jr.: "Nothing seems to satisfy him, especially when it comes to Trip. For example, when Trip was at Northridge, one semester he got 4 As and a B and his father said, 'Why did you get the B?' That infuriated Trip."

Our experience with this firm tended to support the suspicion that the father secretly wanted his son to fail. After we had been working with Trip for about eight months, James Jr. asked to meet with us in order to get a progress report on how his son was doing. Trip approved of the private meeting. We provided a candid assessment, along with our conclusion that Trip was making good progress.

A few days later, Trip called and said that he needed to terminate our work with him and Wallingford Insurance. He said that his father had told him that if he needed a consultant to coach him to be a good CEO, then he was unfit for the job. Trip said that he wanted to continue the coaching process and that he would pay for it personally and not charge it to the business. We worked together for a few more months until one day Trip called to tell us that he had been fired by his father. Trip was shocked and disheartened. The termination led to a lawsuit between father and son. It also led to their estrangement. To our knowledge, Trip and his father never spoke to each other again.

In reflecting on what had happened, we could find no reason for the father's strange behavior except that he did not want his son to succeed. He seemed to be a classic smiling cobra.

During the litigation process, the lawyer representing Trip's father told us that we would be called to testify about the coaching process. We agreed to do whatever was required and noted that our view of Trip as a manager and leader was very favorable and very negative of the father in all respects. We never heard from the attorney again.

The Smiling Cobra Syndrome results from a combination of issues related to family and company leadership and rewards and recognition. Whether consciously or not, the current business leader is in some respect threatened by one or more other family members and so finds ways to undermine their development, sabotage their ability to achieve their goals, or deny them the rewards and recognition they deserve.

Implementing a well-designed performance management system that includes clear goals and links performance achieved with the rewards received is one tool for overcoming this syndrome. For maximum effectiveness, each individual on the team (including the family business leader) needs to have goals that are clear and understood by all other family members. The cobra, if he or she is motivated to change, can benefit from leadership development and coaching, as can the present or potential "victims." This process might begin with 360-degree interviews (like those completed for Trip) for the cobra and his or her direct reports to identify specific developmental issues. The coaching process is described in more detail in chapter 9.

The "I Deserve It" Syndrome

A strong sense of entitlement by one or more family members is the underlying cause of this syndrome. One or more family members feels entitled to more than they are getting and, as a result, takes more than their share from the business because "I deserve it!" When this syndrome is present, it sometimes results in family members embezzling company funds. This ultimate form of betrayal happens more often than one might imagine. Family members tend to trust one another, even when there are conflicts; the opportunity to embezzle funds from a business sometimes occurs when it is least expected, as illustrated in the following case.

At Wilson Marketing & Communications, a small family-owned business, the sister-in-law of the founder served as the CFO. The owner and other family members trusted her and her judgment. Because the company was growing rapidly and all the other family members were busy with clients, in-depth reviews of the company's financials were not conducted regularly. The CFO provided information about revenue and expenses, and seldom were there any questions about the results.

When the economy melted down in 2008, Wilson's revenues declined and new business became more difficult to secure. The family decided to forgo their usual bonuses and use the funds to support continued business operations. Everyone, including the CFO, agreed that this made sense.

During a year-end review in late 2009, the founder noted that expenditures for travel and entertainment were extremely high, given that year's business activities. Since most of these expenses were paid for with credit cards, he asked his sister-in-law to look into it and provide more detailed information. The sister-in-law said that this would require a great deal of time, but that she would do her best to complete the work within the next few months. The founder's daughter, who was also at the meeting, volunteered to complete the analysis because her client services demands at the time were not very high.

As the daughter began going through the credit card statements, she noted that there were charges for restaurants, Internet and in-store purchases for products that she was not aware the company had secured, and excessive charges at a gas station located near the sister-in-law's residence. A review of the general ledger revealed several checks, each for well over $1,000, that could not be reconciled. When copies of these checks were obtained from the bank, the daughter found that they had been hand-written by the sister-in-law to a credit card company that was not used by the family firm. The daughter decided to examine the company's financial records going back several years. It turned out that for nearly a decade the CFO had been siphoning off company funds amounting to over $500,000.

The daughter compiled the information and presented it to her father who, in turn, confronted his sister-in-law. The sister-in-law said simply, "I knew it was wrong." Rather than press charges, the founder asked that she repay the company $250,000, which she did. Although the founder was pretty sure that his brother knew at least some of the details about his wife's actions, the founder and his daughter promised not to disclose what the sister-in-law had done to anyone else, including other family members. The founder also allowed his sister-in-law to resign, rather than terminate her.

The "I Deserve It" Syndrome reflects a perverted concept of rewards and recognition by family members that has little to do with performance. In the minds of those who suffer from this syndrome, family membership "entitles" them to certain rewards, regardless of the contributions that they make or their level of performance. Some may also feel badly treated, which somehow justifies the "I deserve it" mentality.

Effective performance management systems at the company and individual levels can be used to prevent and/or overcome this syndrome. In the aftermath of the problems described above, the founder put in a place a much more sophisticated planning and financial management system. The company set goals, established budgets, and closely monitored performance against goals and budgets on a monthly basis. At the individual level, it is important to establish clear goals and clearly define how individual family member's rewards will be linked to company and individual performance.

The Medea Syndrome

In Greek mythology, Medea, the wife of Jason, killed her own children after he left her for another woman. In the context of a family business, a Medea need not be female, and the actions of a Medea need not be based on a literal betrayal; the betrayal can be figurative, as from a self-inflicted psychic wound. Specifically, a family business Medea is someone who experiences great psychological loss resulting from the impending transition of business leadership from himself or herself to another person. Consciously or unconsciously, he or she does not want to give the business to anyone else and so engages in the destruction of the business that the family has spent a lifetime building.

Motives vary for this seemingly incredible behavior, which is rational only to the perpetrator. One motive is hatred among family members. Another motive is revenge, resulting from a clash between two family members. Or the founder of a firm may not really want to leave the business he or she has created to anyone else in the family. If the founder, whose life's work was building the business, feels unappreciated, hurt, and angry, he or she might start destroying the business so that there is nothing left for the family. Alternatively, the founder might simply not want anyone else to benefit from his or her life's labor. The Medea Syndrome is particularly difficult to deal with when the sufferer's objective is unconscious. Although the behavior can be clear to observers both inside and outside the firm, it might not be clear to the perpetrator.

We have observed this syndrome in our experience as advisors and consultants to family businesses. Most often the perpetrators have been men rather than women, as illustrated in the cases that follow.

Rosebud Fashions was founded by Rose Cohen, with the concept of designing and manufacturing clothing for young women. Rose was the designer, and her husband Charles (known as "Bud") was responsible for business administration. The name of the company was an amalgamation of their two names. Over thirty years, the company grew to more than $120 million in annual revenues and became known for "inexpensive, fashion-forward" designs. Its designers traveled to Europe and Japan to get ideas for blouses and produced knock-off versions of what they saw. Unfortunately, as their company grew, the relationship between Rose and Bud deteriorated. They did not quarrel about the business, but it was well known that their relationship was strained.

Bud's behavior was viewed as erratic. Although he was responsible for the administrative side of the business, he sometimes got involved in purchasing fabrics. He was known to go to lunch with a salesman and return having placed a large order for new fabrics. People jokingly estimated that Rosebud Fashions had enough fabric to go around the globe 1.75 times and Bud was still purchasing more.

The Cohens' daughter, Sandra, who had joined the company after receiving her undergraduate degree from an Ivy League school, had a darker view of Bud's behavior. She believed that her father was trying to bankrupt the business through his profligate purchasing behavior. However, she could not talk to her father about this. She had previously engaged one of us (Eric) to coach her in becoming a better manager and asked if he could assist with this issue as well. The mission was to convince Bud that he had a responsibility to leave the business intact and not destroy it, and that his daughter was capable of ultimately running it.

Eric met with Bud several times to discuss aspects of the business, but chose never to directly address Bud's possible hidden agenda; rather, he discussed the need for a legacy by Bud and Rose, and also described the coaching that he was doing to help Sandra become an effective leader and manager. Bud was a good listener and a smart man, but his vision was somewhat clouded by the anger he had toward his wife (though Eric and Bud also did not discuss this directly). Eric reminded him that more than five hundred people's livelihoods depended on Rosebud Fashions and that those people had placed their trust in his good judgment.

Gradually, over a series of meetings (usually over lunch or dinner), Bud began to ask questions that showed he was thinking about setting up the business for continuation after he and Rose had retired or passed on. He also asked if and how he might be able to assist with Sandra's leadership preparation or whether he should just let Eric handle it. That was the key sign of a shift in his mindset. Eric assured Bud that Sandra would be delighted to have her father's help, and they discussed ways he could participate in the coaching process.

Three years later, Bud and Rose withdrew from the business and Sandra was appointed CEO. She continued her involvement in the business even after she had two children. Her husband, Jeffrey, left his position as VP of marketing in a subsidiary of a Fortune 500 company to join the company as COO. Today, Rosebud Fashions has grown considerably and continues as a successful enterprise.

Although this situation had a happy ending, sometimes the ending is very much darker. One founder of a family business we worked with seemed to want his daughter to be his successor after he retired. He sent her for an MBA, employed her in the firm, asked us to "groom her" for the CEO position, and on the surface did all the right things to prepare his daughter, whom we shall call Janis, for succession. However, we saw some subtle telltale signs that all was not as it seemed. The founder made some casual remarks not directed at Janis, but at "women managers." He seemed overly critical of Janis's work; some of his feedback was justified, but some criticisms seemed "picky." There were also times when Janis's father told her (in one way or another), "I'm not sure that you are ready to lead this company and I'm not sure when you will be." What Janis perceived as "constant" criticism with "little praise" demoralized her. She came to believe that she couldn't do anything right. After a few years, she reluctantly left the business, and her father, Arthur, expressed regret. He said, "All I tried to do was prepare her to be my successor." Arthur eventually sold the company.

The underlying factors that contribute to the Medea Syndrome are treatment of family members and how the leader views the business. Whether aware of it or not, the leader (usually the founder) does not believe that anyone else can or should run the business. This belief becomes a self-fulfilling prophecy as the leader does all he or she can to undermine the development of possible successors. We believe that this syndrome contributes to many family businesses lasting no more than a generation.

Performance management (including clear definition of roles and goals), coaching, and formal succession planning are tools that can be used to overcome or minimize the impact of the Medea Syndrome on the business. The leader (who is the problem) needs to agree to establish and assess company and individual performance (including his or her own) based on specific, measurable goals. In addition, the leader can benefit from coaching that focuses on addressing specific issues related to the development of the business, the development of the leadership team, and succession. Finally, formal succession planning—well in advance of the leader's projected retirement date—can be used to help the leader become more comfortable with turning day-to-day operations over to someone else.

Summary

Over the past thirty-five years, the most acrimonious and dysfunctional conflicts we have seen in our work with businesses of all kinds have been between members of the same family working in a business together. This is "the dark side" of family business. The dark side emerges when family functionality is low and presents itself in a variety of family business syndromes, as described in this chapter. Overcoming each syndrome involves using one or more of the tools described in the last section of this book to increase family functionality. It also involves family business leadership and succession, which we discuss in the next two chapters.

Sometimes it is possible to resolve the underlying issues that lead to the presence of one or more of these syndromes; and sometimes these problems are intractable. When family business dysfunction is not possible to overcome, some family members may leave the business, the business may fail, or the family may choose to sell the business and exit it entirely. Exit (sale of the business) can be the preferred solution when family dynamics have become too toxic to continue as a family business.

8 Leadership

In its hundred-plus-year existence, Bell-Carter Foods has had five generations of leaders, with each facing and effectively addressing very different
challenges. Arthur Bell, the company's founder, was an entrepreneurial
leader who, with his older brother, bought an olive orchard in 1912 and then
expanded into processing olives. In the 1960s, Arthur's stepson, Daniel, assumed leadership of the olive-processing business and continued its growth
and development in a market that included many family-owned businesses
like his own, and where a major goal was to just "stay in business."

Tim and Jud Carter (Daniel's sons) were part of a family business leadership team when they joined the business full-time in the mid-1960s,
working in partnership with their father to make key company decisions
even before being named CEO (Tim) and president (Jud) in 1973. They
faced a market that was consolidating, bringing with it opportunities as
well as challenges. Over the next thirty years, Tim and Jud together built
the infrastructure needed to help the company continue to grow. The next
company leader was a nonfamily member whose role was to continue implementing and refining the processes that Tim and Jud had put in place; as
well as to help groom Tim's son, Tim T. to take over, which he did in 2012.
Tim T.'s focus is on growing the company through new opportunities, while
continuing to promote the success of the core olive business.

One of the most critical functions in family businesses is leadership. Effective leadership is required for managing organizational development and
operations, for dealing with and managing family dynamics, and for helping

to create what we call "family–business equilibrium." Although leadership is demonstrably of critical importance, the typical book on family business does not address the nature and process of leadership. It treats it as a given.

In order to understand effective leadership in family businesses, this chapter addresses several related questions:

- What is leadership?
- What is the nature of leadership in a family business that makes it different from leadership in other businesses, and what can be done to promote effective family business leadership?
- What are the key tasks that leaders in family businesses need to perform to successfully manage day-to-day operations and the long-term development of the business?
- What are the various "styles" of leadership, and when should each style be used?
- What are some of the special challenges of family business leadership?
- What is "effective family business leadership"?

We offer basic concepts, ideas, and research findings related to the leadership of family businesses. The framework we present draws on a combination of leadership research, as well as our own experience working with family business leaders in their organizations.[1] Throughout this chapter, we present case studies of leadership in actual organizations.

What Is Leadership?

Many people tend to view leadership as personified by a charismatic leader—Steve Jobs, founder of Apple; and Richard Branson, founder of the Virgin Group of companies, for example. A better way to think about leadership is as a set of tasks to be performed in a manner that focuses people on setting and working to achieve goals. In this sense, leadership is an ongoing process, not a set of traits that a person possesses. The process involves understanding, predicting, and influencing others' goal-directed behavior. The leader's ultimate objective is to create a goal-congruent situation—that is, a situation in which employees can satisfy their own needs by seeking to achieve the goals of the organization. Leadership, then, is behaviorally oriented and goal-directed.

In the context of growing a business, leaders need to both promote effective day-to-day operations and build an organizational infrastructure that will support the company's continued growth and development. Effective leadership, in fact, is a key ingredient in a company's ability to manage organizational development (defined in chapter 1).

Leadership in Family Businesses: Achieving Equilibrium

Leadership in family business is more complex than in nonfamily organizations because leaders must consider, manage, and balance the needs of the family with the needs of the business. In a nonfamily business, leadership has a single focus: what is right for the business currently and over the longer term. In a family business, virtually all decisions have a dual aspect: what is right for the business and what will be best for the family. Effective leadership in a family business, then, involves working simultaneously to achieve both the goals of the business and the family goals as they relate to the business; effective leaders understand and are able to achieve an optimal "family–business equilibrium."

Effective leaders in family businesses therefore must have two capabilities: (1) the ability to effectively perform as a leader in general (that is, possess effective leadership "skills"); and (2) the ability to effectively manage the family–business equilibrium. When the leader lacks either or both of these capabilities, the kinds of problems described in chapter 7 ("The Dark Side of Family Business") will inevitably emerge. While company leaders are central players in promoting and maintaining family–business equilibrium, they need the support of other family members. That support includes respecting the authority of those in leadership roles, regardless of one's individual role within the family.

The Foundation of Family Business Leadership: Achieving Role Clarity

In the most effective family businesses, there is clarity about what is expected of those in leadership roles (whether they are family members or not) and the role "on the job" is kept distinct from the role "in the family." In other words, there is a clear distinction between "family roles" and "family business roles." A classic example of this comes from sports: Jackie Joyner-Kersee, three-time Olympian and two-time Olympic gold medalist in the heptathlon, was coached by her husband, Bob Kersee. When they were at home, they were husband and wife. When they were at the track, she was the athlete and he was her coach. The results of separating family and business roles, in this case, speak for themselves.

Clearly defining who is in charge and respecting those in leadership roles is as important in family businesses as it is in sports. During the three decades that brothers Tim and Jud Carter served as Bell-Carter's leaders, Tim managed the sales and administrative sides of the business and Jud oversaw production and grower relationships. The two brothers jointly managed the company as a whole, and their family board served as advisors. They were very clear about what each was responsible for and how they would work together in the business.

When role clarity is lacking, conflicts among family members can play out in the business. In one small family service business, the wife (who was the business owner, CEO, and a student in one of the executive education programs that we teach at UCLA) managed sales and service delivery and her husband (the CFO) managed the administrative functions. When the CEO was out with clients, her husband would tell the sales team what to do (much as he would do with the couple's children). Unfortunately, what he told the sales team to do was not always what they should be doing, but they would follow his direction because he was the CEO's husband. This created a great deal of conflict between CEO and CFO and reached a point where the CEO considered firing her husband.

A clear definition of roles is the foundation of effective family business leadership. Achieving role clarity is important at all levels of the company and with all family members. Building on this foundation of role clarity is the need for those in leadership roles to effectively perform certain tasks that focus their teams on both performing effectively on a day-to-day basis and working to promote the long-term development and success of the business. In the next sections, we describe and provide strategies for performing these "operational" and "strategic" leadership tasks, which, it should be noted, can also enhance family functionality.

The Key Tasks of Operational Leadership in a Family Business

Research has identified five specific tasks that need to be performed on a regular basis to promote effective ongoing company operations.[2] When performing these tasks in a family business, leaders (whether family members or not) need to maintain a high level of family–business equilibrium—that is, they need to balance the needs of the business with the needs of the family. This is easier when there is a strong leadership foundation (i.e., clear roles) and when there is a high level of family functionality. The five tasks and strategies for effectively performing them in a family business are presented below.

Task #1: Develop, Communicate, and Monitor Performance against Goals

An internationally renowned behavioral scientist, the late Rensis Likert, argued that to be effective a leader has to set goals and demonstrate a "contagious enthusiasm" for achieving them. "Goal emphasis" is, in fact, the first task of effective operational leadership. When performing this task in a family business, there needs to be a focus on two levels: (1) how the family defines and manages its goals for the business; and (2) how leaders set, communicate, and monitor performance against goals on a day-to-day basis.

Performing this task at the family level requires clearly defining and ensuring that the family is in agreement about the goals for the business. At Bell-Carter, for example, the overall goals that the family has for the business are to keep the family together and continue to grow the company. Performance against high-level goals is shared with the family board, which provides advice when problems are encountered.

The second level of goal emphasis is what happens on a day-to-day basis between managers at all levels and their direct reports. In a high-performing family business, goals for each individual are based on his or her role in the company (not in the family) and are set to support the achievement of overall company goals. Progress against goals is monitored, feedback is given on a regular basis, and rewards are linked to the overall level of performance achieved. In a very successful $40 million manufacturing company with whom we worked for several years, for example, the founder's brother and cousin were members of the senior leadership team, with each managing a specific function. Like all members of the company's leadership team, each had specific goals they were working to achieve within their departments. While at times the owner was a little harder on his brother than he was on other members of his leadership team, all team members were held accountable for and were given feedback on their performance against goals. Family members received no special treatment.

When family functionality is low, problems can emerge in performing this task, including not setting goals for family members or not setting them effectively (too high or too low), not holding family members accountable for performance, and providing rewards to low or mediocre performers simply because they are family members.

Task #2: Facilitate Effective Interaction among Employees

In many cases, goal achievement depends to a great extent on people working effectively and cooperatively together. This second leadership task involves creating and managing effective team and one-on-one meetings and promoting teamwork in other ways (including surfacing and dealing with conflict). In family businesses, this task involves: (1) helping family members work effectively together in and on the business (which, if done successfully, can promote family functionality); and (2) helping family and nonfamily members work effectively together.

Throughout the history of Bell-Carter, the family has worked effectively together in establishing the company's direction and in making key operational decisions. In the early days of Tim and Jud's full-time involvement in running the business, the two brothers and their father met daily. Later, Tim and Jud jointly held formal meetings (typically quarterly or every six months) with the other family members who made up the company's board. The purpose of family board meetings was and continues to be to share progress and solicit advice. There were formal agendas and open sharing of information. Tim T. (Tim's son, who became CEO in 2012) holds regular meetings with his senior leadership team (none of whom are family members)—together and individually—and uses both his father, Tim, and his uncle, Jud, as informal advisors. The family's high level of functionality and ability to recruit and select senior leaders who fit with the company's functional culture have created a situation where formal team-building between family and nonfamily members has not been needed.

From a technical perspective, effectively performing this task involves learning how to use, create, and manage meetings, and developing some basic team-building skills. In a family business, effective "interaction facilitation" means holding family and nonfamily members to the same standards and treating them as equals in the business. When family members are treated differently, it reduces the ability to create an effective team and can lead to employees feeling that it is "us versus them."

Task #3: Facilitate People's Work

Leaders need to provide or help people obtain the resources they need to achieve their goals. This third operational leadership task can be accomplished in a variety of ways, including helping to schedule projects, making suggestions about how work should be done, providing reference materials, and providing resources (financial, human, equipment).

As with the first two tasks, leaders in family businesses need to perform this task within the family and within the business. At a macro level, facilitating people's work involves working with family members to identify and gain support for the investments that need to be made to promote successful company growth. At Bell-Carter, this has traditionally taken place in family board meetings and is primarily driven by the company CEO. The board reviews and discusses company financials, but the board's role is to offer advice and input rather than make decisions.

On a micro level, facilitating people's work involves ensuring that both family and nonfamily members have what they need to complete their work (information, capital, equipment) and achieve company goals. In family businesses where family functionality is low, fighting over resources can be the norm. Information, in particular, is used as power. Instead of providing people with what they need to be successful, the leader withholds information or provides conflicting information to both family and nonfamily employees that report to him or her. This obviously detracts from the ability of individuals and the company as a whole to achieve their goals.

Task #4: Provide Feedback on Performance

This fourth task of effective leadership involves providing both positive feedback and constructive criticism to direct reports on a regular basis about their performance. Positive feedback is important because it reinforces appropriate goal-oriented behavior and thereby increases the likelihood that the behavior will continue. Negative feedback, in the form of expressed dissatisfaction with work and constructive criticism, tends to eliminate dysfunctional behavior.

Family dynamics can positively or negatively influence the feedback process. Feedback to other family members can sometimes be personal. Family members can also be harder on and less professional with other family members than they are with other employees. Examples of this were discussed in chapter 7, "The Dark Side of Family Business." In some companies, there can be a complete lack of feedback from one family member to another. At one large distribution company, for example, the son of the owner was nominally managing the sales function. His practice was to take week-long business trips, spending lavishly on hotels, food, and entertainment. He also bought an expensive company car. Sales were not growing and the company was beginning to suffer. His parents (also involved in the business) were aware of these results, but decided that their son would "eventually figure it out." He didn't, and when sales began to decline, a sister was brought in from another company to take over. As a first step, she sat down with her brother to review his performance and determined that he "needed to be in another role."

In high-performing family businesses, leaders approach and manage this task from both a technical (that is, having the skill to provide feedback effectively) and a family perspective (that is managing family dynamics that might undermine the effectiveness of the feedback process). Both family and nonfamily members are encouraged to provide positive feedback and offer input on ways to improve performance. Family members in leadership roles serve as role models by asking for honest feedback. Having clear goals and agreed upon expectations (effectively performing operational leadership task #1) makes providing feedback easier. In brief, positive feedback recognizes effective performance and constructive criticism helps individuals adjust their actions so as to increase the probability that goals will be achieved.

Task #5: Help People Develop

The final task of operational leadership involves identifying developmental needs and working with direct reports to enhance their skills and capabilities. When there is a high level of family functionality—particularly a willingness to learn and change—this will permeate the company's culture and make learning a "way of life." Family and nonfamily members will be encouraged to improve their individual effectiveness; the company will back this effort by providing financial support for continuing education, in-house leadership development programs, individual coaching, and other training. Every employee, whether family or not, will be working to achieve one or more personal development goals.

At the individual level, each manager/leader needs to focus on developing all members of his or her team. This includes identifying and providing feedback on development goals, providing access to training to enhance skills, and coaching. There may also be some special development issues for family members who represent the next generation of corporate leadership. At Bell-Carter, for example, the development plan for Tim T. Carter to move into the role of CEO included formal education (an MBA and attendance at a Harvard family business program), working in a variety of positions within Bell-Carter, and working closely with Ken Wienholz (a nonfamily member who was then CEO) to understand the business's current operations and challenges, as well as the strengths and weaknesses of the company's leadership team.

Effective leaders in family businesses need to possess the capabilities to develop and coach their teams (the technical side of personnel development), and they need to effectively manage family functionality so that it supports "people development." Low family functionality can have a negative impact on the ability to perform this task. Current leaders may consciously or unconsciously withhold or focus inadequate attention on training and developing family and nonfamily members as a way of retaining control.

·   ·   ·

These, then, are the five tasks that both family and nonfamily leaders need to perform regularly with their teams and with each individual team member to promote the achievement of company goals. In addition, senior leaders need to perform three strategic leadership tasks, as described next.

The Key Tasks of Strategic Leadership in a Family Business

Based on our research, we have identified three key tasks of strategic leadership that must be performed to promote the successful long-term development of family businesses:

- creating the strategic vision for the business;
- organizational development;
- defining and managing the company's culture.[3]

Again, these tasks need to be managed at both the family and business levels, with a strong focus on maintaining family–business equilibrium. Each task and the special challenges faced by family businesses in implementing them are described next.[4]

Strategic Leadership Task #1:
Creating and Communicating a Vision for the Company

This task involves creating a "picture" of the future company and then working to ensure that all team members (family and nonfamily) understand it and are working to make this picture a reality. Company leaders must understand how to create, communicate, and reinforce their vision by developing and implementing a strategic plan; and they need to manage family functionality so that it does not undermine the effectiveness of this process.

At Bell-Carter, the five-year vision for the company from 1994 to 1999 was to "become the leader in the ripe olive category (defined as the company that is able to set prices, have the best cost production, and move toward a dominant share in the branded business) and have a strong regional presence in green olives and olive-based food products." The senior leadership team (led by Tim and Jud Carter) developed the vision and presented it to the family board for input. Everyone at Bell-Carter was focused on this vision, which was made more tangible through the development and implementation of a formal strategic plan. Bell-Carter is now the largest table olive producer in the United States and the second largest in the world. Under the leadership of Tim T. Carter, the founder's son, a new vision is being pursued that focuses on diversification of products.

Although at Bell-Carter all family members and company leaders understood and embraced the vision, there are some family businesses where this is not the case. Family members can covertly or overtly have very different pictures of what the future of the company should be, which can in turn lead to a situation where nonfamily employees are not sure what they should be doing and where not everyone is "rowing in the same direction."

Strategic Leadership Task #2: Organizational Development

As described in chapter 1, as an organization grows, it needs to build the infrastructure required to support it. This leadership task involves focusing on and helping others focus on building the systems, processes, and structure that are required for the company's stage of growth. In a family business, this means leading the effort to successfully manage the conditional stages of growth, focusing on both infrastructure and family functionality.

Bell-Carter's family leadership team performed this task relatively informally up until 1994, when Tim and Jud Carter embarked on a more formal strategic planning process that included a systematic assessment of the strengths and limitations at each level in the Pyramid of Organizational Development and the identification of goals for maximizing company strengths and closing infrastructure gaps. All company leaders at Bell-Carter since 1994 have used the pyramid as a tool for organizational development, and most managers in the company are familiar with it. At Bell-Carter, the family board embraced the changes required and the family was willing to invest in the company's continued development.

In other family businesses, family dynamics can undermine the ability to effectively perform this task. In fact, one reason that some family businesses last no more than one generation is because there is inadequate performance of the organizational development strategic leadership task. In these businesses, the focus is on what the business can do for the family today, rather than on what the business might be or become in the future. The family may be reluctant to invest in the development of the infrastructure needed to support the company's growth and this, in turn, can lead to the business "choking" on its own growth.

Strategic Leadership Task #3: Culture Management

As discussed in chapter 6, culture consists of the company's core values, beliefs, and norms which, in turn, influence people's behavior. In a family business, the company culture will very much reflect the family's culture (and the family's functionality), which can have a positive or not-so-positive impact on overall organizational effectiveness and performance. As described previously, the culture of Bell-Carter, which is very much influenced by the family's culture, has always been one of the company's key strengths. CEO Tim T. Carter is focused on ensuring that Bell-Carter's culture is aligned with the company's goals and the needs of the twenty-first-century workforce.

This strategic leadership task involves defining, communicating, managing, and reinforcing a culture that will support the achievement of company goals. It could also include finding ways to minimize the impact of family dysfunctionality on the business. Strategies for managing company culture in a family business were described in chapter 6. It should not be inferred that because culture management is listed as strategic leadership task #3 it is a lower priority. It could be argued that, in a family business, culture management is Leadership Job #1 because the creation of a strong functional culture is so critical to the overall success of the business.

When this task is not being performed effectively, family dynamics play out in the workplace and undermine the company's ability to achieve its goals. For example, having very heated arguments that include yelling at one another may be the norm. When this behavior occurs among family members in the workplace, problems may not be surfaced and/or may not be effectively dealt with because the norm for nonfamily employees is to "stay under the radar" as a way of not getting involved in the conflict.

Leadership Tasks and Family Business Growth

Leaders of successful family businesses consistently perform the five operational and the three strategic leadership tasks as their companies grow—although in the early stages of growth (i.e., New Venture and Expansion), the strategic leadership tasks may be performed somewhat informally (as was the case at Bell-Carter). In addition, effective family business leaders consistently focus on promoting and reinforcing a high level of family functionality and on creating family–business equilibrium. When the level of family functionality is high, it can promote the effective performance of these leadership tasks and, in turn, contribute to organizational success. When the level of family functionality is low, it can lead to substandard performance of both operational and strategic leadership tasks, which can undermine the ability of the company to continue to grow successfully.

To maximize effectiveness, each operational and strategic leadership task needs to be performed using a style that "fits" the situation. The style that a family business leader chooses can be greatly influenced by the family's functionality, as described below.

Choosing the "Best" Leadership Style

A leadership "style" is the way that leadership is conducted or exercised in an organization. People tend to have their own particular style of leadership that develops naturally over time. However, the style that a person develops is not necessarily appropriate for all situations. There has been a great deal of research trying to identify the elusive "best" or "optimal" style of leadership. But decades of research have failed to confirm that there is one style of leadership that is best for all situations. Rather, there are various styles, each of which may be effective or ineffective, depending on the circumstances.

This conclusion has led to the concept of situational leadership, or what is sometimes referred to as the "contingency theory of leadership."[5] Under this view, there are three key notions:

- There are several different styles of leadership that are available to leaders, constituting a "menu."
- The leader must choose the correct style for the situation.
- The leader must then, of course, be able to use the appropriate style.

Leadership Styles

In our approach, the "menu" of appropriate styles includes the following: (1) autocratic; (2) benevolent autocratic; (3) consultative; (4) participative; (5) team or consensus; and (6) laissez-faire. These represent a continuum of styles that ranges from very directive to very nondirective. In a family business, the style used by a leader in a given situation is influenced by family functionality and by how family members relate to one another. For example, a founder who has children reporting to him or her may adopt an autocratic or directive style of leadership in all situations (acting as the parent rather than the company leader), which may or may not be effective. The six styles and the challenges of using each one in a family business are described next.

The Autocratic Style.   The word "autocrat" connotes *authority*. This style of leadership is very authoritarian or "directive." It involves *telling* people what to do, with the expectation that they will do it. A leader who uses this style promotes the notion that he or she has the legitimate authority to make all decisions and does not feel the need to explain the rationale to direct reports. This "just do it" style of leadership can be characterized by the statement, "I will tell you what we're going to do because I'm the boss."

Sam Walton used this style of leadership in the early years of Wal-Mart, and it is common in family businesses. Sam Steinberg, the godfather of Steinberg, Inc., one of Canada's largest conglomerates, and the "alpha male" among four brothers in the second generation of this firm, was credited as the entrepreneurial genius behind the company's growth from a small family grocery store into a multimillion-dollar supermarket and real estate empire. According to his daughter, Mitzi, he surpassed his brothers in business acumen and used an autocratic leadership style: "When he said sit, they sat down."[6]

The Benevolent Autocratic Style.   The benevolent autocratic style is a "softer" version of the autocratic style. It is sometimes referred to as a "parental" style of leadership, suggesting a family situation where the leader acts on the assumption that he or she knows what is best for the organization and the individuals involved. A manager who uses this style will usually explain the rationale behind decisions, while an autocratic leader will not. Where an autocratic leader might say, "As a condition of coming to work here, you are obliged to accept what I say," a benevolent autocrat might say, "This is what I want you to do and here's why." This is the classic style found in many family businesses during the initial stages of organizational development; it extends to how the leader works with both family and nonfamily members. It can, however, also be used by leaders of family businesses well beyond the early stages of growth.

When the level of family functionality is low, this style can lead to a situation where the leader behaves like Marlon Brando in *The Godfather*—taking care of the "family," but demanding respect in return. When this occurs, both family and nonfamily members spend a great deal of time working to please the godfather and may feel that they are in competition for his or her attention.[7] In turn, the godfather will recognize and reward people for their service to him or her, rather than for their performance in the company.

The Consultative Style.   The third style of leadership is qualitatively different, at least to some degree, from the first two. The consultative style is one of two "interactive styles," in which the manager solicits input from his or her direct reports, but reserves the right to make the final decision. A person using the consultative style presents his or her team with information and asks for their response. Suppose a manager is presenting the organization's goals for the coming year. A leader using the autocratic style might say, "This is what we're going to do. These are our goals for next year." A benevolent autocrat might approach the situation with, "This is what the organization needs, and here is how it will affect you." In contrast, a manager utilizing the consultative style might say, "Here is what I think our goals ought to be for the next year. What's your reaction?" Having asked this question, the manager then needs to make it very clear that while he or she wants input, the decision is still his or hers to make. If this is not clear, problems can arise as direct reports come to believe that the manager is using a nondirective style in which "all votes were equal."

The consultative style becomes appropriate in family businesses as they increase in size beyond the initial stages of growth to include nonfamily and family members in managerial positions. These people will expect to be involved in decision making and not just told what to do. However, they will understand that the family retains primacy over the final decision. Throughout the company's history, the consultative style has been used effectively by Bell-Carter company leaders in working with the family board. The practice has been for company leaders to present and solicit input from the board on their ideas for company development and growth. The family board provides input and advice, but decisions are ultimately the company leader's to make, and the family board has always supported those decisions.

The Participative Style.   A leader using the participative style also reserves the right to make the final decision. The main difference between the participative and consultative styles is the manner in which others' opinions are solicited and used. In the participative style, the group actually helps to develop ideas rather than just providing input on the manager's ideas. In the consultative style, the manager might come into a group and say, "Here is what I think we should do. Give me your reaction." In contrast, the manager using a participative style might say, "Here are the problems. Let's discuss them together and come up with recommendations. Then I'll make the final decision."

There are challenges inherent in using either one of the interactive styles of leadership. First, a manager must be very certain that he or she is open to the ideas and opinions of the team. He or she must be willing to change his or her perspective, based on these ideas. If the manager's mind is already made up, everyone on the team will know this and will be extremely frustrated by having to "go through the motions" of providing input and then have that input ignored. A second challenge is helping team members understand that, although the manager wants their input, the decision is still his or hers to make. This can be difficult to communicate, especially if none of the input provided by the team is used. Whenever this occurs, the manager should make a practice of explaining why he or she decided to pursue a certain course of action, how the information provided by the team was evaluated, and why (in this case) it wasn't used. This will help the team understand that their input was of value and that the manager wasn't simply feigning interest in their input.

As a family business transitions to a leadership team that includes nonfamily professional managers, adopting a participative style can help promote sharing and effective utilization of the knowledge that nonfamily members possess. Functional families understand this and, as a result, look for opportunities to recruit management talent from the outside to support their company's growth.

Daniel Carter used this leadership style in working with his two sons during his tenure as Bell-Carter's CEO. Tim, Jud, and Daniel met every day, and sometimes for dinner, to discuss specific issues. According to Tim, "We were able to disagree," but Daniel had the deciding vote, as was the case when he made the decision (at dinner) that he did not want to "risk the business by going into green olives."[8]

The Team (Partnership) Style.   A leader who adopts the team style is choosing to operate as one member of a team or group in making decisions. His or her vote counts no more than any other team member's. This style can be appropriate in some "partnership" forms of business. There are two versions of the team style: (1) "true consensus" (or jury) style and (2) majority rules. In the former, everyone on the team must agree on the direction to be pursued or the decision to be made. If there is even one dissenter, the "jury" must continue its deliberations until a true consensus is reached. In the latter, majority rules: after a vote, the option receiving the most votes is the one that will be pursued.

This style of leadership is found most often in family businesses where those on the team are highly skilled in their areas of responsibility and where there is a high level of family functionality. Family and nonfamily leaders need to trust that those on the team have the skills to make decisions and that they are focused on what is best for the business. If team members are not that skilled and are motivated by something other than what is best for the business, using this style can be disastrous.

Tim and Jud used the team style as they worked together to lead Bell-Carter. When their leadership team expanded to include nonfamily members—a CFO, a VP of sales, and eventually a VP of operations—the brothers continued to use either this style or the participative style in working with what they called the "executive team." The team discussed issues and worked to reach a consensus. There were a few times, however, when (like Daniel before them), Tim and Jud would use their deciding vote; but these were rare and most often involved the strategic development of the business.

The Laissez-Faire Style.   The most nondirective style of leadership, laissez-faire, places the responsibility for task accomplishment completely on the direct report(s). A leader using this style essentially says, "Do whatever you want to do," or "Do the right thing." The benefit of this style is that the manager does not need to devote a great deal of time to overseeing direct reports' efforts. Instead, the manager's role becomes one of communicating the goals of the company to the people on the team and then letting them determine how to execute them. The manager is still leading the team because he or she ensures that everyone is moving in a direction that will result in the overall attainment of the company's goals.

This leadership style can be used in any type of organization, family business or not. It is potentially a powerful style because it gives the leader a great deal of leverage through the delegation of authority. The key factors in using this style effectively are that each person must have the skills to do whatever needs to be done and is motivated to do it. In businesses where roles are assigned based on family membership, the results of using this style can be disastrous if the family members are not sufficiently skilled or motivated.

During their tenure as company leaders, Tim and Jud Carter effectively used the laissez-faire style in their respective areas of the business. While Jud oversaw the plant and growers and Tim focused on administration and sales, they worked together to manage the business as a whole. They consulted each other on strategic and financial decisions related to their areas of responsibility and seldom disagreed on the right course of action. Both brothers also frequently used the laissez-faire style in managing their direct reports.

Factors to Consider in Choosing a Style

A leader does not always have to use (and, in fact, should not always use) the same style. The most effective leaders have the ability to use the entire menu of styles and the ability to recognize which is appropriate for a given situation. Two factors must be taken into account in choosing a leadership style: (1) the nature of the task, and (2) the nature of the people being supervised.

Nature of the Task. One factor that should influence the manager's choice of leadership style is the degree of programmability of the task. A programmable task is one in which the manager can describe, in advance, all of the steps needed to complete it. A nonprogrammable task is a creative task in which it is almost impossible for a manager to define the steps necessary for its successful completion. If a task is highly programmable, then a directive style of leadership is appropriate. If the task is nonprogrammable, a more participative or nondirective style will be required. In other words, the greater the degree of programmability of the task, the more appropriate it is for a manager to specify exactly how it should be done. Where the task is less programmable, the manager must use a more interactive or nondirective approach.

Nature of the Person Supervised.   This factor is made up of three subfactors: (1) the extent to which the individual has the necessary skills to perform the specific task being assigned or taken on; (2) the extent to which the individual is motivated to perform the task; and (3) the extent to which the individual wants to work alone on that task. Taken together, these three subfactors can be thought of as a single variable called *potential for job autonomy*. The more highly skilled and highly motivated a person is and the greater the person's desire for independence, the higher his or her potential for job autonomy. Conversely, a person with low motivation, low task-relevant skills, and low need for independence has a low potential for job autonomy.

Different leadership styles are appropriate for people with different potential for job autonomy. A nondirective style (consensus or laissez-faire) will be most appropriate with direct reports who have a high potential for job autonomy, while a very directive style is appropriate with people who have low potential for job autonomy. If the "wrong" style is used, the probability of achieving desired results and realizing important goals is reduced. As an organization grows and matures, it will tend to add people who are experienced professionals. These professionals will likely prefer to be managed with a participative or nondirective style of leadership.

Choosing a Leadership Style in Family Businesses

The bottom line is that leadership style is a choice. The choice should be based on the degree of programmability of the task and the nature of the person working on it. In attempting to choose the "best' style," leaders in family businesses face special challenges created by role conflict and other family functionality issues. For example, the company leader—who may also be the head of the family—may use a directive style (as he or she does in the family) in all situations. This may make sense in the context of the family, but not in the context of the business—particularly as the business grows beyond the Expansion stage and professional managers are added to the team. If the leader continues to use the directive style, talented nonfamily leaders may leave the business because they do not like being told what to do. At the other extreme, using a laissez-faire style to manage family members who don't have sufficient skills or motivation to perform the work can be disastrous.

In effective family businesses, both family and nonfamily leaders work to identify and use the most appropriate style when working with their direct reports. And, the choice of style is influenced by the nature of the task and the person performing the task, not by whether the individual in question is or is not a family member.

The Face of the Family

In addition to these generic functions of strategic and operational leadership, there is another leadership function that is specific to functional family businesses—particularly later-stage businesses—in which a family member no longer occupies the most senior leadership position. We call this largely symbolic but critical function "the face of the family"; it refers to the person who represents the family in the business. At GOJO™ Industries, this person is Marcella Kanfer Rolnick.

GOJO™ was founded by Marcella's great uncle and aunt, Jerry and Goldie Lippman, in 1946; their nephew (Marcella's father) became president of the family business in 1973. Marcella worked at the company during high school and college. After college, she worked outside the company before returning when GOJO™ launched Purell™ in the consumer market. She left again in 2002 to pursue her MBA at Stanford.

Over the next several years, she thought about the role that she wanted to play in the family business and, at the same time, learned that she had to manage the assumptions of others about her future role in the company. She admits that, at times, there was some confusion because many people assumed that someday she would become the company's CEO, though that was not her intention. Marcella began to manage these expectations by having what she describes as "frank conversations" with her GOJO™ colleagues about her future role, and she began to focus on answering the question: "How can the family exercise leadership in ways other than through a day-to-day senior management role?" One answer was to make sure that she was "visible"—especially at events to support and promote the company's culture and values. Another was to help the GOJO™ senior leadership team understand what she and her dad, Joe, needed to know to "make the best big decisions" for the company. We provide more detail about GOJO™ and this family business's evolution in chapter 10.

Summary

The nature of leadership in a family business is different from that in ordinary businesses. The ability of family business leaders to perform specific operational and strategic tasks of leadership, and choose and use the "right" style in a given situation, can have a significant impact on whether their businesses will succeed in meeting the challenges they face. In the next chapter, we focus on a special leadership challenge in family businesses: succession.

9 Succession

Over the past century, Bell-Carter has experienced five leadership successions; only one CEO has been a nonfamily member. The first succession occurred when Arthur Bell, then the owner of Bell-Carter's olive processing company, retired and his stepson, Daniel (who had worked in the business for over a decade), and Daniel's half-sister, Mary, became equal co-owners of the business. Daniel became the company's formal leader, while Mary and her husband, Bill, served on the family board as advisors and were not involved in the company on a day-to-day basis. As is true in many family businesses, having a child take over the business seemed like a natural evolution.

When it came time for Daniel to retire in 1973, it was not a given that his oldest son, Tim, would become Bell-Carter's most senior leader. According to Tim, "We always understood that we would give it [the most senior leadership position] to the person who was best equipped. We wanted the business to be a success." When the time came to decide who "the best-equipped person" was to assume the company's leadership, it was not Tim or his younger brother, Jud (both of whom had worked in the business full time since the 1960s), it was both of them! Based on their interests and "passions," Tim would manage the sales and administrative sides of the business and Jud would focus on production and developing/maintaining grower relationships. Tim took the title of chairman and CEO (assuming the title that had been his grandfather's) and Jud became president (assuming Daniel's title). The two brothers would jointly manage the company as a whole.

By 2005, Tim and Jud were ready to retire, or at least cut back. However, the next generation of family had not yet developed all of the capabilities needed to run the company. So they needed to identify someone who could succeed the two brothers. The family (Tim, Jud, and the other members of the family board) decided that, according to Tim, "Ken [Wienholz] had earned the right to be CEO." Ken had been with the company since 1975 and had served in a variety of leadership positions, including vice president of sales, COO, and president of Bell-Carter Olives (during the time that Bell-Carter had its pickle business). Ken represented and reinforced the positive aspects of Bell-Carter's culture and certainly knew the business. It was no surprise when he moved into this role, since the entire organization had been at least implicitly aware that he was being groomed by Tim and Jud to do so. Ken, in a sense, was a member of the extended Carter family; Tim, in fact, says, "He was like a brother to me."

After three years in his role as CEO, Ken (with support from Tim and Jud) began to plan for his retirement from the company, which would occur in 2012. At this time, Tim T. Carter was serving as president of a small but growing food processing company, having left Bell-Carter in 2005. Ken reached out to Tim T. for help with a customer in Los Angeles, and the two started spending time together. Tim T. says, "Ken was starting to retire, and he wanted me included in the succession plan. He was very deliberate about it." In late 2008, Tim T. decided to return to Bell-Carter, with Ken and, of course his father and uncle, serving as coaches. He moved through a variety of positions with the intention, if everything worked out, of becoming the company's CEO upon Ken's retirement, which was scheduled for July 31, 2012. Tim joined the executive team, working closely with Ken to understand how the business was currently operating (including specific challenges) and how the executive team functioned. On July 31, 2011, Tim T. became COO, and shortly thereafter the board approved Tim's promotion to CEO, which took effect on August 1, 2012.

As was true at Bell-Carter, most, though not all, family businesses do not need to face the issue of leadership succession until many years after they have been established. In the classic situation, one or several family members start a business and run it until retirement or failing health requires choosing a successor. Although all companies tend to be built around their

CEO, this is true to an even greater extent in a family business, and this structure increases the complexity of the leadership succession process.

The process of selecting, preparing for, and then actually transferring the leadership authority to a new family (or nonfamily) member—that is, of leadership succession—is one of the greatest challenges to the long-run viability and success of a family business over multiple generations. Research on family businesses suggests that one of the most significant factors in promoting family business continuity is having a succession plan in place.[1] Stated in another way, without effective leadership succession decisions and practices, a family business cannot continue successfully from generation to generation. As Gersick and co-authors state, "SUCCESSION is the ultimate test of a family business."[2]

Leadership of a family business is a key determinant not just of business success, but also of family dynamics. If the leader is chosen wisely, the business is likely to prosper and harmony will be maintained in the family. If a poor choice of leadership is made, the business that took decades to build can quickly unravel.

The purpose of this chapter is to examine leadership succession in family business from the perspective of creating or sustaining family business equilibrium—that is, balancing the needs of the business with the needs of the family. We examine some of the key factors that must be considered in family business succession and propose a systematic process to facilitate it. We use selected cases to provide insight into this crucial process.

Scenarios of Family Business Succession

The overarching challenge of leadership succession in a family business is to create a process or system that continues or achieves family business equilibrium generation after generation. When family functionality is high, the leadership succession process can be close to a dream. When family functionality is low, this process can become a nightmare.

Dream (or Near-Dream) Scenarios

The "dream scenario" in a family business succession is that there is a single competent leader who is ready, willing, and able to replace the current leader; and there is agreement within the family that this is the right person for the job. Unfortunately, the dream scenario is a rare occurrence. Even in businesses with high levels of family functionality, there can be challenges.

At Bell-Carter, for example, the transition to Tim T. Carter was not without its problems. He had worked full-time for the company from 2000 to 2005 and had left under not the best of terms. During this time period, he had rotated through a variety of positions (to help him better understand the company) and had become the head of Bell-Carter's Specialty Products business unit (a unit that developed and sourced new products), where he had responsibility for developing, implementing, and reporting on progress against this unit's strategic plan. This role was very different from those that he had occupied in the past: "From Day 1, I had been out on the road and this was awesome . . . but this role was more internal." When he was given the business unit leadership role he says, "I had very little management experience and I had no functional experience. . . . I was also a little bit of a jerk and was a little bit entitled. I made good business decisions, but I didn't treat people well." The company hired a coach to work with Tim T.; about that, he says, "She taught me how to be a leader. Unfortunately, it was too little too late. I had pissed people off and rubbed them the wrong way."

In late 2005, the company was going through another restructuring and the specialty unit was going to become a full division. The biggest problem for this division, according to Tim T., was the inability to source products from overseas. So the company looked to Tim T. to take a leadership role in sourcing, but in this role he would not be included on the company's executive team. He says, "I saw this as a dead end and as getting stuck in a corner." He met with his father, Tim, and talked about his role and his future at Bell-Carter. Tim T. says, "I told him that I wanted to leave and he said that he didn't agree. So, I left."

Simon Property Group, a very large publicly held business controlled by the Simon family, is one family business that managed to realize the dream scenario and avoid the latent potential for divisiveness within the family. Melvin Simon and Associates, developers and operators of shopping malls, was founded by Melvin ("Mel") Simon in Indianapolis, Indiana, in 1960. Herbert Simon and Fred Simon, Mel's younger brothers, joined the firm later. By 1990, Melvin Simon and Associates had become one of the leading shopping center developers in the United States. By that time, Fred Simon had left the firm and retired, and Mel and Herb were respectively chairman (CEO) and president (COO).

Mel and Herb Simon were talented entrepreneurs and had built a large successful company; but both were beginning to think about retiring and pursuing other interests. David Simon, Mel's son, had an MBA from Columbia University and had worked in one of Wall Street's prestigious venture capital firms. Mel and Herb asked David to join the firm, and he did so in the early 1990s.

The potential pitfalls of the company's proposed leadership transition were obvious. First, David Simon was unproven as a CEO. His focus had been deals, not management. Second, people inside the firm could have objected to David Simon's entry into the business or his becoming CEO. Third, Herb Simon might have wanted one of his own children to run the firm. Fortunately, none of these problems emerged.

In 1992, the majority of the shopping center interests of Melvin Simon & Associates became a publicly traded company under the name Simon Property Group (SPG). In 1995, David Simon became CEO of SPG. Since that time, David has been instrumental in building what is now the largest shopping center development and management company in the United States. In 2013, David Simon was selected as one of thirty people listed in *Barron's* "World's Best CEOs." During his tenure as CEO, Simon Property Group has had an annualized profit of 17.4 percent.[3] In contrast, the return for the Standard and Poor's (S&P) 500 was 8.7 percent during the same period. The company's stock price increased from $24 per share in 1995 to $160 per share in 2013.

Nightmare Scenarios

More common than the dream scenario, however, are a variety of difficult or even "nightmare scenarios" brought about by one or more family functionality issues. These include:

- overt or covert competition between people (family and nonfamily members) to become the family business leader;
- lack of a competent "heir apparent";

  • conflict between family members about who should assume the leadership role.

Competition among Family Members for the Leadership Position. If not managed properly, the presence of more than one family business leadership "candidate" can produce disastrous results, as was vividly illustrated in the experience of Dixon International, dealers for a large global truck manufacturer, which we used in chapter 7 as an example of the Family Business Civil War Syndrome. In this case, two brothers were pitted against each other to assume the leadership role of their business after their father suffered a stroke.

One way to avoid making a choice among family members is to choose a nonfamily member to lead the company. However, that scenario presents its own set of problems and challenges. Another solution is to establish the norm that the selection will be based on the person who is best qualified for the position, as Bell-Carter has done.

Competition between Family and Nonfamily Members for the Leadership Position. This scenario tends to occur when one or more nonfamily members have "assumed" or even been told that they were candidates for the most senior leadership position, which instead is given to a family member (who may or may not have previously worked in the business). We have seen multiple instances of this problem. For example, when the founder of a publicly held bank was planning his retirement, he brought his son into the business, a move that another senior nonfamily leader of the firm resented. In another case, a daughter who was asked to join a truck dealership with the purpose of becoming the CEO upon her father's retirement found that it was difficult to get anything done because the other senior leaders would not respect her authority. They were skeptical about her ability to lead the business, and she believed that nonfamily leaders who aspired to be CEO were trying to undermine her position in the business.

Lack of a Competent "Heir Apparent." This can occur when there are no competent people to replace the current leader, either within the family or within current nonfamily management. It can also occur when the designated successor is unable to develop the skills needed to effectively manage and continue to grow the business. For example, in one $50 million family retail business, there were several family members employed, but none of them had the skills needed to be considered as a successor. The CEO tried to promote a nonfamily member, with less-than-satisfactory results, and then hired an outsider as CEO, who again was unsatisfactory. Finally, the CEO, having reached the age of 70, sold the company.

Conflict among Family Members about Who Should Be the Successor. Overt or covert conflict among family members about who the successor should be can complicate or even prevent the selection of a competent successor. However, sometimes this problem can be resolved, as seen in the case of the King family's leadership succession.

The King family were owners of a $250 million furniture manufacturing company. At 69, Charles King, co-founder (with his wife Rebecca) and CEO of King Family Furniture, was in failing health and decided to reduce his role in the company.[4] Four other family members were employed by the company: his sons, Mark and Stanley (the eldest); his daughter, Barbara; and Barbara's husband, Carl Green. Mark, Stanley, and Barbara had all grown up in the business, working there during high school and on college breaks. Barbara and Carl had met at the University of Southern California when she was pursuing an undergraduate degree in business and he was working to complete his MBA. After graduating, Carl had worked for ten years as a management consultant before joining King Family Furniture.

In family discussions about who should succeed the CEO, it was clear that Rebecca, the matriarch of the family, wanted her son Stanley, the eldest, to take over. Initially she was adamant about this. Stanley, while intelligent and knowledgeable about the business, was not the best choice. He lacked communication skills and was not a natural leader, preferring to solve problems on his own and not deal with people. Carl had less experience in the business than any of the others, but was the best prepared to become the leader because of both his education and his previous management experience. However, while Carl was a family member by virtue of marriage to Barbara, he was not a blood relative.

The situation led to a great deal of heated discussion among the family, and it seemed to settle into a stalemate. Rebecca remained adamant that Stanley should be the new CEO. Her husband was relatively quiet on the issue, not wanting to add to the conflict. Barbara and Mark were very vocal in expressing their belief that Stanley was not the right choice. Carl tried to be politically correct and talked about doing whatever was best for the family and the business. Stanley let the others argue and did not express his opinions.

Unable to achieve a consensus, and with growing sense of foreboding about what might happen to the family as well as the business if the stalemate was not resolved, the family literally retreated to its summer home in northern Michigan for a long weekend. They asked a consultant to join them and help them facilitate the discussion. Before the discussion of the choice of Charles's successor began, the consultant asked them to adopt the principle that there is a difference between "business roles" and "family roles." This notion was accepted by all members of the family.

After much discussion and debate during that three-day weekend, it was finally decided by family consensus that Carl would be the new CEO. All other family members agreed to support Carl, and agreed that it was necessary to separate family roles from business roles on a day-to-day basis. Mark would become COO (a new position), and Stanley would be the vice president of purchasing. Barbara remained VP of business development, and Charles became chairman of the board. Rebecca had no interest in a role in the business. These decisions achieved family business equilibrium and prevented the long-term bitterness that might have occurred as a result of continued debate about who the successor should be.

Three Key Steps in the Succession Process

Promoting a dream rather than a nightmare scenario for family business leadership succession involves three steps:

- Identify the successor or possible successors.
- Provide appropriate training and education to prepare the individual for his or her leadership role.
- Manage the leadership transition.

In implementing these steps, there needs to be a significant focus on managing family functionality and, in turn, promoting family–business equilibrium. The three steps in the family business planning and transition process are described next.

Identify the Successor or Possible Successors

The first critical question that the leadership of a family business needs to address (and a first step in developing a succession plan) is, "Who is the appropriate successor?" In some cases, the best choice for a new leader or successor might be a family member; in other cases, there may be no family members that are or will be qualified to assume the most senior leadership position when the time comes to do so. In these cases, the successor might need to come from outside the family. The term "family business" suggests that leadership will always come from within the family, regardless of the qualities required to run the business. But this is a dangerous notion. A family's livelihood as well as its harmony can suffer if the wrong leader is in place.

Leadership of any business requires a package of competencies and personality traits. If a family member possesses or can develop the necessary capabilities to lead the business, and if (and *only* if) the individual also *wants* to lead the business, that person is probably a good first choice. We say "probably" because there are other factors involved as well, including whether there are also valuable nonfamily members who would like to lead the firm. Although this is not necessarily a decisive factor, it should not be completely ignored.

When there are multiple family members who are being considered to succeed the current leader, there can also be differing perspectives among family members about the criteria that should be used to select the "best" successor. When it is clear that there is no family member with both the desire and the ability to lead the business, then it is necessary to select a nonfamily member as a successor, assuming that the family wants to retain ownership of the business. Although choosing a qualified nonfamily member solves one problem, it can lead to several others, including family members' sense of entitlement about their "position" in the company and resentment of nonfamily members who occupy management positions. This problem can be avoided, to some extent, if family members agree to accept the distinction between "business roles" and "family roles." At Bell-Carter, for example, a nonfamily member became CEO upon Tim and Jud Carter's retirement because the most qualified family candidate was not yet ready to assume the role.

One tool that can be used to as the basis for identifying a possible successor is the Key Result Area–based role description (described in chapter 4).
The role description should identify both the responsibilities and the skills
(competencies) needed to effectively fulfill the role. The successor candidate's qualifications can be assessed using this role description, much as
would be done in hiring for any position. When evaluating a family candidate, family dynamics will need to be managed and may require the use of
an outside facilitator.

Provide Appropriate Training to Prepare the Successor for the Leadership Role

Once the successor (or successors) has been identified, the process of developing the skills needed to become the company's leader needs to begin.
This process should start with an in-depth assessment of the individual's
developmental needs, building on the assessment completed (either formally or informally) during the selection process. We have found that a
"360-degree assessment" is useful in identifying developmental needs. This
involves collecting feedback from the current company leader, peers, and
direct reports about the extent to which the candidate possesses the skills
needed to be effective in the most senior leadership role. Once completed,
the output of this "needs assessment" becomes the basis for creating a development plan.

A development plan—what Ward refers to as a "personal development
plan"—to facilitate succession identifies the specific skills and knowledge
that need to be developed and outlines the methods that will be used in the
training process.[5] For example, if the successor's financial analysis skills are
weak, he or she might be sent to a university-based program to develop that
competency. To prepare a potential CEO for managing a profit center, he
or she might be assigned a small division or strategic business unit of the
family business to run. At Bell-Carter, for example, the development plan
for Tim T. Carter included working outside the family business for three
years after college to gain a broader perspective; rotating through the entire
company to "see how the business really worked"; formal education earning an MBA; working with an outside coach; and coaching from COO/CEO
Ken Wienholz, his father (Tim), and his uncle (Jud).

The development plan for the successor can also include the development of other senior leaders who will need to support this individual once he or she assumes the most senior leadership role. To achieve this goal, the company might implement a formal leadership development program for all of its leaders and managers. Our work and research suggest that the most effective leadership development programs focus not just on skills, but also on behavior and mindset.[6] Therefore, leadership development—whether one-on-one or group-based—needs to focus on what we have termed "the three factor approach" to management and leadership effectiveness:

1. Role Concept: how individuals think about and approach their roles; and how they allocate and invest their time.

2. Management/Leadership Skills: the extent to which individuals have developed the appropriate management/leadership skills (delegation, decision making, planning, etc.).

3. The Inner Game of Management: each individual's "mindset" which, in turn, involves effectively managing the need for control, source of self-esteem, and the need to be liked.[7]

Leadership development programs can improve current effectiveness, as well as prepare leaders at all levels for their future roles. The most successful businesses understand that leadership development—not just for the successor, but for all leaders—is an important ingredient in long-term success.

In 1994 at Bell-Carter, for example, we worked with Tim and Jud to design and implement a four-day leadership development program for managers and leaders at all levels, including the executive team. This program incorporated our "three-factor approach" and focused on such topics as time management, delegation, leadership effectiveness, decision making, and meeting management. Throughout the 1990s, Bell-Carter reinforced and built on this program in workshops conducted by internal trainers. In 2013, Tim T. Carter and his head of human resources launched Bell-Carter University, which was built on the foundation of the concepts presented in 1994 and designed to help the next generation of Bell-Carter leaders and managers maximize their effectiveness. Tim T. says, "This is one of the better decisions that I have made."

Manage the Leadership Transition

The current leader, the successor, and other family members need to support the successor through words and actions. As the great former catcher and manager of the New York Yankees, Edwin "Yogi" Berra, said about baseball games: "It's not over until it's over." Similarly, in the case of a succession, even after the transition of family leadership is made formally, it is not over. Our experience indicates that just as with the appointment of any new CEO, the first two years are crucial. Specific issues that need to be addressed and managed as a part of this transition include how the successor will make his or her mark on the organization, how the current family leader will deal with the psychological loss of position within the business (the "retirement syndrome"), and how other people in the organization will respond to the transition. The successor needs to carefully manage changes within the company by engaging other senior leaders in identifying and implementing them. The successor must also resist the temptation to make changes just for the sake of making them.

For the outgoing leader of the business, succession may bring with it a sense of psychological loss, loss of position and of status within the business and even in the family. Being CEO of a company can be a powerful psychological aphrodisiac. Retirement means loss of control, loss of position, loss of status, and (perhaps) even loss of self-respect. Many people resist retirement for these reasons. In describing the retirement syndrome, Manfred Kets de Vries refers to the difficulties of "letting go" at the end of a career—a concept that is applicable to both family and nonfamily businesses.[8] The leader of a family business might need support and counseling during the process of disengaging from the business in order to avoid creating problems for the business and the family, including becoming a smiling cobra (setting the successor up to fail) or contributing to the Medea Syndrome (destruction of the business).

The successor and the outgoing company leader need to realize that their behavior will be under constant scrutiny, and they therefore need to be hyper-vigilant. Family functionality issues related to the transition should be managed "offline" and outside the business, as it is very important that the successor be given the family's full support.

Some transition issues are created by how company employees respond to and deal with the leadership transition. Some will embrace the change, while others may want to keep things the way they were. Especially sensitive is the perception by nonfamily members that the new leader was given the position by virtue of his or her membership in the "lucky gene club." Even the most qualified successors face the burden of proving that they are the "right choice."

To minimize these and other problems, there is a need to continue *reinforcing* that the new appointee is the best person to lead the business (based on skills, experience, and "fit" with the organization's culture). Just as there is a ceremony of leadership transition in a monarchy or democracy, so should there be a "symbolic transition" in a family business. The late Jim Stowers Jr. did this brilliantly when he transitioned the leadership of American Century Investors to his son, Jim III. The elder Stowers had a bronze mini-statue made showing two hands with a baton being transferred between them. The symbolism was perfect: passing the baton to the next generation.

In addition to the symbolic transfer of power, there is a need for continuing support of the new leader as he or she finds his or her "sea legs," which typically takes one to two years. As Harvey Golub, former CEO of American Express, has said with respect to training for the position of CEO, "You can't really be a CEO until you are one, but you can do a lot of 'flight simulation.'"[9] During this period of transition, an outside mentor or coach can be helpful. The mentor can offer the kind of objective, even critical, feedback that those who report to a CEO are not likely to provide, for fear of jeopardizing their jobs. It is very difficult to tell the emperor that he or she has no clothes, but a good coach can find a constructive way to do this.

Given the complexity of the succession process, a systematic approach to completing the three steps in the leadership succession process will help ensure success. In brief, there is a need to develop a succession "plan."

Developing and Implementing the Succession Plan

Just as the company plan should provide a road map for its continued development, the succession plan should serve as a guide for the development of and transition to the next generation of family leadership. The plan should be documented in writing and should include specific goals and milestones with respect to (1) developing the successor's skills and knowledge; and (2) ensuring that there is support from the organization for the transition.

There is no hard-and-fast amount of lead time required for fully transitioning to the new leader, but a reasonable lead time is typically between five and ten years. This length of time is required to develop a successor, test him or her, and orchestrate the leader's transition in the business.

While it is important to have both the designated successor and the current leader involved in the development of the succession plan, others can also be included. For example, if the successor is going to spend time learning the business by working in several departments, the leaders of those departments need to understand their role in this individual's development. In addition, all family members must support the plan—even if they will not be directly involved in its implementation (e.g., in coaching the successor).

Once the plan is developed, it may be appropriate to formally share all or some of it with the company as a whole or with selected managers. One objective of doing so is to help others support the successors' efforts to develop his or her skills. Another objective is to send the message that leadership development is important, even for the person who will eventually be the CEO.

Performance against the plan should be monitored on a regular basis (at least quarterly), and those involved—the designated successor, the current family business leader, other family members, and the company's leadership team—should work together to address problems as they arise. These problems might be related to the implementation of the development program, progress being made by the successor, or how company employees are responding to and supporting the successor and the successor's development. When there is sufficient planning and effective plan execution, problems in family business succession can be avoided or at least minimized.

Anatomy of a Successful Family Business Succession: Techmer PM

John Manuck, a chemical engineer, began his career working for Monsanto at a polymer production site. In 1981, he founded Techmer PM, which provides design and technical support for colorants and various additives that modify and enhance the end-use performance of plastic products used by automotive, home furnishing, hospital supply, food packaging, and many other industries. By 2013, the company had grown to over five hundred employees and had manufacturing sites in California, Tennessee, Ohio, Illinois, Kansas, Georgia, and Pennsylvania, as well as a presence in many international markets. The company also had a number of family members involved in the business, including John's son, Ryan Howley; Ryan's wife, Marina; John's daughter, Heather Phillips; Heather's husband, Chris Phillips; and John's brother, Rich.

The R-Word and Identifying the Successor

In the spring of 2010, John was having a planning meeting with his executive assistant. As their conversation drew to a close, he asked if she had any questions. "Only one," she said. "What are your retirement plans?"

This question came as a complete surprise to John. He was a vigorous, healthy man who had just turned 60 and had not yet considered retiring. He was having too much fun building Techmer PM. She noted further that if he were to retire she might have to find a new job. John replied, "Don't worry, I am not going anywhere. I expect to be stumbling in many years from now!" A few weeks later at an industry event, John was chatting with company personnel at Techmer's booth, when two of them asked the same question, "John, when are you thinking of retiring?"

When he returned to his office in Tennessee, he called in his executive assistant. "We have known each other a long time," he said. "What is going on with the 'retirement thing'?" She told him that many people were concerned about the future of the company. She said, "People have worked with you through good times and bad; they all feel comfortable approaching you about anything. But what happens if you're not there? Can your son do the job? Will the company be sold?"

John recalls, "Talk about an epiphany! I knew then that I had to do something to get everyone to see the glass half full with opportunity and not threatened by change." He also realized that he had a son who needed some development if he was to lead the company. Even though retirement was, in his view, a long way off, leadership succession needed to become a priority.

There was little question about who John's successor would be. His son, Ryan, had started working in the business while he was in high school and had continued through college. According to Ryan, he had done "everything from sweeping the floors in the beginning to entering data into a computer database to color matching to customer service to tech service assistance." After college, he went to work for Techmer full-time. There was no conflict among the family about this designated successor, and nonfamily leaders supported the choice. Everyone—including Ryan—also agreed that he needed to focus on developing the skills required of an effective CEO.

Planning for Leadership Succession

When John's assistant asked him about his retirement plans, he was also in the process of planning for the biannual Techmer National Meeting, where approximately 100 people from throughout the company engage in team-building and culture-management activities. The company needed to hire an outside firm to help plan and facilitate the meeting, and John thought that this would be a good opportunity to address the leadership succession issue in a positive way.

As he and his wife, Mary, discussed the situation, Mary suggested that they contact us. We had known them as UCLA basketball fans for several years, but had had only limited professional conversations. Over the years, the Manucks had learned a little about our professional practice, but we had never discussed working together. John contacted us and set up a time to talk about the Techmer National Meeting and his desire to implement a leadership development and succession program.

At our initial meeting, we discussed the situation at Techmer and how our firm, Management Systems, could help. We agreed that the Techmer National Meeting would be a good place to start. Among other things, it would provide us with a firsthand experience of Techmer's culture, leaders, and employees. We also agreed that the strategy for leadership succession would focus not only on the successor, but also on building the management and leadership capabilities of all levels of leaders at Techmer—from John and his senior leadership team to front-line managers. The program would also be available to those with leadership potential.

Developing the Next Generation

The Techmer PM strategy for developing the next generation of leaders consisted of two initiatives: (1) a group-based leadership development program for all members of senior leadership, including John and Ryan, and a select group of middle managers; and (2) one-on-one coaching with Ryan to develop the capabilities he would need to begin transitioning into the most senior leadership position.

Group-Based Leadership Development. Drawing on our experience working with managers of similar organizations, as well as what we learned about Techmer at the National Meeting and in interviews with the senior leadership team, we designed a customized leadership development program for the company. Techmer managers were strong operationally, but they needed some advanced training in the strategic and organizational development aspects of leadership. Most of them were focused on their functional or technical roles, and not on the management of Techmer as an enterprise. This is typical of most family businesses.

John wanted this program to be something that people aspired to be a part of. Senior leaders were automatically enrolled; all other managers needed to apply to participate. An application form was developed that needed to be completed and submitted to John. John and the senior leadership team reviewed the applications and selected a first group of twenty participants, in addition to senior management. Those not selected for the first delivery of the program, while disappointed, were told that it would be offered again and that they could reapply.

The five-day program we designed for Techmer used our three-factor approach to leadership and management development: the focus was on skills, behavior, and mindset. It was also designed to help participants understand and use our approach to organizational development (based on the Pyramid of Organizational Development framework). The program was held in two sessions—a two-day session that covered the three-factor framework for management and leadership effectiveness, developing Key Result Area-Based role descriptions, and the Pyramid of Organizational Development. Following this session, all participants (including John, Ryan, and the other members of the senior leadership team) were asked to complete a number of assignments to apply what they had learned. These included tracking their time and working in small teams to complete an organizational assessment of Techmer using the Pyramid of Organizational Development as the lens. During the next session, which was held six months later, participants shared the progress they had made in applying what they had learned and presented their organizational assessment results. This session also focused on developing skills, including time management, delegation, leadership effectiveness, goal-setting, and performance management.

The group program produced several important outcomes for leadership succession. First, of course, it provided the foundation for the development of Ryan's leadership skills. The concepts presented during the group-based training were reinforced and built on in a one-on-one coaching process. Second, the program helped build the skills of other leaders who would be important in supporting the leadership transition. In this regard, the program provided a common language and basis for understanding effective leadership and organizational development—in brief, it gave leaders standards against which they could assess leadership performance and organizational effectiveness. Third, it helped focus John, Ryan, and the rest of the senior leadership team on identifying and working to address key organizational development issues. Finally, it gave Ryan an opportunity to continue developing his knowledge of and ability to work effectively with other members of the senior leadership team, most of whom would eventually report directly to him.

Coaching Program for Ryan Howley.   At the time that the formal succession process began, Ryan had recently returned to the United States. From 2004 to 2007, Ryan worked for Techmer in Germany, where he was mentored by a retired BASF executive who had opened Techmer's first international office there. During that period, Techmer's global sales grew more than 300 percent. Ryan traveled more than 200 days a year and spent time on four continents (Asia, Europe, North America, and South America). He moved to Brazil in 2009 in order to establish a Techmer PM manufacturing presence there. When he returned to the United States in 2010, he was named vice president of strategic growth. In this role, he was responsible for managing two product lines, overseeing Techmer's international business and business development, and managing the company's strategic planning process.

The plan was to strengthen Ryan as a leader, moving him first to COO and later to CEO through formal training (like Techmer's group-based leadership development program), as well as through one-on-one coaching. Ryan was to be mentored by a troika of people: John, David Turner (an experienced senior manager in the firm who had a general management perspective), and Eric Flamholtz.

As CEO and founder of Techmer, John was in the position to guide Ryan's development to a great extent. However, as any parent will attest, certain things are better left to the coaching of others. John asked David, one of his senior managers, to work with Ryan on particular aspects of his development. Eric, who was experienced in coaching not only CEOs, but also younger family members who were in the process of becoming CEOs, was assigned the responsibility for working with Ryan over time, providing him with feedback and coaching that would help him make the transition to his future role.

The coaching by John involved regular meetings focused primarily on helping Ryan understand the CEO role and how John approached it. For example, since corporate financial performance is a critical issue for a CEO, John explained how he approached the analysis of financial results. Coaching sessions also helped Ryan understand and develop ways to effectively manage Techmer's complex organizational structure. Techmer PM has an international joint venture in which it serves as the "general partner" and other investors are "limited partners."[10] John explained how he works with Techmer's partners, implying that Ryan should plan to do it the same way.[11]

David Turner, managing director of the Fibers Division at Techmer PM, also served as an on-site coach. David, who was senior to Ryan in both organizational position and age, began meeting with Ryan approximately every ten days to discuss overall business issues; every six to eight weeks they discussed developmental issues. Thus, David and Ryan were working on two levels: (1) the day-to-day business; and (2) as David put it, "how this is helpful to Ryan's development." This coaching process worked in large part because there was mutual respect. In addition, David was a great selection because he was not competing in any way with Ryan. Some mentors, especially those who are members of the firm, might see themselves in subtle competition with their mentee or might resent a younger individual being groomed to serve at a higher rank than themselves. This was not the case with David.

Eric was engaged to provide an outside perspective, based on his more than thirty-five years of working with senior leaders of growing companies and coaching both executives and family business successors. The coaching process with Ryan began with a meeting to discuss what Ryan wanted to accomplish and by completing a 360-degree assessment that involved asking members of the senior leadership team, including John, to provide input on Ryan's strengths and "opportunities to improve" as a leader. The first set of interviews was conducted in early 2011. The feedback collected suggested that Ryan had some "developmental opportunities." Although it was difficult to hear, Ryan listened carefully to the feedback and made a serious attempt to respond to the criticisms.

Eric and Ryan met periodically to work on specific issues and skills. They also talked by phone as issues came up. The coaching focused on Ryan's work-related interpersonal style, strategic leadership, his role as a company leader, and creating a new role description. A decision was made to help Ryan develop the capabilities needed to be the internal expert on strategic planning. The process also involved discussing the other coaching being done by John and David.

As a way of assessing Ryan's progress, another round of interviews with the same participants was conducted in late 2012. The feedback collected and presented to Ryan in early 2013 was very positive: Everyone interviewed said that he had made significant progress in addressing his developmental issues. Comments included: "It's not the same Ryan as two years ago. He's effective. He's (in) the top tier of effectiveness in the company." "He's come an awful long way. He's done a great job learning. I don't know many people who have improved this much in two years. . . . He's convinced me that he can lead the company."

In David's view, several things contributed to Ryan's improved performance, as measured by the 360-feedback results. First, Ryan had taken over the leadership of a Techmer business unit and had done a good job managing it. Second, David said that the development of a formal strategic plan and Key Result Area–based role descriptions helped clarify what Ryan needed to accomplish. Once Ryan's role was defined using a KRA-based role description, David observed, "It gave us both a 'laser focus' on the things that were important."

Enhancing the Successor's Credibility
as a Way of Managing the Transition

As mentioned earlier, a key aspect of the preparation of a successor in family business is to help him or her achieve credibility. This involves more than just asserting that the designated successor is capable and worthy. At Techmer PM, our strategy to enhance Ryan's credibility was to provide opportunities for him to make significant and positive impacts on the company. For example, Ryan was given the assignment to develop the marketing function at Techmer, which was essentially nonexistent. In addition, he was trained by Eric to facilitate the company's new strategic planning process. His role in leading strategic planning had the dual benefit of creating the competence Techmer needed, as well as giving Ryan a unique role in the firm. In fact, Ryan enthusiastically became very competent at strategic planning, and was recognized as Techmer's expert in this important process. He accomplished this through a combination of his participation in the process, self-study, and one-on-one coaching. These things gave Ryan a platform to make a difference and demonstrate that he was worthy of the future role of CEO.

Results of a Successful Transition

As Ryan continued to make progress, John decided that his role should evolve as well. In February 2013, Ryan began to assume more responsibility and was named president. The leadership transition at Techmer is still a work in progress, but from all indications, it has been highly successful. The founder's son has been promoted to president and continues to work toward taking on the ultimate role of CEO. As David Turner stated, "Ryan has gone from being a very junior member of senior management to become a leader. He is a different person. Specifically: His judgment is good. He is good with information. He is able to gather his own information faster and better than most other members of senior management. He's more confident. He is the voice of the next generation at Techmer." David also observed: "By whatever means used to get here, this was a success for him and for the company."

These results were achieved in a period of eighteen months, an unusually short time period for development and transformation. The senior management team also improved its capabilities. All told, the leadership capabilities of Techmer have become significantly stronger. Of course, Ryan Howley is the person primarily responsible for his own successful development. Each of his coaches made a contribution, but Ryan's own efforts were the foundation for his success.

Lessons from Successful and Unsuccessful Family Business Succession

Drawing on the scenarios and examples in this chapter, we can derive some lessons about family business leadership succession.

First, succession in family business requires a dual focus on what's good for the business and what's good for the family. In our view, the optimal choice is to *do what is right for the business over the long run.* As Hess states, "Succession is a dual leadership change. A change in the leadership of the business and in some cases, a change in leadership of the family."[12] This is because harmony in the family depends on the health of the business. However, doing what is right for the business over the long term is not always what is right from the family's perspective, and some choices can lead to problems.

Second, the process of selecting the successor needs to be managed effectively. In some family businesses, such as Bell-Carter and Techmer, the choice of successor is obvious and accepted by both family and nonfamily members. In other family businesses, however, there is a lack of agreement about who the successor should be. In these cases, family dynamics need to be managed so that they support the "best" choice of successor. One useful decision-making tool to identify a candidate's specific developmental needs is a Key Result Area–based role description, which clearly identifies the responsibilities and the skills/competencies needed to effectively fulfill the role.

Third, there needs to be a development process/program in place to prepare the successor for his or her new role. Although there are exceptions, our experience suggests that most successful leadership transitions include a development process. The process helps the successor understand the business and its operations, improve his or her leadership skills, and develop effective working relationships with the people that he or she will manage. The process should also be designed to help the successor continue promoting the positive aspects of the company's culture.

Fourth, the formal transition process from the current to the new leader needs to be effectively managed. It is not correct to see succession as an "event." It is a process that requires time to unfold. As Gersick and his co-authors state, "Succession always takes time. Even in those cases in which sudden illness or dramatic events lead to abrupt changes in individuals' titles or roles, there is a period of preparation and anticipation, 'the actual handing over of the keys,' and the period of adjustment and adaptation."[13]

Finally, success requires preparation and planning. As the in-depth description of succession planning at Techmer PM demonstrates, planning and preparation for succession are critical contributing factors to a successful transition.

Summary

Leadership succession is a crucial issue that family businesses must manage to support continued success. When done effectively, leadership succession keeps a successful family business on the path to becoming a family business champion. When done ineffectively, it can quickly destroy a family business that was painstakingly built over a lifetime of work.

10 Lessons Learned

Throughout this book, we have presented a framework and tools for creating family business champions—that is, family businesses that will continue their success for multiple generations. In order to be considered a true family business champion, the family business must have undergone at least one, and ideally more than one, successful leadership transition, while simultaneously demonstrating considerable growth and remaining profitable. As Hess has stated, "Most family businesses end at the founder's death and few make it through two leadership successions."[1]

In this final chapter, we step back from our discussion of individual companies and tools to offer our thoughts, insights, and conclusions about what is required to become a true family business champion. Throughout this book, we have used Bell-Carter Foods to illustrate a family business champion in which the family continues to actively manage the company's day-to-day operations. We conclude with one more example of a family business champion, GOJO™ Industries, a company in which the family has taken on a more strategic role as the business has become part of a larger portfolio, including an array of new ventures.

Lessons for the Family Business That Wants to Become a Champion

We have distilled our exploration of what determines success and failure in family business into seven lessons, as follows.

Lesson 1: The Family and the Business Must Be Viewed as Distinct Entities

The key to creating a family business champion is treating the business as a business and the family as a family. The Bell-Carter model of keeping family roles and business roles separate, and of not allowing family needs and requirements to dominate the business, is the key to long-term success, generation after generation.

Lesson 2: Successful Family Businesses Are Able to Create Family–Business Equilibrium

Family–business equilibrium is the optimum balance between the business needs and the family needs. Successful family businesses create and sustain family–business equilibrium over the long term. This is a family business culture issue.

Lesson 3: Family Functionality Is an Intangible but Real Asset for a Family Business

A functional family is a prerequisite to a successful family business. Although family functionality is not in itself a guarantee of family business success, it is always a contributing factor. As such, it is an asset of the enterprise. Where family functionality does not exist, the business is much less likely to succeed; and rarely, if ever, will it become a family business champion.

Lesson 4: All of the Classic Management Tools Have a Dual Aspect: The Technical and the Family

Managerial tools—including planning, structure, performance management, and culture management—cannot be used in isolation; their use must take into account the family circumstances and the level of family functionality.

Lesson 5: Sustainably Successful Family Businesses Have Some Things in Common

All sustainable successful family businesses have a common set of attributes:

- strong business and family business foundations: family members have a high level of agreement about the business they are in, the role that the business plays for the family, what they want to achieve with the business, and how they want to achieve it;

- an infrastructure that supports current and anticipated future operations; and
- a high level of family functionality: family dynamics in the business promote, rather than detract from, effectively managing and growing the company.

Lesson 6: A Low Degree of Family Functionality Puts a Family Business at Risk

There are two key variables that account for family business success: (1) a high degree of family functionality; and (2) a high degree of organizational development. All of the family business champions that we have worked with have had a high degree of family functionality. Most of these companies have had to achieve a high degree of organizational development. It is *much* easier to develop a strong organizational infrastructure than it is to "fix" family functionality problems. Accordingly, we conclude that *the family businesses that are at risk are those with either a low degree of family functionality and/or an underdeveloped infrastructure.*

Lesson 7: Formal Systems of Management Are Required as a Family Business Grows

During the early stages of family business development, management processes can be very informal. However, as a company grows in size and complexity and the number of family and nonfamily employees increases, there is a corresponding need for a more systematic, formalized system of management.

A Road Map to Becoming a Family Business Champion

There are four action steps to creating the road map for family business development. What is most important is the "perspective" or ultimate objective of the process, which is to create family–business equilibrium. Each step in developing and following the road map should be undertaken with this overarching purpose in mind.

Step 1: Organizational and Family Assessment

The purpose of the assessment is to identify the degree of family business functionality and the degree of organizational development; and the specific aspects of each dimension that must be improved. Assessment results are the foundation for the preparation of a family business development plan. The framework and survey tools discussed in chapter 1 can be used to complete this step.

Step 2: Prepare a Family Business Development Plan

This plan must consider both family functionality and organizational development. The plan can be presented in general terms, or better yet, it can use the planning approach described in chapter 3. This plan should also "drill down" to action plans for achieving specific goals, which are not typically included in strategic plans.

Step 3: Execute the Family Business Development Plan

This involves implementing the plan by working to achieve the family business's goals.

Step 4: Monitor Progress and Make Adjustments, as Needed

Progress in achieving plan goals should be assessed regularly, at least quarterly. This progress review should also include identifying and working to address any problems being encountered. If needed, adjustments should be made to the plan to enhance the probability of achieving the family business (and business) strategic mission.

Progress can be monitored using the survey tools we provide in chapter 1. Monitoring and measurement are the keys to making progress. They strengthen accountability and are critical to converting ideas into action. Without them, a plan is just a plan.

To illustrate the process of building family business champions "in action," we present as our final case the story of a family business, GOJO™, that has evolved successfully for three generations. We have used aspects of this family business's evolution as examples throughout the book; here, we provide a more detailed look at this family business champion.

GOJO™ and the Lippman and Kanfer Families

Founded in 1946 by a husband and wife, Jerry and Goldie Lippman, GOJO™ is the world leader in institutional hand hygiene and healthy skin, best known today for the invention of PURELL™ hand sanitizer. The idea for the company's first product came when Goldie worked in one of Akron, Ohio's rubber plants during World War II. Many of the male rubber workers had gone off to war, and the women who replaced them wanted a better way to remove dirt from their hands than the harsh industrial chemicals used at the time.

Jerry, who had only a tenth-grade education, sought out chemistry professor Clarence Cook at Kent State University, and together they invented a product that would remove dirt without irritating the skin. This was sold as GOJO™ Hand Cleaner, and the couple's first customers were Goldie's co-workers in the rubber factory. The name, GOJO™, is taken from the founders' names: GO for Goldie and JO for Jerome.

The Lippmans made their original hand cleaner in the washing machine in the basement of Goldie's parents' house. Unable to procure cans because metal had been directed to the war effort, Jerry asked local restaurateurs, whom he knew from his former job as a cookie salesman, to save their empty glass pickle jars. He collected them once a week, washed them, and packed them with his product, despite their fragility and variation in size.

With Goldie handling administrative matters, Jerry began selling to automotive service and manufacturing distributors and, within a few years, a new product category, heavy-duty hand cleaner, was established. The market remained small because of the high cost of the product, relative to the "free" cleaning solvents readily available. Jerry solved this problem by developing a portion-control dispenser and adopting a "razor/razor blade" approach to placing dispensers and selling proprietary refills.

The Second Generation Enters the Business

Jerry and Goldie did not have any children, but were like second parents to Goldie's sister's son, Joe Kanfer. According to Joe's daughter, Marcella Kanfer Rolnick, "Dad was basically raised as an only child of three sisters." By the time he was 10 years old, Jerry and Joe had become what Marcella describes as "soul mates."

Joe wasn't sure about joining the business. He had graduated from the Wharton School at the University of Pennsylvania in 1968 and anticipated a Wall Street or legal career. But Joe had a deep respect for Jerry and had spent the summers of his childhood working long hours at the factory. Jerry had taken Joe on sales trips by the time he was 7, and Joe had developed a strong attachment to the business. By the time Joe was a young adult, there was, according to Marcella, a significant degree of mutual respect, with Joe marveling at Jerry's resourcefulness and Jerry at Joe's intellectual abilities. This remained true as their combined talents fueled the company's growth over the ensuing years.

Joe was in his twenties and pretty confident when he told Jerry that he wanted the opportunity to earn ownership of half the business if he stayed and did not go off to Wall Street. Jerry agreed. But first, Joe wanted to get his law degree, and in 1973 at the age of 26, he enrolled at the University of Michigan. His plan was disrupted by the Arab-Israeli Yom Kippur War of 1973. The oil embargo imposed by the Arabs meant that the company could not get the petroleum-based raw materials it needed to produce its products.

Joe stepped into the breach. He began buying and trading petroleum products on the black market from a phone booth at the law school in Ann Arbor, four hours from the company's facilities. He bought used tanks and began buying and selling an array of chemicals until the company wound up with the ones it needed, and a nice profit to boot.

Joe traveled the 200 miles between Akron and Ann Arbor every week until he graduated. He recounts that with three days at GOJO™ and four at law school and two 200-mile trips every week, he went three years without reading a newspaper or seeing a TV program.

When Joe returned to the company full time after law school, Jerry made Joe president. Jerry told Joe, "You make the decisions now. You have half the company, so don't screw it up! I am here if you need me."

In doing estate planning, Jerry suggested that Joe have control. But a trusted advisor suggested that Jerry should always own 1 percent more than Joe so that Jerry would know he had the final say after working his whole life to build the company. "This worked out perfectly," said Joe. "Jerry let me do what I wanted and make a lot of mistakes, and I think he did so more easily because he knew he could say no, even though he never did. When I did make a mistake, Jerry always called it a 'blessing in disguise' because I could have made a worse mistake and I learned something. This idea of learning has been central to the GOJO™ culture since the beginning." It should be noted that this is an excellent example of how to manage the succession process.

Within a few years, it became obvious to Joe that the nature of employment in America was changing and that the very dirty hands of the manufacturing era would no longer be a growing market. Recognizing the success of an installed base of dispensers in industrial markets, he broadened the markets served by offering specialized skin care products in proprietary dispensers for virtually every business to business market. By serving the needs of many markets, the company was able to learn faster than its single-market competitors and spread the cost of product development and capital.

Over the years, Joe and Jerry developed a high-functioning partnership marked by dialogue, mutual respect, collaborative decision making, and creating space to learn. They gave each generation just a little more responsibility than they were ready for and then were there for them, never looking back. Their approach set the tone for how Joe and Marcella operate together, as well as for how they work with the leadership team at GOJO™. It remains a defining characteristic of this privately held enterprise to this day. It is also an excellent example of how the family culture infused the business culture in a positive way and how the family effectively managed issues associated with leading the business.

The Third Generation

Joe's oldest child, Marcella, describes her relationship with the family business like this: "My first sibling was GOJO™. I was always there . . . and I grew up with GOJO™ at the dinner table." As she grew older, Jerry regularly told her that she had a future in the business, implying that her destiny was to become one of its leaders. She worked at the company during high school and college—in market research, in the microbiology lab, on the factory floor, and doing special projects like "building a library system for my grandpa [Jerry]."

After college at Princeton, Marcella went to work for a consulting company in New York City because, as she puts it, "I didn't know if I wanted to be or if I was trained to think I wanted to be in the business. Plus I thought it would be important to get some outside experience, even though that was never something my grandpa or dad thought was important."

By this time, Marcella had concluded that she wanted a more entrepreneurial environment and that she "didn't feel at home in the corporate world." It was the late 1990s and GOJO™ had become very focused on consumer marketing to support the sales of PURELL™, which was originally a health care product. So Marcella "created a job" for herself that involved talking to the media, attending conferences, and working on experimental programs, all to promote the new hand sanitizer concept. She says, "It was around that time that the company articulated its first purpose statement that reframed GOJO™ from a chemical or soap company to a hygiene and well-being company [that is, the company changed its business concept]. And working on PURELL™, I felt I was coming back to do something important."

Marcella decided to use her return to GOJO™, now that she was a post-college professional, to learn the company from a middle management perspective without yet knowing her ultimate aspirations. She says that she wanted to manage her involvement in the company at that point so that she did not prematurely send the signal that she had returned "forever."

She had planned to go to business school and left for Stanford University's MBA program in 2002. During her time in business school, she and Joe traded daily phone messages about the business (using the GOJO™ voicemail account she had had since she was 18 years old and had used in the same way when she was in college). In those messages, Marcella and Joe shared their visions, hopes, and concerns about working together in the business. According to Marcella, "We knew we never wanted business to interfere with our father-daughter relationship and were committed to going in eyes wide open. My dad was just as encouraging of me and willing to take a chance on me the way Grandpa Jerry was with him." This is an excellent example of lesson #1 for business champions: Keep the business and family separate.

After Marcella received her MBA, her husband was accepted to the University of Iowa's Writer's Workshop MFA program. So they moved to Iowa City. Marcella says, "I spent those two years working on special projects, as well as preemptively thinking about what it means to be a family business with four sibling-owners after it was only Jerry and Goldie in 'Gen 1' and

Joe in 'Gen 2.' It felt like it could get complicated if we weren't thought-ful." It was at this time that Marcella's younger siblings were entering young adulthood. According to Marcella, even though they had had summer jobs at GOJO™ in high school, they were not destined to work in the business: "They love the company and are proud of all the good it does, but having careers at GOJO™ wasn't their passion."

Through the various experiences that Marcella had —both within and outside of GOJO™—she was developing an idea of what her career path would be. She says of her family: "We are a family that likes to create mean-ing and value in the world, not just enjoy each other's company on holidays. And we are at our best when we are working together." By the time she earned her MBA, she had been exposed to GOJO™, to "corporate America," to consulting, to Silicon Valley startups, to retail, to merchant banking, and to nonprofit organizations and philanthropy. She began to wonder: "Maybe there is more that I can contribute that starts with GOJO™ but doesn't end with GOJO™?" It was in Iowa that she came up with a "multifaceted family enterprise concept," which she describes as including "for-profit compa-nies [GOJO™ and, as of 2007, a handful of early-stage ventures], nonprofit/philanthropy, and the family itself," to create a variety of opportunities for everyone who wanted to opt in.

Marcella says that, as the oldest and the only one working in the family business, she was becoming "the next generation's key decision maker in partnership with my dad," a partnership influenced by and reflective of the way Jerry and Joe had worked together a generation earlier. As her siblings were coming of age, she was beginning to "feel the significance of making decisions that could impact the family's well-being and the well-being of the many families that depended on GOJO™ and our activities for their livelihoods."

Jerry had asked Marcella to be the co-chair of their family foundation around that time. Through her work in the nonprofit world, Marcella was receiving a lot of opportunities to serve on boards, which she valued. But she realized that she could not simultaneously serve on boards, build out the family enterprise beyond GOJO™, and be the CEO of GOJO™, which "was becoming increasingly complex as a business." She found that her pas-sion was in both "ensuring that the preconditions for long-term success of

GOJO™ are in place" and, as she puts it, "working to build out a portfolio for and with the family that generates meaning and value." Marcella, in effect, was beginning to reconceptualize the family's business foundation.

While the vast majority of the family's investment is in GOJO™, Marcella began to view her role as working to create a more balanced, multiclass portfolio that would allow the family to "apply what we learn at GOJO" to support other companies' growth. To this end, the Kanfer Family Enterprise has invested in a number of startups in Israel, as well as in many innovative nonprofit organizations. But, as Marcella puts it, "GOJO™ is still the 'mothership' and we love it. We love the people, we love the GOJO™ Purpose, and we love the culture."

As Marcella worked to identify her role within the family business, she started to realize that she was not managing the expectations that many of her GOJO™ colleagues had for what she would become within the company. She began to better manage her leadership role, in part by "ensuring the preconditions for long-term viability and vitality are in place" and in part as the "face of the family" within GOJO™ (described in chapter 8).

Development of the Board

As a privately held company, the board of directors historically had consisted of family members who were closely involved with the business—Jerry, who passed away in 2005, Marcella, and Joe—and Mark Lerner, GOJO™ president and COO. "Our board meetings would often start to feel like another management discussion," said Marcella. In 2011, a decision was made to expand the board to include independent directors. Marcella says that this was driven by her recognition that she would be the person tasked with making key decisions in the future and that she would not have the benefit of Joe's and Mark's wisdom and perspective forever. She wanted a significant period of overlap between new directors and the leadership that had made GOJO™ so successful over the past quarter-century. She believed it was prudent and necessary for her to "be able to look my siblings in the eyes down the road and say we're making the best decisions we can." In brief, Marcella was practicing effective strategic leadership and strategic thinking.

The GOJO™ board now has six independent directors—with expertise in finance, human resources/organizational development, private equity/

investments, health care, family businesses, strategy consulting, and global marketing. One board member was selected because he is a member of the fourth generation of his own family's business. Joe and Marcella invited Mamie Kanfer Stewart, Marcella's younger sister, to be a board observer in order to learn and grow her own skills and, with them, to represent the family on the GOJO™ board. The board meets quarterly and, according to Marcella, "We attracted people that could, and in some cases already do, serve on boards of companies much larger than ours. We made them full directors with decision-making authority—not just advisors. Notwithstanding that board members of private companies serve at the pleasure of the owners, in our case, our family as represented by Joe, Mamie, and me, we established the expectation that they would speak their minds—and they do!"

GOJO™ board meetings frame and discuss topics in three different modalities, based on where they are in their lifecycle and what kind of input would be most valuable from directors: generative, strategic, and fiduciary. Joe explains, "The generative sessions, those where subjects are new and not yet fully developed or even understood, are the ones with the big payoff because board members with dramatically different experiences and knowledge open up our thinking. And as the family migrates away from day-to-day involvement, having independents serve as oversight 'belts and suspenders' is also very important to us."

Planning for the Future

When Jerry was still alive, the family proactively planned for what would happen to his estate in order to avoid business disruption at GOJO™. The decision was made to put family assets in a trust for Joe's lineal descendants. Having the vast majority of GOJO™ shares owned by trusts means that, upon the death of any family member, the family would not have to sell the business to pay estate taxes. Also, the family's intent is for family dynamics to not interfere with the success of GOJO™, just as they don't want business to interfere with the healthy functioning of the family.

There is what Marcella describes as a "family business foundation" that details the vision, purpose, and values for what has become the Kanfer Family Enterprise. As stated earlier, the portfolio of the family's businesses and activities include GOJO™, early-stage ventures, nonprofit entities, and resources that facilitate what Marcella calls "family member competency development and growth." The family's early-stage ventures have full-time leaders who closely collaborate with and are overseen by Joe and Marcella. The strategy for this part of the portfolio, according to Marcella, is "to support promising businesses that can generate both significant societal and financial value."

Resources that facilitate family members' growth and development include what Marcella describes as "investments in the next generation's businesses" because the family culture is one that nurtures entrepreneurship or, as Marcella describes it, a "go at it, see what happens, and learn" sensibility. As of 2014, Mamie, brother Jaron Kanfer, Mamie's husband R. Justin Stewart, and sister Ketti's husband Donny Zigdon are all being coached and supported in their respective business ventures. In addition, the entire family is regularly invited to an annual meeting where the performance of their overall portfolio—including GOJO™—is reviewed. All are invited to collaborate through the family's philanthropic foundations, as well. Marcella says that "doing business together enriches family relationships."

Marcella's Role and the Future

Marcella continues evolving her role as a leader of her family's enterprise—and it is truly a multi-dimensional one. In her role as vice chair of GOJO™, she is focused on company strategy and performance, in particular major investments to support GOJO's continued strength and growth in the mid- to long term, on helping to maintain the positive aspects of the company's culture, on championing priorities like the enterprise commitment to sustainability, and on representing the family and its commitment to the company. She regularly travels to corporate headquarters in Akron from her home in Brooklyn, New York.

From her Brooklyn office, she connects with GOJO™ daily using Cisco Telepresence videoconferencing technology, works with a small team that supports all of the multi-generational family's for-profit and nonprofit activities outside of GOJO™, and actively advises Mamie's startup, which is developing strategy management solutions that enable growing organizations to scale up. Joe and Marcella continue to look for opportunities to invest in and build purpose-driven businesses. Inspired by the purpose-driven learning organization that is GOJO™, she says that their goal is to "ensure that the infrastructure is in place to grow the family's personal capabilities and investments, leveraging years of accumulated wisdom and ways of working, so that it can live on for future generations, engaging in activities that benefit society."

Results at GOJO™

During GOJO™'s three generations of family business success, the role of the family has evolved, especially from the second generation to the third. Since the Lippman-Kanfer family was and continues to be a functional family, family members are able to explore their own interests and find their own place in the family business. This is especially true of the third generation, which has created defined nontraditional roles. In addition, liquidity and diversification of assets was created for the family by using earnings to make other investments. A great deal of credit for the functional environment at GOJO™ is attributable to the values and behavior of co-founder Jerry Lippman and his nephew, Joe Kanfer.

What GOJO™ Did to Become a Family Business Champion

In its evolution from small family business to family business champion, the family behind GOJO™ behaved consistently with the seven lessons we presented at the beginning of the chapter.

First, the family has kept the business distinct from the family and has established family–business equilibrium. The family dynamics don't interfere with the success of GOJO™, and the business doesn't interfere with the healthy functioning of the family. In addition, the family has invested in startup companies outside of GOJO™.

Second, the family behind GOJO™ and the Kanfer Family Enterprise has a highly functional family culture that is and has been a tremendous asset. It has promoted collaboration, learning, and constructive resolution of conflicts. As noted earlier, after the entry of Joe Kanfer into the business, "Joe and Jerry developed a high-functioning 'partnership' marked by ongoing dialogue, mutual respect, collaborative decision-making, and creating space to learn by giving the next generation just a little more responsibility than they are ready for and being there for them, but never looking back."

Third, the family has a very high level of agreement about the purpose of its businesses (GOJO™ and others) and the role they play within the family. They meet periodically to revisit and discuss their purpose and roles, with Joe and Marcella serving as the leaders of this process.

Fourth, the family is focused on ensuring that they have developed and are using the best systems and processes to support current operations and overall growth of their portfolio of businesses. They are open to change and willing to learn. This value is also very much a part of the GOJO™ culture.

Finally, the family has effectively dealt with and managed leadership and succession issues. They have transferred the management of GOJO™ to a team of professional managers, are effectively using a board to support effective decision making, and have clearly defined the roles of and support the leaders of their family business portfolio.

Final Thoughts

The development of a family business champion is an ongoing and never-ending process; this is because family business champions are *not* perfect companies. A perfect company, like a unicorn, does not exist.

Most of the family business champions—including Bell-Carter (which has been successful for more than 100 years) and GOJO™ (which has been successful for three generations)—would candidly admit that they have their problems. But family business champions are able to identify and address their problems, and as a result, they get stronger and stronger.

We wrote this book to help you do what family business champions do—get stronger as a family business. If you apply the concepts, tools, and methods we describe to any family business, they will make a positive difference and put the organization on the path to becoming a family business champion.

Appendix
Family Business
Self-Assessment Tools

These questionnaires can be used to evaluate the strengths and weaknesses of your family business management "tools." Each questionnaire addresses a specific tool: strategic planning; structure; performance management; and culture management.

Interpreting the Scores

A score of less than 20 on any part of the survey indicates that there are opportunities to improve your company's effectiveness by developing and using that specific tool. A score greater than 30 indicates that your company's use of this tool is reasonably effective; and a score greater than 40 indicates that your company's use of this tool is contributing to its success.

Part 1
Family Business Strategic Planning Effectiveness

Item	Score				
	To a very slight extent	*To a slight extent*	*To some extent*	*To a great extent*	*To a very great extent*
1. Our business has a strategic plan that views the business separately from the family.					
2. Family and nonfamily members of our team understand the company's direction and goals.					
3. The strategic plan articulates a clear business concept.					
4. The strategic plan articulates a clear strategic mission.					
5. The strategic plan articulates a clear core strategy.					
6. All goals are SMART.[a]					
7. SWOT analysis findings are used effectively in creating our company's strategic plan.[b]					
8. The strategic plan includes goals for infrastructure development.					
9. The strategic plan is supported by all family members.					
10. The strategic plan for the business achieves family–business equilibrium.					
Number of responses in column					
Multiply column total by the number indicated.	×1	×2	×3	×4	×5
Subtotal					
Total Score					

a. SMART = Specific, Measurable, Actionable and builds in Accountability, Results-Oriented and Realistic, and Time Dated.

b. SWOT = Strengths, Weaknesses, Opportunities, and Threats.

Part 2
Family Business Structural Effectiveness

Item	Score				
	To a very slight extent	*To a slight extent*	*To some extent*	*To a great extent*	*To a very great extent*
1. Our organizational structure supports our business strategy.					
2. Roles of family and nonfamily members are clearly defined.					
3. The formal (on paper) and informal (how things really work) structures are aligned.					
4. All family members occupy "real" roles; that is, there are no artificial roles created for family members.					
5. All family members occupy roles for which they have proper qualifications.					
6. No family member has a dual reporting relationship in which they report to both a nonfamily supervisor and another family member.					
7. There are no "organizational silos" caused by family dynamics.					
8. The structure has been designed to meet the business's needs more than the family's needs.					
9. There is no conflict between family members' "family role" and their "business role."					
10. Overall, the organizational structure achieves family–business equilibrium.					
Number of responses in column					
Multiply column total by the number indicated.	×1	×2	×3	×4	×5
Subtotal					
Total Score					

Part 3

Family Business Performance Management Effectiveness

Item	Score				
	To a very slight extent	*To a slight extent*	*To some extent*	*To a great extent*	*To a very great extent*
1. People know what is expected of them.					
2. People feel that their performance is appreciated.					
3. Performance against goals is regularly measured.					
4. Rewards received are clearly linked to the performance achieved.					
5. When plans are made, the desired results are achieved.					
6. Performance standards are the same for family and nonfamily members.					
7. The family has a high level of agreement about what our goals should be.					
8. There is a high level of accountability for performance among family members.					
9. The results people achieve are more important than being a member of the family.					
10. Overall, the performance management system achieves family–business equilibrium.					
Number of responses in column					
Multiply column total by the number indicated.	×1	×2	×3	×4	×5
Subtotal					
Total Score					

Part 4

Family Business Culture Management Effectiveness

Item	Score				
	To a very slight extent	*To a slight extent*	*To some extent*	*To a great extent*	*To a very great extent*
1. People have a clear understanding of the company's core values.					
2. The company is customer oriented.					
3. Family members are treated appropriately in the business.					
4. Nonfamily members are treated appropriately in the business.					
5. Our company focuses on holding people accountable for performance.					
6. The organization is open to innovation and change.					
7. Processes are valued.					
8. People's behavior tends to be consistent with our stated values.					
9. Leaders serve as role models for our values and our culture.					
10. Overall, the culture achieves family–business equilibrium.					
Number of responses in column					
Multiply column total by the number indicated.	×1	×2	×3	×4	×5
Subtotal					
Total Score					

Notes

Preface

1. See Edward D. Hess, *The Successful Family Business: A Proactive Plan for Managing the Family and the Business* (Westport, CT: Praeger, 2006), ix.

2. See John L. Ward, *Keeping the Family Business Healthy* (Marietta, GA: Family Enterprise, 1997), 1.

3. An article in the *Wall Street Journal* referred to Bank Santander, successful for four generations, as a "family business 'dynasty.'" For simplicity's sake, we use the term "family business champion" throughout this book, even for companies that have been successful for four or more generations.

4. This case example was developed from published sources, including M. G. P. A. Jacobs and W. H. G. Maas, *The Magic of Heineken* (Amsterdam: Heineken NV, 2001). The authors gratefully acknowledge the assistance of Mr. Brett Hundley who, as an undergraduate student at UCLA, prepared an earlier version of this case while serving as an intern at the authors' firm, Management Systems Consulting Corporation, in 2012.

5. Jacobs and Maas, *The Magic of Heineken*, 1.3.

6. Ibid., 2.3.

7. Heineken refers to Henry Pierre Heineken as the second-generation leader, though one could also view Peterson and Gerard's wife as the second generation. Jacobs and Maas, *The Magic of Heineken*, 4.5.

8. Ibid., 4.7.

9. Ibid., 9–4.

10. Ibid., 9–7.

11. The story of how Freddy reacquired control of HBM is interesting, complicated, and beyond the scope of this book. For a discussion, see ibid., 9.10–9.18.

12. Ibid., 9.27, 9.14.

13. Yvonne Randle was the lead consultant for almost all of that period. Eric Flamholtz

was involved for the first few years and remained involved by proxy, along with other consultants from our firm.

Chapter 1

1. Mark Leenders and Eric Waarts, "Competitiveness and Evolution of Family Businesses: The Role of Family Orientation and Business Orientation," *European Management Journal* 21, no. 6 (December 2003): 686–697.

2. The need to manage both the business and the resulting family issues have been explored by other researchers and consultants, including Edward Hess, *The Successful Family Business: A Proactive Plan for Managing the Family and the Business* (Westport, CT: Praeger, 2006), and John L. Ward, *Perpetuating the Family Business: 50 Lessons Learned from Long-lasting Successful Families in Business* (New York: Palgrave Macmillan, 2004).

3. Exceptions include News Corp, Cargill, Mars, Samsung Electronics, TATA, Westfield, and Melvin Simon & Associates (now Simon Property Group).

4. John L. Ward, "The Special Role of Strategic Planning for Family Business," *Family Business Review* (Summer 1988): 106–107.

5. Rodrigo Basco and María José Pérez Rodríguez, "Studying the Family Enterprise Holistically: Evidence for Integrated Family and Business Systems," *Family Business Review* (March 2009): 22, 82–95.

6. Our concepts of family functionality and organizational development are similar (but not identical) to Leenders and Waarts's constructs of family orientation and business orientation. See Mark Leenders and Eric Waarts, "Competitiveness and Evolution of Family Businesses: The Role of Family Orientation and Business Orientation," *European Managements Journal* 21, no. 6 (December 2003): 686–697.

7. See Eric G. Flamholtz and Yvonne Randle, *Growing Pains: Transitioning from an Entrepreneurship to a Professionally Managed Firm* (San Francisco: Jossey-Bass, 2007).

8. Although the original concept was to sell products for "99 cents only," the concept later changed to sell products for 99 cents or less.

9. See Eric G. Flamholtz and Yvonne Randle, *Corporate Culture: The Ultimate Strategic Asset* (Stanford, CA: Stanford University Press, 2011).

10. Eric G. Flamholtz and Zeynep Aksehirli empirically tested the proposed link between the organizational development model and the financial success of organizations measured in terms of ROI; see Flamholtz and Aksehirli, "Organizational Success and Failure, An Empirical Test of a Holistic Model, *European Management Journal* 18, no. 5 (2000): 488–498. The R^2 for this model was found to be 0.39 at a significance level of 0.01. Eric Flamholtz and Wei Hua provided additional empirical evidence of the hypothesized link between the organizational development model and financial performance; see Flamholtz and Hua, "Strategic Organizational Development and the Bottom Line: Further Empirical Evidence," *European Management Journal* 20, no. 1 (2002): 72–81.

11. Treatment of family members is a primary focus of some researchers. See, for

example, John L. Ward, *Keeping the Family Business Healthy* (Marietta, GA: Family Enterprise Publishers, 1987).

12. See Edward D. Hess, *The Successful Family Business Plan* (Westport, CT: Praeger, 2006), pp. 48–49; Hess discusses the impact that treatment of family members can have on nonfamily members.

13. See also ibid.

14. John L. Ward identifies "inflexibility and resistance to change" as a key challenge in growing family businesses; see "Mastering the Basic Principles of Growth," in *The Family Business Growth Handbook*, ed. Howard Muson (Philadelphia: Family Business Publishing, 2002).

15. Kelin E. Gersick, John A. Davis, M. M. Hampton, and I. Lansberg discuss the dynamics associated with family business leadership throughout their book *Generation to Generation: Life Cycles of the Family Business* (Boston: Harvard Business School Press, 1997).

16. We provide several examples of businesses with "battling brothers" throughout this book. It is a pervasive phenomenon in family business.

Chapter 2

1. See Kelin E. Gersick, John A. Davis, M. M. Hampton, and I. Lansberg, *Generation to Generation: Life Cycles of the Family Business* (Boston: Harvard Business School Press, 1997).

2. See, for example, Howard E. Aldrich, *Organizations and Environments* (Englewood Cliffs, NJ: Prentice-Hall, 1979); Danny Miller and Paul Friesen, "A Longitudinal Study of the Corporate Life Cycle," *Management Science* 30 (1983): 1161–1183; and Eric G. Flamholtz and Yvonne Randle, "Successful Organizational Development and Growing Pains," *Management Online Review* (March 2007), www.morexpertise.com.

3. John L. Ward, *Keeping the Family Business Healthy* (Marietta, GA: Family Enterprise Publishers, 1987).

4. Gersick et al., *Generation to Generation.*

5. See, for example, Donald H. Thain, "Stages of Corporate Development," *Business Quarterly* (Winter 1969): 33–45; Robert E. Quinn and Kim Cameron, "Organizational Life Cycles and Shifting Criteria of Effectiveness: Some Preliminary Evidence," *Management Science* 29 (1982): 33–51; Ichak Adizes, *Corporate Lifecycles: How and Why Corporations Die and What to Do about It* (Carpinteria, CA: Adizes Institute, 1990).

6. See, for example, Danny Miller and Paul Friesen, "Archetypes of Organizational Transition," *Administrative Science Quarterly* 25 (1980): 268–299; and Eric G. Flamholtz and Yvonne Randle, *Growing Pains* (San Francisco: Jossey-Bass, 2007).

7. See, for example, Larry E. Greiner, "Evolution and Revolution as Organizations Grow," *Harvard Business Review* (July–August 1979): 37–46; and Neil C. Churchill and Virginia L. Lewis, "The Five Stages of Small Business Growth," *Harvard Business Review* (May–June 1983): 30–50.

8. Yvonne Randle, *Toward an Ecological Life Cycle Model of Organizational Success and Failure* (PhD diss., UCLA, 1990); Eric G. Flamholtz and Yvonne Randle, "Successful Organizational Development and Growing Pains," *Management Online Review* (March 2007), www.morexpertise.com.

9. For a more in-depth discussion of this model, see Flamholtz and Randle, *Growing Pains*.

10. The "Manneken Pis" is a small bronze fountain sculpture depicting a little boy urinating into the fountain's basin; it is a landmark in Brussels, Belgium.

11. Brad Rehrig, *The Rehrig Pacific Company Story* (Los Angeles: Rehrig Pacific Company, 2013).

12. Leadership succession can occur at any stage of development—later than or earlier than the Professionalization stage. The exact timing depends on a number of factors, including the company's growth rate, the age and health of the founder/entrepreneur, and the skills and experience level of potential successors.

13. As noted, some businesses are ready to move to the next stage earlier than the stated revenue numbers would indicate.

Chapter 3

1. John L. Ward, "The Special Role of Strategic Planning for Family Business," *Family Business Review* 1, no. 2 (Summer 1988): 105.

2. In this chapter we develop the distinction between a "family business plan" and a "strategic plan" for the business per se.

3. Ward, "Special Role of Strategic Planning for Family Business," 105.

4. Ibid., 107.

5. John L. Ward, *Keeping the Family Business Healthy: How to Plan for Continuing Growth, Profitability, and Family Leadership* (San Francisco: Jossey-Bass, 1987).

6. Ward, "Special Role of Strategic Planning for Family Business," 109.

7. Ibid.

Chapter 4

1. See Eric G. Flamholtz and Yvonne Randle, *Growing Pains: Transitioning from an Entrepreneurship to a Professionally Managed Firm* (San Francisco: Jossey-Bass, 2007), 191.

2. See the classic article by George A. Miller, "The Magical Number Seven, Plus or Minus Two," *Psychological Review* 65 (1956): 81–97.

3. See Flamholtz and Randle, *Growing Pains*, chapter 8; and Jay R. Galbraith, *Designing Organizations: An Executive Briefing on Strategy, Structure, and Process* (San Francisco: Jossey-Bass, 1995.

Chapter 5

1. The term "performance management" has replaced the earlier term "control," because of the negative connotations of the concept of control.

2. Corporate culture and the role of performance management are examined further in chapter 6.

3. See Marshall McLuhan, *Understanding Media* (Boston: MIT Press, 1994).

4. See, e.g., Marshall Meyer, *Rethinking Performance Measurement: Beyond the Balanced Scorecard* (Cambridge, U.K.: Cambridge University Press, 2002).

5. See the classic article by Steven Kerr, "On the Folly of Rewarding A, while Hoping for B," *Academy of Management Journal* 18 (1975): 769–783.

6. This is public information that was reported in the company's reports to the Securities and Exchange Commission.

7. Some might say that the salaries were unrealistically low.

8. For further discussion of performance management, see Eric Flamholtz, *Effective Management Control: Theory and Practice* (Dordrecht, The Netherlands: Kluwer Academic Publishers, 1996).

Chapter 6

1. Eric G. Flamholtz and Yvonne Randle, *Corporate Culture: The Ultimate Strategic Asset* (Stanford, CA: Stanford University Press, 2011); Eric Flamholtz, "Conceptualizing and Measuring Human Capital of the Third Kind: Corporate Culture," *Journal of Human Resource Costing & Accounting* 9, no. 2 (2005): 78–93.

2. John L. Ward and Craig E. Aronoff, *Family Business Values: How to Assure a Legacy of Continuity and Success* (New York: Palgrave Macmillan, 2001), 2.

3. See, for example, Linda Smircich, "Concepts of Culture and Organizational Analysis," *Administrative Science Quarterly* 28 (1983): 339–358; Terrence E. Deal and Allan A. Kennedy, *Corporate Cultures: The Rites and Rituals of Corporate Life* (Reading, MA: Addison-Wesley, 1982); Joanne Martin, *Cultures in Organizations: Three Perspectives* (New York: Oxford University Press, 1992); Edgar H. Schein, *Organizational Culture and Leadership* (San Francisco: Jossey-Bass, 2004).

4. Ward and Aronoff, *Family Business Values*, 8.

5. Kelin E. Gersick, John A. Davis, M. M. Hampton, and I. Lansberg, *Generation to Generation: Life Cycles of the Family Business* (Boston: Harvard Business School Press, 1997), 149.

6. See also Edgar H. Schein, *The Corporate Culture Survival Guide* (San Francisco: Jossey-Bass, 1999), 15–20.

7. See Gersick et al., *Generation to Generation*, 149.

8. See Edward D. Hess, *The Successful Family Business* (Westport, CT: Praeger, 2006), chap. 3.

9. Eric G. Flamholtz, "Corporate Culture and the Bottom Line," *European Management Journal* 19, no. 3 (2001): 268–275; Eric G. Flamholtz and Rangapriya Narasimhan-Kannan, "Differential Impact of Culture upon Financial Performance: An Empirical Investigation," *European Management Journal* 23, no. 1 (2005): 50–64.

10. Flamholtz, "Corporate Culture"; Flamholtz and Narasimhan-Kannan, "Differential Impact of Culture"; Flamholtz and Randle, *Corporate Culture*.

11. In our review of the literature of culture management, we have not found any other set of variables that has been identified as empirically related to or drivers of financial performance. All other variables are proposed with face validity rather than empirical validity. Admittedly, this is difficult research to do and requires a "special research site."

12. Flamholtz, "Corporate Culture."

13. This section draws from a company document, "Overview of Taylor-Dunn Manufacturing Company," by permission of Jim Goodwin, chairman and CEO.

14. This section draws on Flamholtz and Randle, *Corporate Culture*, with the permission of the publisher.

15. Steps 1 and 2 can be reversed, with the identification of the desired culture occurring first, followed by the identification of the current culture. This can be necessary in companies where there is no strong preexisting culture.

16. Hess, *The Successful Family Business*, 25.

17. A generation of employees is defined as a cohort of people who enter an organization at about the same time and therefore share a common set of experiences as the company grows.

18. Hess, *The Successful Family Business*, 48.

19. Ibid., 49.

20. Flamholtz, "Conceptualizing and Measuring the Economic Value of Human Capital of the Third Kind"; Flamholtz, "Corporate Culture."

Chapter 7

1. See Eric G. Flamholtz and Yvonne Randle, *Growing Pains: Transitioning from an Entrepreneurship to a Professionally Managed Firm* (San Francisco: Jossey-Bass, 2007).

Chapter 8

1. Throughout this chapter, we reference others' research and theory in discussing key concepts. There are a number of "classic" and recent works on leadership effectiveness, including: Joseph L. Badaracco, *Leading Quietly: An Unorthodox Guide to Doing the Right Thing* (Boston: Harvard Business School Press, 2002); Edgar H. Schein, *Organizational Culture and Leadership* (San Francisco; Jossey-Bass, 1985); Craig L. Pearce and Jay A. Conger, *Shared Leadership: Reframing the Hows and Whys of Leadership* (Thousand Oaks, CA: Sage, 2003); David E. Heenan and Warren Bennis, *Co-Leaders: The Power of Great Partnerships* (New York: John Wiley & Sons, 1999).

2. This conceptualization is a slight modification of the four-factor theory of leadership proposed by D. Bowers and S. Seashore in "Predicting Organizational Effectiveness with a Four-Factor Theory of Leadership," *Administrative Science Quarterly* 11 (1966): 238–263. The four factors that Bowers and Seashore identified are goal emphasis,

work facilitation, interaction facilitation, and support. In our approach to leadership, we divide "support" into two dimensions: supportive behavior and personnel development.

3. Eric G. Flamholtz and Yvonne Randle, *Leading Strategic Change: Bridging Theory and Practice* (Cambridge, U.K.: Cambridge University Press, 2008).

4. See Eric. G. Flamholtz and Yvonne Randle, *Growing Pains: Transitioning from an Entrepreneurship to a Professionally Managed Firm* (San Francisco: Jossey-Bass, 2007), chap. 11.

5. For a discussion of the contingency theory of leadership, see the classic work by Fred E. Fiedler, *A Theory of Leadership Effectiveness* (New York: McGraw-Hill, 1967).

6. Kelin E. Gersick, John A. Davis, M. M. Hampton, and I. Lansberg, *Generation to Generation: Life Cycles of the Family Business* (Boston: Harvard Business School Press, 1997), 43.

7. There are women who occupy this role, but the term "godmother" does not have the same connotation. For a discussion of the Godfather Syndrome, see chapter 4 in Eric G. Flamholtz and Yvonne Randle, *The Inner Game of Management: How to Make the Transition to a Managerial Role* (New York: AMACOM, 1987).

8. The green olive business is very different from the black olive business.

Chapter 9

1. Ivan Lansberg, "The Succession Conspiracy," *Family Business Review* 1, no. 2, (Summer 1988): 120.

2. Kelin E. Gersick, John A. Davis, M. M. Hampton, and I. Lansberg, *Generation to Generation: Life Cycles of the Family Business* (Boston: Harvard Business School Press, 1997), 193.

3. Andrew Bary, "World's Best CEOs," *Barron's*, March 24, 2013, S32.

4. King Family Furniture is a real company, but it has been disguised for the purposes of this case.

5. John L. Ward, *Keeping Family Business Healthy: How to Plan for Continuing Growth, Profitability, and Family Leadership* (Marietta, GA: Family Enterprise Publishers, 1987), 192–193.

6. See Eric G. Flamholtz and Yvonne Randle, *Growing Pains: Transitioning from an Entrepreneurship to a Professionally Managed Firm* (San Francisco: Jossey-Bass, 2007), chap 9.

7. Eric G. Flamholtz and Yvonne Randle, *The Inner Game of Management: How to Make the Transition to a Managerial Role* (New York: AMACOM, 1987).

8. Manfred Kets de Vries, "The Retirement Syndrome: The Psychology of Letting Go," *European Management Journal* 21, no. 6 (2003): 707–716.

9. See David Garvin and Artemis March, *Harvey Golub, Recharging American Express*, Case Study (Boston: Harvard Business School Publishing, 1996).

10. The general partner has overall responsibility and power to make decisions; it also has the highest risk. The general partner has personal risk; whereas limited partners,

as the words imply, have risk only up to the amount of their investment in the company. Limited partners have voting power only if the company is "in trouble" as determined by specific financial ratios.

11. As part of his management process, John explained to Ryan that John usually sends communication to the LP saying "We are planning to take X action, if you have objections please reply by X date."

12. Edward D. Hess, *The Successful Family Business: A Proactive Plan for Managing the Family and the Business* (Westport, CT: Praeger, 2006), 77.

13. Gersick et al., *Generation to Generation*, 193.

Chapter 10

1. Edward D. Hess, *The Successful Family Business: A Proactive Plan for Managing the Family and the Business* (Westport, CT: Praeger, 2006), 77.

Index